The
Diary
of
Anaïs Nin

Works by Anaïs Nin

The
Diary
of
Anaïs Nin

1939–1944

Edited and with a Preface by Gunther Stuhlmann

A Harvest/HBJ Book
Harcourt Brace Jovanovich
New York and London

Preface

Anaïs Nin, we learn from her gradually unfolding *Diary*, has had to come to terms with America, with the experience of a "new world" as it were, several times in her life. Each time this encounter took place at a different stage in her own development. Each time it produced a response, a reflex, that had far-reaching consequences both for her life and for her art.

The *Diary* itself, Miss Nin's basic stance vis-à-vis the world, had its origin in her first journey to the United States. Her ultimate choice, two decades later, between the profession of psychoanalysis and her commitment to writing—between a "life of action" and a "life of the senses," as she phrased it—was triggered by her New York experiences, as we have seen in the second published volume of the *Diary*. The present volume is the record of her third crucial confrontation with the New World, during the difficult years of the early 1940's, which eventually determined her career as a writer.

When Miss Nin arrived in New York for the first time, at the age of eleven, with her mother and her two younger brothers, she was not prepared to share the unsettling immigrant experience of so many of her fellow passengers. America, she had been led to believe, represented merely a "temporary" dislocation. The painful separation from her beloved father, the celebrated Spanish composer and pianist, Joaquin Nin, was to be of short duration. In the notebooks she had begun during the lengthy passage from Barcelona on the S.S. *Montserrat,* as a "letter" to her father, she anticipated an early resumption of the enchanted life in his orbit that had been disrupted, inexplicably to her, by a family crisis. So she stepped ashore clutching her brother's violin case—a symbol, perhaps, of her "artistic" past—proclaiming visibly her distinction from those who had obviously come to embrace a new life, to start out, again, as "Americans."

New York, the sprawling, angular hub of what was then a provincial frontier country, presented a sharp contrast to the tree-lined, residential charm of Paris, where she had been born. It offered none of the mellow grace of Brussels, Arcachon or any of the Old World places her father's virtuoso career had previously taken the family. Settling into the dreary middle-class gentility of Manhattan's West Side, attending a Catholic school, where she was made conscious of the peculiarities of her newly acquired English, or being exposed to the sweatily proletarian boardwalk in Coney Island—all these manifestations of "American" life compared rather unfavorably with her memories of Europe. "I would prefer to return to Barcelona," she confided to one of her early notebooks. "I hate school. I hate New York. It is always noisy, everything is somber, shut-in, severe." As a transient stranger, she also felt ambiguously isolated. "I make no friends and the reason is this: One is never sure to stay anywhere."

Clinging to the hope of an eventual release from her American exile, obedient to her mother, the young Anaïs earnestly tried to cope with the new environment. But after an uncomfortable year in New York, a terrible realization began to dawn on her: "The veil is torn and I must tell myself: Father is never coming back. Now a thousand things I did not understand become clear. I forgive Mother for deceiving us, letting us believe Father had not gone away forever. She did not want to destroy our youth with tragedy. But now I find reality more terrible as I was not prepared for it."

The loss of her father, this central, traumatic experience of Miss Nin's youth, which was to haunt her for so many years (as we have seen in the two previously published *Diary* volumes), perforce also heralded a significant change in her own status. The return to Europe, to the familiar, aristocratic Bohemia of her father, had definitely been cut off. Now truly "displaced," she regarded herself as an odd, precocious "foreigner" amidst her American contemporaries, whose formative backgrounds, ambitions and expectations she did not share. "Why," she asked her budding *Diary*, "am I not like everybody?"

"When a child is uprooted," Miss Nin wrote many years later, "it seeks to make a center from which it cannot be uprooted." Her center, as we know, became the monumental *Diary* she is still keeping today. It served as the confidant of her maturing years, the precious mirror of her intimate self. It turned into the multi-leveled novel of her life, the ultimate instrument of her art. In New York, she carried the *Diary*, tucked away in a straw basket, like an astronaut, enduring an alien environment, linked to his life-sustaining survival pack.

Cut off from retreat into the past, except in memory, Miss Nin now embarked upon the exemplary process of pioneering which was to become one of the basic themes in her life. Instead of "giving in," of conforming to the prevailing standards and expectations of American life, or of rejecting them altogether in futile rebellion, she opted for a third alternative. In the midst of the concrete wilderness she began to construct, to preserve, her own "livable" world. It became, essentially, a world of attitudes rather than objects, of personal values rather than abstract ideologies, of aesthetic appreciations rather than material ambitions. Almost instinctively, she grasped for what was perhaps the only workable answer to permanent displacement of any kind: the creation of an intimate, individual world, an "un-uprootable" personal bastion in a fluid, potentially hostile and destructive environment.

Unlike many native-born Americans who never experienced a climate concerned with or even appreciative of cultural values, who first had to "escape back" to Europe, to get away from the "drab sameness"—as Brooklyn-born Henry Miller called it—of a parochial, materialistic immigrant society, Miss Nin had been brought up in a cosmopolitan world of art. The experience had been firmly implanted in her as a child. It had been preserved, like a treasured icon, in her mother's brownstone in the West Seventies, where Spanish and Cuban artists found a hospitable gathering place. And she herself had rejoined this world, a few years later, by becoming a model, a Spanish dancer, by gaining access, on her own, to those enclaves in New York where other "foreigners"—real or imagined—pursued their "foreign" trade of artistic creation. Thus, before Miss Nin returned to France eventually, in the 1920's, she had already re-established, in America, a link, an umbilical cord, to the boundary-transcending world of art and artists which forevermore was to remain her sanctuary on both sides of the Atlantic.

When Miss Nin disembarked again in New York, almost twenty

years later, in November 1934, she approached the New World in a different mood, as we have seen in the opening section of volume two of the *Diary*. Her relationship to America—as that of post-World War I Europe in general—was undergoing decided changes. What once had been a remote, obliterating melting pot for the tired masses of Europe was now emerging, in its own right, as the probing ground of a fascinating technology, as a harbinger of a New Era. The advent of better communications—faster ships, airplanes, radio, newsreels, the export of American jazz, of Hollywood films, the emergence of a fresh, indigenous literature—had carried a new image, a new awareness of the United States to Europe. It was an image of vitality, and vitality, the possibility of growth, the opening of new perspectives, had always attracted Miss Nin.

Thus, she landed in New York with a sense of elation, no longer an anxious child, an inexplicably exiled stranger. New York held promise, it was a bracing antidote to an aging, perhaps moribund Europe. The once oppressive, sky-obliterating towers of Manhattan now appeared to her as symbols of the modern world, of the potentialities of progress. New York, she wrote, was "pointing upward, into ascension, into the future."

France, like most of the Old World, had witnessed the birth and initial development of psychoanalysis with benevolent reserve. But America, it seemed, had reacted to the promise of this new "science," as to so many other things, with genuine enthusiasm. Thus, when Dr. Otto Rank moved his practice from Paris to New York, Miss Nin decided to follow, to assist him, for a while, in his pioneering work. After the richly textured years in the small village of Louveciennes, on the outskirts of Paris—so intensely described in the first published volume of the *Diary*—the prospect of change, of a new involvement with others, apparently appealed to Miss Nin's creative sense of adventure.

New York, indeed, offered a fertile ground for analysis, as Miss Nin was soon to find out in her room in the "Hotel Chaotica," in Dr. Rank's Central Park office. Beneath the "plastic brilliance, hard metal surfaces, glare and noise" of Manhattan, which had seemed such a hopeful contrast to the constrictions, the smallness of Europe, she encountered different kinds of constrictions, of smallness, of inhibitions in the tales of her patients which soon overwhelmed her. Her search for human potential had become a destructive nightmare. When the onslaught of unearthed neuroses threatened to devour her own creative work as a writer, Miss Nin returned to France, in June 1935, forsaking—as it turned out—forever the practice of psychoanalysis.

Paris, Europe, in the 1930's, had not yet succumbed to the syndromes of the new age of skyscrapers and highway culture. Despite its own political and economic turmoil, it was still a "humane" city, lived-in, worn down to a comfortable human pace. The myriad cafés lining its tree-shaded boulevards still offered room for the talker, the walker, the genuine artist and the genial fraud. One could still live, as Miss Nin did, in a houseboat, *La Belle Aurore,* tied to a city *quai,* or find a reasonably priced apartment in Passy, overlooking the Seine. The sometimes miserly, provincial Parisians still respected the *artiste,* even when he was not affluent economically. Her friends—Henry Miller, Antonin Artaud, Jean Carteret, Lawrence Durrell, Conrad Moricand—were not subjected to the dignity-crushing yardstick of "making it." There was, perhaps, less room for "mobility," for the kind of phenomenal success attainable almost overnight in America. But there were, perhaps, also fewer people who felt as deeply dissatisfied as those "successes" Miss Nin had encountered in her psychoanalytical work in New York.

When Miss Nin was forced to leave Paris, in December 1939, after the outbreak of World War II, she left behind a city that had nourished her artistic and human growth for almost two decades. She had published her first book there, in 1931, a study of D. H. Lawrence, and her latest book, *Winter of Artifice,* had just come off the presses, only to disappear in the turmoil of war. In Paris, she had become reunited and reconciled with her father, and she had seen him collapse on stage during his thousandth concert. In Paris, she had undergone psychoanalysis with Dr. René Allendy and Dr. Rank. She had built her lasting friendships with Miller, Durrell, with Gonzalo, the Peruvian revolutionary who had tried to acquaint her with Marxian ideology, who himself perhaps symbolized some of the noble futility, the dilemma of political action, which emerged as one of the hallmarks of the 1930's. In Paris, she had tended to the ever-swelling ranks of refugees from the Spanish Civil War, to the escapees from political and religious persecution in Nazi Germany. And throughout, she had tried to preserve the personal island she had created against the growing dark sea of misery and destruction.

Her farewell to Paris, to Europe, expressed once more a deep sense of loss: "We all knew that we were parting from a pattern of life we would never see again. It was the end of our romantic life."

Miss Nin's third arrival in New York—this time, appropriately, by the novel conveyance of a "flying boat," a hydroplane from Lisbon—inevitably opened up some of the old wounds of her first encounter with the United States. Once again she arrived as a "foreigner," an English-language writer published only in France, as a "refugee." Uncontrollable events had once more separated her from a vanishing Europe, from an enchanted past, from a "romantic life."

Much of this volume reflects the discomfort, the sense of isolation Miss Nin at first experienced in New York. "The tragedy is that just as we were about to enjoy our maturity in Europe, which loves and appreciates maturity, we were all uprooted and placed in a country which only loves youth and immaturity." She echoes her childhood feelings: "There is an atmosphere of separatism. The foreigner is an outsider. I seek to mingle with American life, but I feel a suspicion, a mistrust, an indifference."

Most people, she finds, turn away from the unfamiliar. They are not interested in dreams, visions, in Europe, in the "past." They profess cultural interests, cultural ambitions, but they lack a receptivity for subtleties, sophistication. "I ask myself where am I now? In a place which denies myth, and sees the world in flat, ordinary colors."

Confronted by the glacial aspects of New York life underneath its façade of uncomplicated hospitality, she seeks out other "outsiders." The only ones who have preserved a naturalness in their lives, she feels, in spite of all deprivations, are her Negro and Haitian friends. In Greenwich Village she discovers a backdrop for "genuine artists and genuine relationships." But even there many of the small amenities of European life are missing, the climate is barren.

"I used to live in the streets," Yves Tanguy, the exiled French painter, complains to her. "Here I never want to go out." Henry Miller, who had been forced to return from Greece, other Europeans —Max Ernst, André Breton, Marcel Duchamp—voice similar sentiments. There are no comfortable cafés, no casual meeting places. There is no real sharing of life, only shallow prattle or egocentric monologues. And though Miss Nin tries to establish around her some of the old cosmopolitan life, she seems frozen in the New York environment.

Parties here seem only pale reflections of those in distant Paris. Refugees, she notes, tend to repeat themselves after a while. Valiantly, she tries not to act "like the White Russians in Paris," to bridge the gap.

She meets American poets, but she finds them "confused about their roles. They set themselves up as philosophers or men of action. I do not think a poet should preach, seek to convert, philosophize or moralize." She reads and meets American writers, yet she feels that "life and writing here are boxed-in, as monotonously symmetrical as the architecture. It is a dreary order, a mechanical structure, a functional practical servant." She finds the "mature here are tough intellectuals, harsh, rigid . . . they are only interested in ideas, politics, science, not in art, aesthetics or life." Their harshness runs counter to her feminine sensibilities. "American literature," she writes somewhat prophetically, "needs expansion of consciousness."

She is, again, sought out by the young, the unknown, who sense in her, perhaps, a kindred spirit, an unusual, receptive woman who has achieved independence not by trading on her femininity, a fellow visionary who is not part of the grinding cultural machine that consumes rather than nourishes. But she still feels ill at ease among them. She is aware of an essential, separating difference. She misses in them, perhaps, a sense of continuum. "They are busy trying to find their own style, their own art. But they borrow and imitate as we did when we were young, only we were grateful for our influences." The razing of the past, the obliteration of memory, rejection rather than organic growth seems at the root of their enthusiasm. "America," she notes, "is rejecting all European influences, like children who reject their parents."

Suddenly, she is keenly aware of the passage of time. "I am watching Henry age, and Gonzalo age, and I feel the weight of their aging."

Her work, in New York, falls upon deaf ears. Nobody seems interested in "European" writing, in what some editors believe is "unhealthy," decadent "surrealism." Write something like *The Good Earth*, she is told. Cut out the poetry, the dream, the vision. Give us the facts, Ma'am. "In being deprived of publication," she writes early in 1941, "I am deprived of existence, forced back into solitude, disconnected from life." She does not want to be a "foreigner" forever. "Being published would have been a bridge between myself and America," but "by rejecting me you throw me back into my small personal world."

When nobody within the established publishing scene offered to bring out some of her work, she decided to go it alone. Communication, to her, was an essential necessity. "It was my first bridge. To reach my father. To reach Europe. To keep the people I love from vanishing. Writing against loss, against uprooting, against destruction." In January 1942 she sets up her own small press in a loft on Macdougal Street.

Work on a new edition of *Winter of Artifice* is slow, cumbersome, and exhausting. But it is also a "marvelous cure against anger and frustration." It is an act of defiance, an assertion of independence. "At the end of the day, you can see your work, weigh it. It is done, it exists." Her words have become tangible.

Challenging indifference evokes a new sense of vitality in her, a new determination, a new solidity.

She has become more chary of psychoanalysis as a panacea. "If one can get lost in the labyrinth of emotion one can also get lost in the labyrinth of analysis. I found this out with Rank." But she maintains that psychoanalysis "is our only way of gaining wisdom because we no longer have religion."

She has arrived at a different assessment of her relationship with her father: "If, for example, my father had not been my father but a friend, I would have appreciated his scholarship, his musical erudition, his gift for creating an atmosphere, his wit in the world, his talent for storytelling, his charm. But because he was my father and a certain role was assigned to him, a certain expectation was created in me. It was by measuring his behavior according to the expectations of a daughter that I found him wanting."

She regards her rebellions with a different eye: "Very often I would say I rebelled against this or that. Much later it occurred to me to question this statement. Instead of rebellion could it be that I was merely asserting my own belief?"

Her introspection shifts from her own emotions to the emotions of her friends, to a clearer assessment of her craft, her search for new forms to embody a larger consciousness, new symbols to be found in science and technology.

In the face of the spreading war, of the annihilation of the Old World, she also clings to the course set for her own life by her first American experience: "The worse the state of the world grows, the more intensely I seek to create an inner and intimate world in which certain qualities may be preserved." It is her steady, unswerving answer to chaos, loss, and destruction.

In reviewing the small, handset edition of *Under a Glass Bell*, in 1944, Edmund Wilson remarked that these stories "take place in a special world, a world of feminine perception and fancy which is all the more curious and charming for being innocently international." Two of the keystones of Miss Nin's lifework, indeed, are feminine perception and a true internationality. Both were born of the special circumstances of her life. In her struggle for independent creation as a means of survival, she employed, rather than rejected her strength as a woman. ("Contrary to most creative women of our time," she notes in these pages, "I have not imitated man, or become man.") In her fight against dislocation, she also rejected neither the past nor the future—Europe or America—but fused them into a genuine artistic internationalism, a bridge from yesterday into tomorrow. (Ironically, while until recently America regarded her as a "foreign" writer, her novels were published in France, in the 1960's, as *romans Americains*.")

The present volume, drawn from the original volumes 60 to 67 of the *Diary*, links directly with the two previously published volumes, covering the years 1931–34 and 1934–39. Personal and legal reasons made the omission of certain persons again obligatory and a few names were changed or eliminated. Pseudonyms are indicated as such in the index. The dates in brackets supplied by the editor are again merely intended to indicate the passing of time since the dates given in the originals are sometimes confusing, due to later elaboration of events, and an actual chronology seemed preferable.

As the *Diary* unfolds, as new sections of Miss Nin's lifework become available, a thought she jotted down here as a theme for a future book might serve, perhaps, as an epigraph for the *Diary* itself: "There are few human beings who receive the truth complete and staggering, by instant illumination. Most of them acquire it fragment by fragment, on a small scale, by successive developments, cellular, like a laborious mosaic.

New York
April 1969   GUNTHER STUHLMANN

The
Diary
of
Anaïs Nin

I left a Paris lit in a muted way like the inside of a cathedral, full of shadowy niches, black corners, twinkling oil lamps. In the half mist hanging over it, violet, blue, and green lights looked like stained-glass windows all wet and alive with candlelight. I could not have recognized the faces of those I was leaving. My bags were carried by a soldier whose shoes were too big for him. I suffered deeply from the wrench of separation. I felt every cell and cord which tied me to France snapping in me, the parting from a pattern of life I loved, from an atmosphere rich, creative and human, from intimacy with a people and a city. I was parting from a rhythm rooted very deeply in me, from mysterious, enveloped nights, from an obsession with war which gave a bitter and vivid taste to all our living, from the sound of anti-aircraft guns, of airplanes passing, of sirens lamenting like foghorns on stormy nights at sea.

I could not believe that there could be, anywhere in the world, space and air where the nightmare of war did not exist.

On the train to Irún. On the way to take the hydroplane from Portugal. It seems as if I will never tear myself away from France. Each mile of the journey, each landscape, each little station, each face, causes a painful separation. I carry with me only two brief-cases filled with recent diaries. At the last moment, when I had taken all the volumes out of the vault in the Paris bank and packed them in two suitcases, I found that the cost of excess weight far exceeded the money I had. So the bulk of the diaries went back into the vault. And now, in the train, I feel despondent, ashamed to be saved from catastrophe, to abandon my friends to an unknown fate.

For the second time in my life, America looms as a refuge. My mind is journeying backwards in time. I think of the Maginot Line, which crossed near Louveciennes, in the Forest of Marly. We stumbled upon it one day on a hike. A young soldier took us through part of it. He was very proud. A cement labyrinth with apertures only for gun barrels. He showed us a vast empty pool, which he explained would be filled with acid to dissolve the bodies of the dead. I think of my concierge, who lost her husband in the First World War and might lose her son in the Second. I think of the Pierre Chareaus in danger because they are Jews, and those who escaped from Germany and are now once more afraid for their lives.

At Irún there was a period of waiting, a change of trains. I took a walk. A wall behind a church, at the top of a hill. I turned my back on it to look at the church. I felt pains in my back. I turned around. Suddenly I noticed that the wall was pitted with bullet holes. A passer-by said: "Thousands of Spaniards were executed here." Vestiges of destruction all around me. Children playing in the ruins of buildings.

The train again. Portugal. I cannot smile at the sun. I cannot smile at the white buildings, the women in black, at the wild flowers and the singing in cafés. I am in mourning for France.

The hydroplane is poised on the water. The refugees cheer. Escape! A woman takes me to the ladies' room to search me, to see that I am not carrying a revolver, a camera, or gold. To get inside the hydroplane we walk on its wing and enter through an opening in its belly. The metal is the same color as the sea. It seems too heavy to fly. As it courses along the water with one engine starting, then another, gathering speed but bumping against the waves, I feel as if in a nightmare when one cannot fly upward even though menaced by great dangers.

Strange that when we finally fly, the separation from the past seems easier to achieve. Height and distance from the earth seem to stabilize the spirit, to liberate it from its sorrows. We enter the consciousness of the cosmos. The face of Europe grows smaller. Now there are only sky and clouds.

We land in the Azores. Legend says this is the part of Atlantis which did not sink. Black coral rocks, black sand from volcanic eruptions. Pastel-colored houses clinging to the rocks. A soft grey drizzle. The houses lean against each other, shaky and frail, like

Utrillo's houses. Women pass by in long dark capes, their faces hidden in large hoods supported by frames, like nuns' hoods inflated by the wind.

When we leave the Azores after refueling, the hydroplane again seems too heavy. The sea is stormier, and we have difficulty in taking off. The waves buffet the windows. We rise after a great struggle.

Night. The stars and the moon impassive, undisturbed, eternal. A little of their impassivity flows into me. They are consoling. They reduce the intensity and acuteness of human sorrow. I feel less strangled, less oppressed. I transfer to the moon and the stars some of the trust in God I once had, and realize that serenity comes from an acceptance of death. Man's life span is short. There is an end to pain.

After dinner the bunks are pulled down. I lie down and open my briefcases. I lie awake, rereading the last letters I received, and writing in the diary. The essence of all I have lived in the last ten years rests in these briefcases. I have run away with a part of my treasures, my memories, my obsession with preserving, portraying, recording. All of us may die, but in these pages we will continue to smile, talk, make love.

The first letter I reread is from Conrad Moricand. He wrote in pencil, while with the Légion Étrangère, before they discovered he was too old and sent him back to Paris. He wrote after reading *Winter of Artifice:*

At one time I might not have appreciated your novel because of its temporal quality. Its concern with what Max Jacob once defined cruelly as "those tales about Adam and Eve." This in spite of your gift for analyzing quarter tones and your lucidity which makes me tremble at times. This human world you explore with so much skill was an unknown world to me, voluntarily repudiated by me. I was very young when I detached myself from life in the raw, when I became disincarnated. All I wanted then was to rise above contingencies, to be able to distill an essence. I accepted the role of a spectator (which is all I have been, a passive spectator), not a participant. Today, old and worn out, I am no longer proud of my attitude. I begin to suspect my own heart, which I had

5

thought to be warm, and ask myself if as a cold observer in the face of *la vie saignante,* which alone contains the pulse of life, I did not commit a sacrilege, a blasphemous indifference and detachment. Perhaps I deserved the death-dealing lightning blows of Anteros, the god who punishes those who have not loved. Witness this old naturalist studying the phenomenon of life under his astrologic microscope, and being now miraculously moved by your closeness to life. The poet in me, which you so charitably discerned, was precisely the instrument I used to keep life at a distance, a distance which I now believe was far more than an abdication, a sort of cheating, of evading life, because one must respond, one must feel. One must know tenderness, but with my temperament, a man incapable of love, as I have been, as I am, my somersaults towards heaven were only a derivative, an ultimate cheating. I took refuge in a cosmic existence. It was a very cold region, dear Anaïs, and the great Pascal was aware of this long before I was. To define you I can find no better adjective than emotional cosmic sense, when I observe this many-faceted heart of yours, its multiplicity of contacts, its ramifications. Your book gave me a nostalgia for an earthy life, earthy and consuming, which I missed in my chimerical quest for wisdom and serenity, my no man's land peopled only with the ugly cactus of solitude. If I had a choice, I would choose your way. Your weighing machines, so precise when it comes to weighing the imponderable . . .

Woman has to be reminded constantly of the vaster, mythical and cosmic worlds. That is where man finds his strength. Jean [Carteret] sought to remind me of this in Saint-Tropez. He asked me not to look upon painful events and experiences which beset me as death-dealing or withering, but as mere storms which carry away dead leaves without destroying the trees. . . .

You must not get trapped in humanity and its struggles. You must keep alive your contact with all things, your relationships to all kinds of people. When you are too much invaded by others' discords, when you are driven by scruples or guilt to retrogress in order to help others live, and when they try to crystallize you in one role, you lose your ability to maintain and sustain the flow, you arrest the turning of the bigger wheels, you get caught in the spokes.

The last letter from Lawrence Durrell, written from Greece:

DEAR:

This is so long overdue that it is past all apology; I have been writing you a portmanteau letter for some time, but have decided not to send it. Such a void yawns when we turn our mind northwards and think of you entombed in the European cities with your gas masks and thoughts. It is something that the war does: Dissolves and untightens purpose, so that one's friends move about in the still places of the imagination like candlelit fellows, not quite belonging to the past, but without future and form. There is a little leafy square opposite the Closeries des Lilas, where sometimes I wait for you to pass in your cloak, going homeward. Darling Anaïs, I do feel for you in your cutoffness; and there seems nothing to say to you that will make you less conscious of the distance of light and air which lies between us; the war goes deep and bitter in me—it makes everything taste of ash. The success of the three musketeers,* the success of your book, above all, which just rode the crest in its gay cover, the third musketeer; a success which is swallowed suddenly in the blackout and the alarms. I was writing a long thing to you about how we lost the island; how the autumn came down in a sudden sweep of pearl and black—a terrific slow augur as war was breaking. I can never really recapture the way we stood on the balcony and watched the green rain falling in the sea, a kind of pitiful last will and testament ending the summer. The sea tossing its mythological blue like the mane of horses. The island went down in the smoke and here we are in the city, no less fabulous but built in heavy ringing strokes of white and red; all the contour and curvature of the world which gave us a sea outside our house is gone. We left Henry. He is in a strange state, pitched in too high a key, a little hysterical with light and air, but physically fit as a drum. There is something deeply wrong about his attitude towards the world, but I cannot say what it is. He himself feels it, and takes pains to justify his "egotism" as you call it; perhaps if it were unconscious of itself his egotism would become true detachment. In some inner way he refuses to grow; but it is only a phase of his growth. There always was that lovable myopia in him to everything except his own processes. And the war is too big a thing for him to swallow; he must reject it. He is enchanted by Greece, the air is so kind to him, and the scenery so crystalline; but it has made him dumb. He cannot speak any more.

For my part I feel completely hopeless inside; it is so good to be working at the trivial all day and drinking retsina at night. My heart shrinks when I read the manifestoes of the leaders, when I really see the pygmies at work in the world with their hysteria and violence. We do not speak

---

* Henry Miller's *Black Spring*, Lawrence Durrell's *Black Book*, and Anaïs Nin's *Winter of Artifice* had been published in sequence according to a joint plan—Ed.

about the war here, but it is a kind of weight we carry among us, among our frivolities. The radio pours in its news all day; we file and counterfile political theories; we write long and meaningless memoranda on official paper about the number of pens in the office. Tomorrow it all ceases. A new specimen of civil servant has arrived from London and has closed down this department, believing that propaganda is not necessary here. I shall be left to my own devices tomorrow; I don't know whether writing is any kind of anodyne. I must try. We have a balcony here also from which the Acropolis shines in the mist all day; but the war eats into one slowly, symptom of the inner war of Europe, the pragmatist's disease. I feel entitled to none of this clear, poignant, peaceful Attican country, the blue and the white and green; or the curved sky at night with its brilliant stars. I would like to break you a morsel of this land and send it to you to keep under your pillow like a wedding cake.

The money question is going to be a problem unless I find some other job; a serious, a laughably serious question. In fact, if I don't we shall be en route for France very shortly. Life is very black for us all; no hopes, no solutions in sight. Only there is a kind of imperative at the bottom of things which tells me that we must bear our tears gracefully.

I was asleep when a storm awakened me. Hail, snow, lightning. Gradually everyone awakened and dressed, chose to sit up, clutching at some precious possession. One cannot see the ocean. The clouds are black and dense.

Why does the dialogue with Moricand continue through the voyage? He was not the most important of my friends. Was he a symbol of old forms I would never see again? All my life, it seems, first with my father, and at the end with Moricand, I admired form and discipline and rejected them as interfering with life and nature. I loved form, but not formality. I loved discipline, but not rigidity. Yes, of course, the dialogue with Moricand is a continuation of my dialogue with my father. The icy formality an insulation from feeling. Yet in the midst of chaos and hysteria in Paris I sought form in Etsu Inagaki Sujimoto's *Fille de Samurai*. Style. I loved Jeanne because she was a poet, I followed her into her world and bruised myself against her social conventions, class distinctions, upper-class taboos, so contrary to her own essence. And the same with Rebecca West. This formality, all the things one could not say, or do, or enter, irritated me in Moricand, too. At some point this formality would break down (with my father, with Moricand when he read *Winter of Artifice*).

Moricand's letter was a cry of sorrow at having missed human life out of overrefinement, squeamishness. But he confessed his unnaturalness, and when he did so, I also became aware of the beauty of this form, this stylization, this discipline, which may have been, beyond social forms and rigid etiquettes, an attempt to control nature. I was not only saying farewell to Moricand but also to a form of culture personified by Moricand. Grace of bearing, grace of the spirit, the masking of one's failings, anguishes, to present to the world only a smiling face and witty façade. *Poetry become a heroic act.* Sense of ceremony and ritual a sacred duty, to add to the beauty of the world. Henry [Miller's] courage consisted in immersing himself in all experience, without repulsion. My father's and Moricand's courage lay in resisting ugliness, sordidness, in selectivity, in repudiating the lower depths.

I wish I had all my diaries with me, for if we sink they would sink with me and no one would ever be hurt by the truth.

I had to leave Helba and Gonzalo in Paris, waiting for their consulate to repatriate them. I left Gonzalo my first edition of Proust to sell in case of need. I left my furniture and books in storage.

They say the war will be over soon.

To continue living in the past I read another letter from Moricand:

We are stranded in a snowstorm. As we have not yet received our uniforms, and our woodcutting chores, digging trenches, and eating keep us out of doors, we look like sordid hobos. My raincoat is a rag, my shoes a stew. We chopped wood in freezing weather. We sleep in barns, on the straw. Two men were jailed for keeping their hands in their pockets.

Will the customs officer read the diaries? They were not examined at the frontier. What will they say when I land in America? Contraband?

We fly through dark masses of muddy clouds. I feel the loneliness, the smallness, the helplessness of man. Four years of intensity, love, and fervent living lie there within these notebooks, fragile, ephemeral in the immense night and space. The hydroplane trembles. I feel its weight struggling against the wind, the straining of its heavy body piercing through the storm clouds. I lie back, feeling light and unreal.

Bermuda should have appeared at dawn but it was sighted five hours late because of the storm and contrary winds. Everyone was happy to step on land, into a luxurious hotel where, it was announced, we were obliged to wait for twenty-four hours on account of the weather.

We drove through the island to visit the stalactite caves. Far below a rather pale nature, a subdued tropical life, lay a scenery of dreams, a dream born out of a continuity impossible to an artist. We were never given a million years as the lime and water were to achieve such castles, spirals, turrets, flowers, gems. All carved of time and stillness. The earth enclosed this creation, safe from change, cyclones, disruptions, and created out of endless patience an enchantment whose only music was the falling drop of water. Earth closed the doors of daylight and fabricated a castle such as man never could; reversed candles shedding tears instead of wax, nuns, gargoyles, gnomes, mummies, anemones of snow, cream, lace patterns, spirals of dew like hanging pearls.

A dream from which all violence was absent.

Here lay a dream entombed, reflected in pools of water. Atlantis itself at the bottom of an awesome crevice; a mummy of its inhabitants stands in a sea born of darkness, the statue of an unknown cult.

Nothing breaks or falls here until man makes an opening to the corrupt air of his dreamless world and the stalactites near the opening dry up, crumble into colorless dust, while deeper in the cave they are luminous and seemingly eternal.

Up on the surface again, the roofs of Bermuda homes seem covered with snow. But it is only lime to repel rain water. The

Negroes are soft and beautiful like the climate. I saw a plant called the "plant of life" which can live without roots. Its leaves throw off foamy hairs. Wherever a piece of this plant falls it flowers richly. I kept a leaf of it as a reminder in my many uprootings.

The next day the plane took off again. We came down gently at Port Washington. My mother was there alone because my brother Joaquin was giving a concert in Boston.

I landed with my diaries but empty, feeling like a ghost. I entered a hotel palace of Byzantine luxury. Luxury anesthetized me. At the same time it made me more aware of my misery, as a sick person is more aware of his fragility when exceptional care is taken of him. America presents its overwhelming luxury, incredible comforts, and this increases my concern for those left in the cold and dangers of war. The softer the velvet box, the deeper the rugs, the warmer the rooms, the greater the abundance of food, the more I miss what I have lost, the lonelier I feel.

I can ring the bell for a regal breakfast, but I am dying of homesickness and half of me is having a meager breakfast in a Paris bistro, half of me sleeps in unheated rooms, half of me loses a son, a father, a brother, to war, to a camp, to a prison. *Send for the doctor!* I need a medicine man who will solder my body and soul together, which splits at every separation. The doctor says it is the flu. He cannot see the body is empty, the fire is gone, I am a king without a kingdom, an artist without a home, a stranger to luxury, to power, to bigness, to comfort. I lost a world, a small human world of love and friendship. I am no adventurer, I miss my home, familiar streets, those I love and know well.

Made a superhuman effort to come back to life. Visited Frances Steloff [of the Gotham Book Mart] who played for us the role Sylvia Beach played in Paris. She has befriended our books, and she receives me with a gentle, warm smile. She is busy among her books, boasting not of learning so much as of her love for them. She welcomes those who stand for hours browsing, she welcomes unknown magazines, unknown poets. The James Joyce Society meets in her shop. She gives tea parties for authors on publication around one. The place is filled with photographs: Virginia Woolf, James Joyce, Whitman, Dreiser, Hemingway, O'Neill, D. H. Lawrence, Ezra Pound.

She believes in health foods, and invites me to the Theosophic Society.

I met Dorothy Norman, who published my story "Birth" in *Twice a Year*. Dark eyes and a smile that is not happy, serious, intelligent, strong. She took me to her small office in the Stieglitz Gallery. I met Alfred Stieglitz, the photographer, dressed like an old European artist, cape and soft hat, talking like a man accustomed to respect. Admired his photographs of New York, his sensitive approach and wisdom. "Make me love New York," I said as he took my hand to show me what he loved: a bridge's span like a spider web in strength, shadows under the Elevated, a spire, a street.

The illumined skyscrapers shine like Christmas trees. War seems distant. Greece a dream. Henry far away. Gonzalo hazy in the fogs of Paris. I live externally, superficially. The luxury after the tender human scale of Paris is overpowering. Where are the cafés with only three small tables, and tottering chairs? This is Gulliver's country. But I, who love human scale, small objects, small intimate cities, small trains, small cars, small restaurants, small concert halls, do not respond to giant scales.

I visited Joaquin at Williams College, where he teaches as a full professor of music. He has a comfortable home. He is independent. He takes care of Mother. The students like his sense of humor, even though he demands much of them. He composes standing up beside his piano, whistles gaily when things go well, and asks the same question he did when he was small: "Do you love me?" Then, as if this were the fuel he needed to continue, he resumes his intensive long hours of composition, of piano study. He distributes in all discussions or talks a mellow tolerance, a love of harmony, a dislike of hostilities. He is in spirit a peacemaker, but also much concerned with justice. He is indulgent, kind to other composers, generous. There is in his music, composition, and playing, a classic beauty and purity, a luminous clarity.

A few copies of *Winter of Artifice* have escaped censorship and are selling. It is snowing. I work on the story of "The Mouse." I can see that a loving care goes into my writing, which has nothing to do with writing as such but with the desire that what I have seen and known should not die, a sense of the preciousness of experience.

I wear the same fourteen-year-old astrakhan coat, fitted, with a high collar, a muff and hood I made myself.

The telephone has begun to ring. Invitations and engagements.

Receptions for French war relief, exhibitions, cocktails at the French Consulate, lunch at the Cosmopolitan Club with Katrine Perkins.

Cable from Henry. He is sailing this week. The United States Consulate advised him to leave Greece.

In Paris, Jean Carteret and I talked about anxiety at separation and divisions. I felt a conflict between poetry and realism. I felt a conflict between understanding others by osmosis, identifying with others, and my fear of loss of identity, integrity.

When through sympathy I flow into others I feel anguish over what will become of my real self. Jean said it was a fear of the passageways, of the bridges between them breaking, and so I would be cut off from a part of myself. This stemming from the initial bridge breaking between myself and my father.

Now anxiety prevents me from feeling, from entering a new life which might annihilate the past one in my memory and I rush to describe it.

Tomorrow a party for Joaquin and me at an art gallery.

I cannot shake off my mourning.

I write to Moricand, to Gonzalo, to Jean. I shop for my mother's and Joaquin's Christmas presents.

The shops are a feast, the decorations fantastic. A Christmas tree at Jaeckel's (where I once worked as a model) is made of white fox furs. Candles burn at every window of the million-eyed Radio City. Green holly hangs lavishly on façades of buildings. There is ice skating in the evenings, in the open air. The whole spectacle is regal.

Dinner at Dorothy Norman's apartment on Park Avenue.

In Paris, when entering a room, everyone pays attention, seeks to make you feel welcome, to enter into conversation, is curious, responsive. Here it seems everyone is pretending not to see, hear, or look too intently. The faces reveal no interest, no responsiveness.

Overtones are missing. Relationships seem impersonal and everyone conceals his secret life, whereas in Paris it was the exciting substance of our talks, intimate revelations and sharing of experience.

Dorothy Norman is intellectual but cold as a human being. She lives by a rigid pattern. She shocked me deeply by saying: "Europe is decadent. You must be happy to be in a healthy country."

"What you call decadent," I said, "is the courage to experience all of life."

Great sadness last night as I heard the New Year's celebrations in the street from my bed.

All around us there is excitement in place of exaltation, rush and action in place of depth, humor in place of feeling.

At the Gotham Book Mart I met the old mystic Claude Bragdon. He took me to lunch. He is a tall, austere man, a rigid, petrified man like an ancient dead tree or a long-preserved mummy. I did not realize that there are still real, dogmatic Puritans in America, a type as definite, as fanatic as the religious men of India.

After lunch in his hotel he took me to the top floor, to a glass-enclosed garden of artificial plants. It seemed suitable that he should be sitting among unnatural plants, in a make-believe garden, at the top of twenty floors of concrete. And there he delivered his sermon:

"You are one of the Delphic women. I knew that as soon as I

heard about you and knew it even more so after I met you. But you will destroy your powers of divination and your psychic intuition unless you separate yourself from human life, and above all things from sensuality. There is too much sensuality in you. You need to be purified. Let me help you. I have been able to renounce everything. You will need my help."

I renounced being a Delphic woman.

Party at Kay de San Faustino's and Yves Tanguy's. Caresse Crosby enters with the bouyancy of a powder puff, a caressing voice (was this how she gained the nickname of Caresse from Harry Crosby?), her fur hat, her eyelashes, her smile all glittery with animation. The word on her lips is always YES, and all her being says YES YES YES to all that is happening and all that is offered her. She trails behind her, like the plume of a peacock, a fabulous legend. She ran the Black Sun Press in Paris, lived in a converted windmill, knew D. H. Lawrence, Ezra Pound, André Breton, painters, writers. At the Quatre Arts Ball she once rode a horse as Lady Godiva.

The life of certain women dresses them in anecdotes which become more visible than fur coats or silk dresses. Stories surround Caresse like a perfume, a necklace, a feather. She always seems fresher and younger than all the women there, because of her mobility, ease, flowingness. D. H. Lawrence would have called it her "livingness." A pollen carrier, I thought, as she mixed, stirred, brewed, concocted her friendships by a constant flux and reflux of activity, by curiosity, avidity, amorousness.

Yves Tanguy is the painter of deserts and white bones. He loves to paint bleached bones lying dead in the sun of emptiness. He teases Kay by calling her lovingly: "My dear widow, my dear widow." There is a certain affinity in their painting. He has a clownish face, ironic and at the same time candid. A tuft of hair seems determined to stand up by itself in the middle of his head. He acted out a man in a fit of epilepsy so realistically that he frightened me. Then he exposed his trickery: soap lather coming out of his mouth. But then he told a somber story. When he was seventeen, in France, he did not want to be drafted for military service. So he learned to simulate epilepsy. He was not drafted, he did not have to go to war in 1914. But from then on he had real attacks of epilepsy. Dr. René Allendy told him it was out of guilt. He had to make his alibi real, to exonerate himself.

"One can never escape one's childhood," Tanguy said.

I told him one could, by way of psychoanalysis.

We talked about our regret for a dying France. Kay said she wished she had died there, with them. I reacted by saying we must stop behaving like the White Russians exiled from Russia, who spent all their evenings in Russian night clubs with caviar and champagne, dancing, talking, and weeping about their past.

James Cooney and Blanche, his wife, who printed their magazine, *The Phoenix,* by hand, were among the first in America to show interest in my work. We corresponded for a long time. They published some of my stories. Now I visited them in Woodstock.

James Cooney, red-haired, Irish, with his hair falling over ingenuous green eyes, humorous and romantic, emotional and generous. They live in a log cabin in the woods. They wanted to go back to the earth, live a Lawrencian life, but a community one, gathering together people with the same interests. The guesthouse is the woodshed. He believes in living simply, working with his hands. Blanche is gentle, self-effacing. Robert Duncan—a strikingly beautiful boy, who looked about seventeen, with regular features, abundant hair, a faunish expression and a slight deviation in one eye, which made him seem to be looking always beyond and around you—read one of his poems. I visited the press. Humanly I liked them, but in their evaluation of writers they seemed confused, immature. I awakened early because of unfamiliar noises and surroundings. Jim was already chopping wood for the fire.

Returning from Woodstock, crossing the half-frozen Hudson at Kingston, I was chilled by the largeness, emptiness, loneliness of the landscape. Siberia. Great blocks of ice colliding with a great noise. Something desolate about the atmosphere, grandiose and impersonal.

Party at Mabel Dodge Luhan's on Fifth Avenue. When I arrived at the door, her husband was sitting on the doorstep, squatting rather, as if he did not want to be a part of what was going on inside. He is an American Indian, handsome, quiet, withdrawn. I wanted to talk with him but his attitude intimidated me. I would have preferred to stay outside and talk with him.

A grotesque evening. Mabel Dodge Luhan, small, rotund, with fierce blue eyes, a hypnotist's eyes, all WILL as she had revealed herself in her book on D. H. Lawrence. "I willed him to come." She had tried to will him into writing a book about the Indians, and she had also tried to will him away from Frieda.

She moved like a commanding old Queen Elizabeth or Christina, pushing her guests in the direction she wanted, introducing them. Photographers from *Life* magazine were hiding from her in corners. But she caught up with them, pushing through the crowd; took the cameras and hurled them down the stairs. The photographers rushed after them to collect the fragments.

I read over my old diaries. I sit by the fire of my life in Paris and wonder when this life here will start to burn brightly. So far it looks like those electric logs in artificial fireplaces burning with moderate glow and without sparkle or warmth.

Henry sailed from Greece on December twenty-seventh. Gonzalo and Helba sailed from Marseilles on January fifth.

My father is living in Havana, with rheumatism in his hands, no longer able to give concerts. My mother is growing old and has to be treated with care. Her superb energy is dwindling.

Henry arrived alone. I had the flu and could not meet the boat.

I moved to the Hotel George Washington. It is served entirely by Filipinos. It gives the place a warm, friendly glow.

Henry gives me Nijinsky's life to read, the one written by his wife. I feel she helped to increase his insanity. Because she had no empathy, he complains that she never feels anything, only thinks. She tried to make him something he could not be: a husband;

whereas Sergei Diaghilev protected Nijinsky's dreams, protected the artist, made no demands on him except that he should dance.

The snow is falling.

Robert Duncan comes with Virginia Admiral, a painter who is working with Hans Hofmann. He is shy. He enters obliquely, as if to avoid collision. He talks as if under hypnosis. He invites me to contribute to a magazine called *Ritual*, and says: "Your *House of Incest* inspired me with the courage to state the visionary experience of the poet, his sense of ritual. I wrote 'Arctics' after I read it last fall. If there is a link between your 'Birth' story and your magnificent *House of Incest* it is in the profound sense of ritual, in the act and in all experience."

They are both children out of *Les Enfants Terribles*. But they are children. She says: "You are much kinder and sweeter than I imagined from *House of Incest*."

[February, 1940]

Robert Duncan writes a diary, too. This is his portrait of me:

She is a very delicate woman, you know, sharp, she has such tiny bones and eyes that would break, I am sure, and she moves sideways through glass. Can you guess when she washes them, her eyes, where she dries them, fox, princess, daughter? And her feet? What sort of polish she uses over the cool pewter of her feet—nails of isinglass, brittle, like they would cut clear through . . .

As long as I'm not made of plastic!
He gave me his poems to read. I wrote him:

What you have shown me I call prose. Poetry is a transmutation. It cannot be so direct. It is not the primitive images I object to, but even a penis in primitive myths becomes different, a symbol. In your poetry you reach this at times, at other times you do not. Some of it is too clear, too direct. It is not an issue between vulgarity and style, colloquialism and literature, but a matter of atmosphere and transmutation. The physical aspect in poetry has to be transfused with meaning. Incandescent and transparent only to show the meaning within and one simply cannot do that with flat-footed words, prosaic or one-dimensional. Prose is pedestrian, poetry is flying. Poetry is the myth created out of human elements. In the "Maze" poem it seems to me you were successful. Don't misunderstand me. I do not wish to eliminate daily language but untransmuted reality.

When Gonzalo discussed his talks with Antonin Artaud, the period of working for his theater, the long walks through Paris after the evenings of rehearsals, when they were staging *Beatrice Cenci,* and he described Artaud in a fever of ideas and projects; or when Henry described his nights with June and Jean in the cellar room on Henry Street, I always listened with a kind of jealousy and envy, as if I had never known, or would ever know such nights. This was because their way of telling their experiences heightened them so much that they seemed to bear no resemblance to any experience in my own life.

Today I became aware that I had known many similar experiences; they lay modestly ensconced in the pages of the diary.

But there still remained a difference between the effect of Henry's and Gonzalo's stories and the extraordinary talks or nights I actually experienced, and this difference lay in the separation between the realm of life itself and the dramatization of this life. What I listened to was a dramatization because both Henry and Gonzalo had a gift for this. It was the dramatization that caused what I believed to be an insurmountable contrast to my own experiences. I felt at the time that nothing could parallel them even while I was experiencing similar moments in my own life. It was not until I achieved the same power of dramatization of my own life that I could begin to live it with a sense of the extraordinary. It was this which made me so restless, this disparity between the imagined and the actual.

But now I see that the extraordinary was in my own vision (as it was in Henry's and Gonzalo's visions). I see my life in Paris with the added elements of fiction: lighting, focus, the gold patina which memory adds to it, and they appear to me more vividly, more separated from the quotidian details which dilute it, from the unformed, the excrescences, the dust or dullness of familiarity. They are highlighted in this case by poignant memory and a desire to relive it all, now that it is forever lost.

For this I suddenly cut myself off from my social activities, and pursued in the dark the flashes of beauty and uniqueness I had once held in my hand without awareness of their preciousness.

I thought about Dr. Otto Rank, and wondered how he was. I had had no news of him for some time. When I telephoned this morning I could not believe the voice that told me he had died of a throat infection, not too long before I landed in America. The death of Rank did not seem believable, because he was only in his fifties, because of his vitality and love of life.

He had been about to fulfill his wish to live in California. His new wife had a ranch there. She had fulfilled his need of a collaborator, had translated his writings, worked with him. He had been happy, about to escape from individual therapy. He had finished a new book.

No flowers, no announcements, no letters of consolation. A void. But memory can invoke a figure, and because of its own vividness, it appears clear and sharp; eyes both soft and penetrating, his curiosity and interest, his abundance of ideas, his fecundity. He did have sorrows, profound depressions, disappointments, frustrations, but he never became bitter or cynical. His faith never died, nor his capacity to feel, to respond. He never hardened, never became calloused. I trusted and accepted his thought, but did not fully understand its ramifications.

I wanted to know whether he had died easily, painlessly. Whether he had known he was dying. I had no one to ask. Rank, perhaps due to the professional ethical habit of secrecy, rarely mixed his friends, rarely talked about them. He was discreet and secretive even about his life. He imparted little. The small but intense joys of his childhood came from nature. The only grievous bitterness from the attitude of his colleagues after his break with Freud. His sadness from his first marriage. I knew he felt analysis and therapy separated him from life rather than fulfilled his personal needs. Analysis creates illusory attachments. He must have been caught in the illusions of love more than other men. Because he was spiritually rich, he was preyed upon, used. What had he intended to do with his leisure in the California sun? Fulfill the writer, the poet and playwright he once was? Who really knew him intimately and well?

In the face of death, one asks oneself invariably: Did I see enough, hear enough, observe enough, love enough, did I listen attentively, did I appreciate, did I sustain the life? Did Rank die not knowing perhaps how much or how deep was his gift, how vivid his human presence?

I visited Hugh and Brigitte Chisholm in their East River apartment. The place is so near the water that it gave me the illusion of a boat. The barges passed down the river while we talked. The river rippled and shimmered. Brigitte is a flawless beauty, so perfect she seems unreal; abundant, loose dark hair, clear-cut classical features, large dark eyes set wide apart, full mouth and perfect teeth. She is tall, full-breasted, long-legged, boyish in her directness, feminine in her rich voice, boyish again in her gestures, feminine and voluptuous when she lies down. Hugh is small in stature, with curly hair, soft greenish eyes, an impish air. He is a good poet.

As I enter they treat me like an *objet d'art*. They walk around me, push me into the room, examine me, exclaim over my Goyaesque hood, and the red flower in my hair. Hugh loves *House of Incest*.

Brigitte sat cross-legged on a satin divan, wearing slacks and tinkling bracelets. She shines steadily, under any circumstance. Not intermittently as I do, because I can only bloom in a certain atmosphere, a certain warmth. Otherwise I retract, retreat from the scene. That afternoon, in the warmth of their appreciation, I blossomed.

The apartment was full of things I would individually find ugly, silver candelabras, tables with nooks in the center for trailing plants, enormous mulberry poufs, rococo objects I saw often in French and English aristocratic homes, objects such as Jeanne collected, to be amused by, to play with. They were ornate, gathered without consistency or unity from antique shops, with the same light, snobbish playfulness—not to be taken seriously. All whims and caprices, amusing, full of chic; they would lose all their charm if put together by anyone else. Here they retained their Dadaist impertinence. They were made beautiful by an aristocratic boldness which dared bad taste.

From the objects I could divine their life in Rome, Paris, Florence; Brigitte's mother; the famous *haute couture* designer, Coco Chanel; *Vogue*; the pompousness of their family background and their effort to laugh at it. Frontiers overlapping into surrealism, and the key word, the obsessional society key word: amusing.

I could sense all kinds of refinements, of elegant *laisser-aller* and *laissez-faire*, audacities and adventurousness.

There are only two kinds of freedom in the world: the freedom of the rich and powerful, and the freedom of the artist and the monk who renounce possessions.

I love to encounter these freedoms, here expressed in casualness of whimsical objects, but finding poetic expression in Hugh's poems.

Small talk is like the air that shatters the stalactites into dust again. I do not participate. I wait. I laugh. I am aware that shallowness disintegrates the deeper undercurrents everyone seeks. The underground rivers of dreams, of deeper and deeper selves running underneath.

My reward is that I am often taken into those realms, and I find a far more fascinating personage.

Yet at night I am tired, not, as before, from my own pretenses and roles, but from loneliness, from my inability to stay on the periphery. This need of a deeper life pulls me away from the most perfumed, the most decorative, the most attractive and aesthetic atmospheres, makes me each day renounce some pleasure, some floating garden, some frivolity, some glittering object. I would have liked for a few days to live within the pages of *Vogue* and *Harper's Bazaar*.

But I prefer my submarine regions.

I first met Beth at a party. She spoke softly. She was eloquent with her body. She lay on the couch as if it were time to go to bed rather than to talk or drink together. She placed her hand in mine as if we were old friends drawing comfort and companionship from this gesture, and the rest of the people were strangers. We agreed to meet again. She was the first flowerlike, plantlike woman I had met in New York, with a yielding, pliant, sensuous quality quite rare in a place filled with wiry, nervous, high-strung women.

She had plenty of leisure. She liked to shop, to linger over lunch, to talk. Our only difficulty was that I would be pulled away by my work.

In French museums I saw countless paintings of women about to step into their bath, pink-fleshed, fleshy, fresh-out-of-their-clothes, with the dew of coverage still clinging to them. Beth, all dressed, evoked these paintings, but being American she evoked far more the glow and roseate dewiness of after-the-bath. She was full-fleshed, transparently clean, with clear blue eyes as if a little water had been gathered in a white porcelain cup. Her mouth was so full and ripe it reminded me of one of Man Ray's canvases, on which he had painted only a mouth, leaving the rest the chalk-sandy, off-white canvas desert. Beth appeared sensuous in every strand of her shining hair, in the pink lobe of her ears, a flesh made for nudity as naturally as a fruit. I could only imagine her in a bedroom, about to undress, or already undressed. This image of her fruitlike skin not made for clothes may have been partly created by her recurrent talk: "At that time I was sleeping around with everyone, or with everybody." So I assumed she lived, breathed, existed in a constant atmosphere of erotic pleasures. It would have taken the most expert accounting to keep track of her sexual activity. She deceived me.

When she once told me she most enjoyed sleeping with men for money I concluded she was never satisfied, could not obtain enough men (I knew it was not money she needed).

She tried to persuade me to accompany her to an apartment where a certain lady took care of distributing girls according to taste and type. (I could not envisage any charm in this because I could only enjoy sexuality when I was in love.) When I questioned her about the quality or variations of the pleasures obtained she confessed she had never known an orgasm.

I knew no woman as easily persuaded to go to bed who had obtained so little from her play-acting. The extent of her frigidity appalled me, and I persuaded her it would get worse, and finally become incurable if she so deadened her contact with men. I gently took her by the hand and led her to an analyst.

But this woman, who could undress at the request of any man, make love with anyone, go to orgies, act as a call girl in a professional house, this Beth told me she found it actually difficult to *talk* about sex!

Waiting for Gonzalo and Helba at the dock, in the most cruel Siberian cold. After three hours I was told he was detained and that I should telephone his consulate. While waiting for a consular representative we shouted at each other, Gonzalo leaning over the deck railing, and I on the dock.

Finally, someone arrived from the consulate and freed them. There they were—trunks, baskets, paper packages, cartons, and all. Helba wanted to go straight to her room in my hotel, but Gonzalo was so keyed up he wanted to walk the streets. The last time he had been in New York, Helba had stopped the show at the Ziegfield Follies with her Peruvian Indian dances.

I took Gonzalo to the top of the Empire State Building, the most lyrical view of New York.

Gonzalo was in high spirits. After the mournful days in Paris, New York seemed like a musical comedy.

We returned to find out if Helba needed anything. We bought her food and left her again. We sat at the bar and talked about his last days in Paris. Do you remember so and so? He had to return to Cuba. The ones who had not been able to return home ended up in the Légion Étrangère, and some in concentration camps.

Helba sent a message: she needed salt for her sandwich.

We went up again. Returned to the bar. I wanted to know what had become of all the people I knew.

Helba wanted fruit. Gonzalo shook his hair despairingly: "On my first day in New York, I can't lock myself in with a sick woman!"

Alfred Perlès writes the best interpretation of *Winter of Artifice* in an English magazine, and Ralph Utley the most obtuse in a Washington paper.

Conrad Moricand's article on "Paracelsus and Astrology" appears in the *American Astrology* magazine.

Jean Carteret writes me a desperately lonely letter.

Henry took me to visit a friend of his who was once in charge of American censorship. He had banned Henry's *Tropic of Cancer,* but when he visited Paris he sought Henry out and took him out to dinner. He now has the most complete collection of Henry's works. He has the greatest collection of erotica and of criminal annals in the country.

A monolithic woman met us at the door, quoting Plato. So little humanity, warmth or femininity in her that she seemed made of stone. He looked like a happy, rotund priest who eats and drinks too much.

Henry looks frail and sad. He is anxious over the meeting with his parents, whom he has not seen for eleven years. He was going to see them the next day. He dreaded the reunion. His father was ill. Perhaps they would need his help and he had no money to give them. I offered to give him whatever they needed. Henry said it would not be the same thing, it was not his, and why should he deceive them? I said: "Some illusions are life-giving." But Henry does not believe this.

When he visited his parents he found them as he feared, poor, his father ill with cancer of the prostate. But not in pain. Henry came back and sobbed all night with pity and guilt. The next day when we met he sobbed again. He was altogether changed, human, quite broken and soft. He said he understood now all that he had mocked in me, my care of my mother and Joaquin, that one could not really escape one's karma, and that by his evasions all he had done was to accumulate guilt.

As it happened, that day a rare book collector had given him fifty dollars for a manuscript, and it was this money Henry took to his family.

All of Henry's intoxication with Greece vanished. He suddenly softened and began to visit his family every week, taking gifts to the three of them, visiting his aunts, cousins, etc. The days passed while I shared his new phase of pity.

Henry was staying in a hotel room, and was unhappy. When I visited Caresse in her furnished apartment on Fifty-third Street I had an intuition it would be a place Henry would like. I mentioned this to her. Sometime later she informed me there was a bachelor apartment for rent in the same house. It was just what he wanted, a large room to work in, peaceful and secluded because the windows gave on a back yard.

He settled there and began to work.

[April, 1940]

Gonzalo found a large room for himself and Helba on the West Side, near the docks. In the daytime the neighborhood is colorful, with the big markets, the ships unloading, the bars, the trucks, but at night it is sinister, deserted, full of darkness, with only the bars open, and shadowy figures hiding under the highway.

When I was very ill with bronchitis I was happy to rediscover Dr. Max Jacobson, the German *émigré* doctor, whom I had helped indirectly to reach America. He rushed over with his miracle bag and cured me instantly. Max Jacobson takes care of me while he is getting his license to be able to practice here. He is becoming known for the amazing doctor he is. Intuitive, alert, observant. He has almost no need of the laboratory. I have never seen a human eye so like an X-ray when he scans a human being for signs of illness.

I danced until five A.M. at the Savoy Ballroom. I love Harlem. The Savoy is the only genuinely joyous place in New York.

Gonzalo lives only in the here and now. His pockets are full of newspapers and he sits most of the time glued to the radio. At the movies he wants to see only the newsreels.

He makes fun of me. "For days and days I will be digging into newspapers for news, digging away for data so I will understand what is happening. You come floating out of nowhere. You say: 'Well, how is it?' You listen to what I have to say. You look over the whole scene briskly, attentively, get the gist of it, grasp it in general terms, and in a few minutes you are off again into some other realm where you live, all wrapped in clouds and mysteries, while I feel I'm left with my feet on the ground, on earth, trapped in the present."

My answer was: "It isn't good to stay too long in the polluted air of history."

The truth is I am escaping discussions, because I no longer believe Marxism is a solution to the miseries of the world. Because it does not cure man of violence. And it is only a solution to material needs. In the process, as in the process of American pragmatism, all other values are destroyed. Both countries exclude spiritual needs. America is in even greater danger because of its cult of toughness, its hatred of sensitivity, and someday it may have to pay a terrible price for this, because atrophy of feeling creates criminals.

Paul Rosenfeld is a most likable man, enthusiastic, warm, learned. He is a discriminating music and literary critic. His house is overflowing with good books and good music. We often have lunch together in the Village. He is small in stature, but his manners are so elegant it gives him distinction. His face is always pink, alert, and playful. He has a gift for enthusiasm.

He invited me to meet Sherwood Anderson. French writers manage to look like writers. Sherwood Anderson looks like a doctor, a businessman, a banker. He was practical and literal in his talk. But very human, full of wisdom and tenderness.

"In France," I told him, "my first friend was Hélène Boussinesq, your translator. She not only translated you, but she loved you as a human being and talked about you so much that I felt as if I had known you. I knew which restaurants you liked in Paris, which cafés, which drinks, which writers. You became so familiar a figure to me that when people mentioned you and asked if I knew you I would say I did. I felt I did. The French loved you. And *Dark Laughter* was an exotic book for them and for me. Through you I became familiar with the way little towns were, and little people felt. I hope you don't mind my saying I knew you well!"

Sherwood Anderson laughed at this and did not look displeased.

A few minutes later, he was sound asleep. He remained asleep for the rest of the evening.

My young friends John Latouche and the Chisholms said they would call for me to go to a party. I dressed in my Indian sari and fell asleep all dressed and made up. When they came, because I had been asleep, the whole evening took on the atmosphere of a dream.

I had been told I would meet the Greek poet Kalamares. As soon as I arrived I saw a tall dark man with burning eyes, who came over and sat at my feet. It was Kalamares. Eventually he changed his name. Perhaps he knew that kalamares with a C means squid in Spanish, and that I made fun of *calamares en su tinta* (squid in its ink sauce), a most appropriate name for a writer!

John Latouche is delightful, full of playfulness and fantasy. He made up a language which sounds like French but is a gibberish equivalent. He talks to me in this at length, and I answer in fake Japanese. We deliver fervent speeches, outdoing Joyce with our double talk.

When people tell me it is my own fault that everyone over-burdens me, I tell them the story of my trip to London. It was a rough crossing of the Channel, and so everyone stayed on deck. I did not feel too well and I fell asleep on my chaise longue. Someone pulled at my sleeve and awakened me. A man was talking: "Excuse me for awakening you, but I looked all around first, at all the other passengers, and I decided you were the one I must talk to. I have to talk to someone. I am a *grand blessé de guerre,* and I am in great pain. When it is damp I suffer a great deal. The doctors can't help me. But if you will let me talk with you . . ." And he talked to me all the way to London. Karma? Destiny? Fatality?

My ideas usually come not at my desk writing but in the midst of living. It was while dancing in Harlem that I resolved the duality of my houseboat story. There were two ways of telling the story, and as I could not choose between them, I am telling both. A story on two levels. What happens by day and what happens in dreams at night. One story begins when I am sitting at the Café Flore and I see an advertisement in the paper: Houseboat for rent.

But the other version is of a visit I paid ten years earlier to the house of Maupassant in Étretat, Brittany. A storm had swept a fishing boat right into the garden and left it there. It had been turned into a tool shed. I had a dream about living in it, which later became a short story of a twenty-year journey in this boat which had suddenly started to sail during the night. The night dream, the story, and the realism must now fuse for a complete story. Realism: I saw the boat turned into a tool shed. Dream: I dreamt of sailing down an endless river in it. I wrote the story of the dream. I then began my search for a real houseboat, because I took the dream for an indication of a wish. I had so often dreamt about boats which were stranded for lack of water. The boat in the Maupassant garden left high and dry, unable to sail any more, stirred the memory of the recurrent dream. To exorcise the dream, or fulfill it, I sought a real houseboat and lived in it (also dreamt in it).

The symbolic or prophetic short story which described a journey of twenty years and a return to the point of departure was strangely fulfilled when my houseboat was ordered back to Neuilly, where I was born.

This story was not lost in my unconscious. It waited in the darkness of my memory to be fulfilled. It probably influenced my search for a houseboat, my renting one, occupying it, finding the river life I had dreamt of. In the Café Flore, when my eyes fell on the advertisement, dream burst into reality. I rewrote the story. It became stylized, it became mythical. A poem. The poem is a process of evaporation and distillation. To reach the quintessence is to reach the deepest meaning of a story.

I found a hearing aid for Helba. Gonzalo, Helba, and I went to try it out together. Gonzalo translated for Helba. When the earplug was in place and she was told to turn on the battery, she mimed the greatest amazement, like a primitive who had never heard music before. The salesman placed a watch next to her ear. Her face expressed maximum elation. Gonzalo was moved by her pleasure. "Now," he said, "she will be able to go out alone, to hear music, and to dance again." Did she hear him? One week later the hearing aid was stored away and the tragedy of Helba's deafness once more compared with Beethoven's.

Henry admires Kenneth Patchen's work. He sent Patchen to visit me. He loomed at my door, large, heavy, pale, and out of his small tight child's mouth a muttering that may have been a greeting. He sat heavy and stony in my small room. His eyes were soft, brilliant, but like those of an animal, with no recognition, no sign of personal focus, merely watchfulness. He saw the papers scattered on the desk, evinced no curiosity or interest. Conversation was arduous. There was an impenetrable wall of sullenness, a desire not to talk. He knew none of the books I knew. He said so little that later I had the greatest difficulty remembering whether he had spoken at all. I tried to understand him. I did not share Henry's enthusiasm for his writing. To me it seemed like the mumblings of a prisoner, inarticulate, repeating again and again without hitting the target, a dimly unfocused obsession.

He had come because I was the woman who had helped Henry. He wanted my help. Even though he saw the modesty of my room, with barely space for a table by the window, and even though I explained that my situation had changed because when I returned to America I had no longer the benefit of exchange from dollars to francs, and my income was reduced by half. I also explained that I was overburdened, still committed to friends in France, and that life in New York was far more expensive than Paris. "I paid ten dollars a month for my houseboat," I said, laughing. But Patchen did not smile. He did not hear me. A brooding, inert, heavy man. We could not talk. I was baffled by his sluggishness. I had never before encountered such an inarticulate man, without a spark of life or responsiveness.

I reread his manuscript with care, seeking to understand. It gave me a feeling of a force devouring itself, some process of destruction the opposite of Lawrence's phoenix rising from the ashes, of Henry's rebellions which gave birth to new forms of life. There was in the pages of Patchen a perpetual suicide and no rebirth.

Inert and blighted. Henry told me that when Patchen was young he worked as a laborer, cleaning the insides of gas tanks, and that he had fallen from a ladder and injured his back.

I went to visit him in his cold-water flat. His wife was big and strong. I wondered why she did not work for him, as so many wives of artists worked for their husbands. Sometime later in the evening

Patchen said, in connection with Abe Rattner's wife, who works very hard at fashion reporting: "No wife of mine will ever take a job."

I was working on *Under a Glass Bell*. I could no longer face the weight of Patchen's presence, the laborious, one-sided effort at communicating. I no longer answered the bell.

I am in debt again.

Something has happened to all of us who have been uprooted. Human beings wither at first like plants at a rough change of climate. We look for places to sit where one is not rushed out, told to drink our coffee and leave as others are waiting for the table. We found an Italian expresso place on Macdougal Street, with only eight or ten small tables, where Italians linger and play chess, and there we are allowed to sit and talk over a coffee.

The war news is so terrible that it causes a kind of catalepsy. To revive I plunge into writing.

Jean Carteret was mobilized. But Jean won't die. Though I think of him as a magical being, my last image of him in Paris I would like to erase. His passion for objects was carried to the extreme, so that when he came to my apartment to pick up the record player I was giving him, and a few books, he began to rummage through my wastepaper baskets like a ragpicker, collecting broken boxes, combs, rags, worn-out zippers, strings, empty medicine bottles, old magazines.

Poor Jean, my opium dreamer, dragged into the inferno of war. And Moricand begging, begging with elegant letters and literary images, and I unable to answer all the needs any more.

It was always more difficult to believe in Moricand's suffering because of the mysterious alchemy which makes the poet turn his life into a symbol, bread into wafer, and cover his poverty with literary glamor, literary associations, with the poverty of William Blake, of Erik Satie, of Modigliani. The relation of his life to the history of other astrologers, poets, mystics, the death by starvation of other gallant figures, situated him in a realm which seemed beyond human compassion, but was in reality an act of courage known only to stage people, to actors and performers.

Great changes in Henry. In Greece it was poetic intoxication and detachment. Here the meeting with his dying father completely humanized him, touched off a deep source of pity so that now he is acting as I acted: he is full of sympathy. He gives me absolution for the sacrifices he once made fun of.

A private collector offers him a hundred dollars a month to write erotic stories. It seems like a Dantesque punishment to condemn Henry to write erotica at a dollar a page. Henry rebels, because his mood of the moment is the opposite of Rabelaisian. Because writing to order is a castrating occupation, because to be writing with a voyeur at the keyhole takes all the spontaneity and pleasure out of his fanciful adventures.

[May, 1940]

Invasion of Holland.
Invasion of Belgium.
Five-hundred-thousand dead.
The Germans cross the French border.
Impossible to think of anything else, to feel anything else.

No place to sit and talk. You are rushed by the waitress. The radios blare so loudly one is deafened. The lights stun you. Noise and light are amplified until the senses become dulled.

The news is terrible.

In Europe the machines are killing people. Here the machines seem to have dehumanized people. There are few amenities, the softening use of courtesy to palliate the cruelties of life. Under the guise of honesty people are brutal to each other.

"The court was stunned by the man's calm description of six killings."

The voices over the radio are flat and toneless. The white people's dancing seems like a parody of Negro dances. Beauty is missing. Writing is flat and one-dimensional. Each political party outdoes itself in hurling low-brow insults and fanatical accusations.

I rented a furnished apartment on Washington Square West. The Village has character, atmosphere. The houses are old, the shops small. In the Square old Italians play chess on stone tables. There are trees, patios, back yards. It has a history. The university was built by the Dutch. I love the ginkgo trees, the studio windows, the small theaters, Bleecker Street with its vegetable carts, fish shops, cheese shops. It is human. People stroll about. They sit in the park.

My bed is convertible, which means it vanishes into a closet. I am always afraid it will do this while I am asleep.

Millicent Fredericks, the cleaning woman, is full of dignity, pride and spirit. She comes from Antigua, where she was a schoolteacher and where there was no prejudice against the Negro. She is half-Portuguese, half-African. She has fine features, which a Gauguin would have enjoyed painting. She tells me about her life in Harlem, about her four children, about her American Negro husband, who was a tailor but who grew "careless" (meaning he would not work any more). She has a beautiful face, gently curling hair, fine big eyes, a generous mouth. She has fine manners, and is deeply religious.

She was one of many children. When they did not have enough to eat they went to the sugar factories and ate the molasses discarded by the refineries. When she came to America and married, she could not get a job as a teacher. She is not a United States citizen.

She is resigned to doing housework. She works in my neighborhood for several families.

She tells me how she could not sleep the night before because of the neighbors' brawling. Their apartments are so badly built and so close together they hear radios and quarrels even from the house next door. The police had come.

In the subway, on her way downtown, a white woman had insulted her. In the bus, when she takes a seat, white passengers move to another seat.

Dark, tragic days. The Germans thirty-six miles from Paris. Italy invaded France. I turn against Russia because she believes war will hasten the revolution, and have bitter arguments with Gonzalo.

Desperate at the news. Paris encircled. Near surrender. Ill with pain, darkness, horror, chaos.

One evening Caresse telephoned: "You must come and see two young poets who have come all the way from Des Moines to meet you and Miller."

Henry and I had dinner in a Chinese restaurant first, then we went up to Caresse's apartment. Lafe Young was short and almost anonymous behind huge dark glasses, all stuttering and nervousness. John Dudley was tall and lean, handsome, with curly blond hair, brilliant blue eyes, a skin as clear as a woman's, a rich voice, sensitive hands. I could well believe him when he told me he was a descendant of the Earl of Dudley, the favorite of Queen Elizabeth. His ancestors owned the Kenilworth Castle of Walter Scott's novel, which once enchanted me. He has vitality, an alert, leaping quality, faith, fervor, humility. He draws and writes, and plays jazz. His drawings were studies of jazz musicians. Lafe and John are starting a magazine called *Generation.* I invited them to visit me. We all went up to Harlem to hear a drummer he liked. He joined the musicians and played with them.

Later, instead of dancing, he wanted to talk with me. We sat on one of the window sills so the music would not drown out our talk. He was like a radiant vision of the future, the symbol of another life. He knew intuitively I was hovering between two worlds, one dying, the other yet unknown. "Anaïs, stay here. We need you. I drove all the way from Des Moines just to know you."

I answered, "You can help me enter American life."

"Anaïs, read my writing, look at my drawings. Listen to my drumming." Nimble hands. Quick tempo. Eagerness. Laughter. The world of jazz, the language of jazz musicians, a certain rhythm he has acquired from them.

"If I were American born," I said, "I would write the equivalent of jazz. You're a white Negro, you have their rhythm and their warmth."

John does not know Europe. He is young and without a past.

I invited him to Kay and Yves' housewarming. But first he wanted to make a drawing of me.

While he worked I noticed he was wearing a ring too tight for his finger. I could not bear to see the constriction. I asked him to take it off. He took it off and as a symbol of his expansion never wore it again.

Lafe and John are staying near Caresse. They were leaning out of their window when I arrived. They sat surrounded by cans of beer. We talked while John worked.

He is explosive, active, with an electric personality. This was his first visit to New York. He was finding it difficult to interest anyone in the magazine, or to raise money for it. So they cannot stay.

He repeats: "What can I give you? What can I do for you?"

I said: "You rescued me from living in the past."

He initiates me into the history of jazz.

Henry took all of us to 662 Briggs Avenue in Brooklyn, where he spent nine years of his childhood. Henry talked about his childhood. The night was beautiful. *Black Spring,* the pages of *Black Spring* were coming to life. Henry's rich and bursting past. Games, terrors, disillusions, fears, drolleries. They sound more human in the summer night, less heightened but more moving.

[July, 1940]

Caresse invited me to her home in Bowling Green, Virginia.

I flew to Richmond and was met by John Payne and Henry. We drove through soft rolling hills, richly covered fields, past small lakes, trees heavily draped with moss, profusion of ferns, flower bushes, trailing vines.

As we arrived, Caresse was supervising the tying up and loading of wheat sheaves. As they were thrown into the truck, the wheat dust flew around her, lighted by the sun like a gold Venetian halo. She wore a huge straw hat and moved in her typical way with airiness and freedom.

The car continued along a circular driveway and there stood Hampton Manor, a Southern version of the enchanted house of *Le Grand Meaulnes,* the enchanted house of Louveciennes. White, classical, serene, symmetrical, with its tall graceful columns, its terraces of tiles, and the noble proportions of doors and windows, a little taller and a little wider than ordinary windows.

Weeping willows arched over it, moss grew like soft carpets at its feet, trailing vine embraced it. The rooms were high-ceilinged, large, harmonious, uncluttered, with shining parquet floors. Negro servants glided gently about. The dream of *Under a Glass Bell* in American Southern style.

Outside, in the twilight, whippoorwills, other bird calls, a concert of crickets buzzing with delight at the heat, at the waves of heat rising from the perfumed ground.

The library a treasure room. Caresse showed me a few of the Black Sun Press editions, with their sun symbol stamped on the book covers. The diary of Harry Crosby, published in 1931.

On the wall hung Max Ernst's portrait of her, an abstraction composed of a curled, frilled flower heart which might have been the heart of a starched, undulating petticoat, the heart of a ballet skirt, the heart of a sea shell. With this he had portrayed the femininity and charm of Caresse, the honeyed, consenting, inviting, assenting, agreeing, receptive, yielding flower heart which drew everyone around her.

I would have painted her as a pollen grain flying through the air and seeding one personality with another, as she loved to encourage all forms of insemination among her friends. She liked artistic and creative copulation in all its forms and expressions, interracial, sexual, spiritual. Caresse the pollen bearer. She never looked back, she was never turned to stone, she wept over Paris but she had already created the first place of beauty I had seen in America, the first hearth, the first open house. She felt that everything could be transplanted and would thrive. This would be another Mill, and where before there were Paul Éluard, René Crevel, D. H. Lawrence, Ezra Pound, Hart Crane, James Joyce, now she had invited Henry, Salvador Dali, other artists, and she opened her house to those yet unborn, the young, being also the mother of potential artists. Now with all of us sitting around her table she was happy.

Her gift for friendship was the central link. She seemed innocent of all diplomacy or ingenuity as she sat at the head of the table, rubbing her eyes, smoothing her face burned by the sun, flicking her tongue, her small pink tongue, with epicurean delight at our projects and activities.

In the morning everyone worked. It was the freshest moment of the day. The hypnotic heat would come in the afternoon when all of us took siestas. In the late afternoon it was wonderful to walk through the fields and woods. Around the big manor house were small cabins inhabited by the Negro farmers and their families. The children were shy and hid behind trees, but now and then we would come upon them playing naked by the side of a pond. The little girls' hair was braided in dozens of small braids, tied at the tip by bright ribbons. Their eyes were soft, round, startled.

Henry was adding pages to the second part of *Tropic of Capricorn.*

The Dalis arrived but were tired and went up to their room. The next day John Dudley and his wife, Flo, arrived.

The Dalis appeared for breakfast. Both small in stature, they sat close together. Both were unremarkable in appearance, she all in moderate tones, a little faded, and he drawn with charcoal like a child's drawing of a Spaniard, any Spaniard, except for the incredible length of his mustache. They turned towards each other as if for protection, reassurance, not open, trusting or at ease. Dudley was suspicious. Was Dali truly mad? Was it a pose? Was he spontaneously eccentric or calculatingly so?

They wanted me to solve this riddle because I could speak Spanish, but they had not foreseen the organizational powers of Mrs. Dali. Before we were even conscious of it, the household was functioning for the well-being of Dali. We were not allowed to enter the library because he was going to work there. Would Dudley mind driving to Richmond and trying to find odds and ends which Dali needed for his painting? Would I mind translating an article for him? Would Caresse invite *Life* magazine to come and visit?

So we each fulfilled our appointed tasks. Mrs. Dali never raised her voice, never seduced or charmed. Quietly she assumed we were all there to serve Dali, the great, indisputable genius.

I cooked a Spanish dish, hoping to establish a Spanish atmosphere in which he might expand. But Mrs. Dali does not care for Spanish cooking.

One morning we heard that Caresse's publishing plans had failed. So we sat around and discussed the possibilities of setting up a press at Hampton Manor. We walked to the barn to look it over as a possible print shop, but it was too open, windy, and unprotected. We would not be able to heat it. Then we examined a small house once built for the servants, a lovely little white house with natural, unpainted wood inside, and many rooms. It was perfect. This would solve John Dudley's problem too; he was penniless and had nowhere to go. He was a good craftsman and would run the press.

Caresse wanted to publish *Nadja* by André Breton, translated by Eugene Jolas, a novel of Kay Boyle's, Memoirs of Marianne Oswald, a book by Blaise Cendrars, Raymond Radiguet, Miller, and myself.

One evening when everyone was out, Caresse and I talked intimately. She told me delightful stories. One about her second marriage. Soon after the honeymoon her husband was drafted. She went to visit him during one of his leaves. But the town was so full there were no hotel rooms to be found. They did not want to separate, and so they walked through fields and woods. Deep inside of a trench in an exercise area he put his coat down and they made love and fell asleep together. Early in the morning, they were awakened by a thundering noise. Over their very bodies horses were leaping across the trenches. Cavalry officers were practicing at dawn!

After Harry Crosby committed suicide, she stayed at the Mill and the house was full of guests. Three of the guests were her lovers. This did not dismay her. She placed each one in a different wing of the house, and visited them at different hours.

When I went again to Hampton Manor, Caresse was away, the atmosphere had changed. The meals were marred by undercurrents of hostility. Mrs. Dali did not speak much English so conversations were in French, which humiliated Flo and John Dudley. Mrs. Dali's demands were overpowering. John was tired of running errands. Flo felt alienated from the international art talks. John was irritated by Dali's cheerful and continuous industriousness. Dali painted every day, whistling and singing.

Henry was irritated by Mrs. Dali's cuddling of Dali. Henry resorted to his favorite weapon: contrariness and contradiction. Everything Dali said was wrong. There was something wrong even with his preference for lamb! I liked to hear Dali talk. He was full of inventions and wild fantasies. John and Henry were annoyed when we talked Spanish. Mrs. Dali was on her guard against me. Dali liked me and lost his shyness when I came. He showed me his work.

Henry was writing about Greece.

But the enchantment was vanishing. The plan for publication was abandoned. Caresse did not have the money for the initial cost. John did not want to do all the work. I could not come often enough to be useful.

On the day of John's birthday we found a pack of cards strewn around his Model A Ford. I picked up only the ones with their faces up and asked the Negro cook to read his fate. He said they were all lucky ones.

The Negro gardener had an evil-looking boil on his thumb. John and I offered to take him to the hospital.

Driving along, the distant roads look wet, and as one approaches them they are absolutely dust dry. Mirage. Branches of the trees are wrapped in cocoons, spider webs, dried leaves and dried insects lying tangled in gowns of white fog and dew, and threads of silver fluid hang down, from which the cocoons will weave their silvery pockets, their snowy-white wings of crystallized saliva.

There was a pool crowded with headless trees.

The air was languid. The trees were languid. Negro children stared at us and grinned. The cicadas sang with drunken exhilaration.

While the gardener was at the hospital, we swam in the Potomac, and then sat in a café to wait for him.

John had been writing about the death of Europe, of Europe's artists. I listened and then I said: "John, if you want to make air and space and room for your own work and work for the future, do so, but don't bury us prematurely because as you can see from Dali's work, from Henry's writing, and from my own which you say nourishes you, we are far from dead. In fact, we are more alive and more productive than you. You are preparing to live, preparing to work. Don't deny the sources of your nourishment. Even if your work is totally different, as well it may be, even if you invent a new kind of painting, a new kind of writing, it is more generous to salute your ancestors. Can you imagine your future?"

"It is true, I cannot imagine my future."

"Possibly because you are rejecting the past. The future takes its nourishment from the past and then converts it, produces a new alchemy. Feed on us before you bury us."

This hurt him, because he had been feeding on Henry's work and mine, but he also was angry and wanted to be free of us because he could not overcome his confusions, his chaos, his uncertainties, his abortions, his need of us, his need of standing alone.

His eyes filled with tears: "You came from a sunken Atlantis." (Again! How eager they are to imagine Europe sunken, and they able to create a new world!) "A lost world, you are a survivor of a lost world. You have seen death, but you have not died. You and Henry are more alive than the artists of my age."

At night, as we walked out of the house, the lighted rooms look like the rooms in Chirico paintings, and the ponds like Max Ernst's scenes of stagnant pools. Our bare feet in sandals feel the wet grass tickling. At night insects beat their wings against the screens. The nights lie around us like an abyss of sensual warmth, awakening the senses, almost palpable. They are like a caress on the skin. Wherever the earth can breathe, our bodies breathe, too, and the pulse of nature sets our own pulse beating. Tropical nights are hammocks for lovers.

[September, 1940]

While I was away *Life* magazine came to photograph the place. A piano was hauled up with pulleys to the top of an ancient tree. Levitation must be encouraged. Dali was at his easel.*

While I was away there were other happenings. Caresse was divorcing her Southern gentleman husband. He had heard that Caresse had filled her house with artists. He arrived one night, opened all the doors and turned on all the lights. Alas, there was no orgy! He found Mr. and Mrs. Dali asleep in one room, Caresse asleep in another room, Henry alone in another room, John and Flo Dudley asleep in another room. He ordered everyone to leave, but as no one paid any attention to him, he rushed down the stairs, shouting that he would destroy all of Dali's paintings. At this the Dalis became alarmed, they dressed, ran downstairs, packed all the paintings and drove away.

The general obsession with observing only historical or sociological movements, and not a particular human being (which is considered with such righteousness here) is as mistaken as a doctor who does not take an interest in a particular case. Every particular case is an experience that can be valuable to the understanding of the illness.

There is an opacity in individual relationships, and an insistence that the writer make the relation of the particular to the whole which makes for a kind of farsightedness. I believe in just the opposite. Every individual is representative of the whole, a symptom, and should be intimately understood, and this would give a far greater understanding of mass movements and sociology.

Also, this indifference to the individual, total lack of interest in intimate knowledge of the isolated, unique human being, atrophies human reactions and humanism. Too much social consciousness, and not a bit of insight into human beings.

* The photograph appeared in *Life*, April 7, 1941.—Ed.

44

As soon as you speak in psychological terms (applying under-standing of one to the many is not the task of the novelist but of the historian) people act as if you had a lack of interest in the wider currents of the history of man. In other words, they feel able to study masses and consider this more virtuous, a sign of a vaster concept, than relating to one person. This makes them, as I observe in Dorothy Norman's salon, inadequate in relationships, in friend-ships, in psychological understanding.

Around her, talk is entirely of ideas, not of people. And if art is our relation to the senses, then they have none. They argue. Mean-while, their human reflexes are totally absent. A Negro is an idea, a concept. To me he is a person, Millicent perhaps, who becomes a symbol of what they have to endure.

There is a harshness, too, a hard surface from which I shrink. I feel no sympathy or empathy. Just concepts. Any sign of feeling affects them like a breach of morality. The constant relation to figures (masses) seems to destroy the sense of humanity, very much, I imagine, as a general loses his feeling for his soldier as a man, and sees him only as a number in an army. The artists are a good antidote to inexpressive, deadpan faces.

I wrote the story of Hans Reichel, the painter, from notes in the diary. Strange days of loneliness and inner fire. What is memory? Can it be inherited over centuries? My love of Hampton Manor inherited from the first relatives who came to New Orleans from France? If we inherit character traits, why not also memories?

What I like in John Dudley is his rhythm. Rhythm is what I most like about America. The language of jazz musicians has savor, color, vibrancy. The reflectiveness, reverie, of Europe is not possible because of the tempo. This tempo prevents experience from seeping in, sinking in, penetrating.

I respond to intensity, but I also like reflection to follow action, for then understanding is born, and understanding prepares me for the next day's acts.

My social consciousness is different from that of the Americans. It is not expressed in group work, in collective activity. It consists in giving help to the exceptional person who is struggling to educate himself, who is gifted but has no opportunities, no guidance.

My lack of faith in the men who lead us is that they do not recognize the irrational in men, they have no insight, and whoever does not recognize the personal, individual drama of man cannot lead them.

Psychology has ceased to be for me a mere therapy for neurotic moments. It is not only the neurotic who lives by irrational impulses rooted deeply in his experience, but everyone. This may be more or less masked by outward conventionalities. This individual irrational should be isolated and understood before it becomes an aggregate. The masses are merely an accumulation of such blind impulses. Nations, leaders, history, could be analyzed and understood as nonrational behavior can be.

In fact, most of the time the leaders have been those who symbolized nonrational emotions for the masses and therefore their negative, or destructive tendencies.

After much searching I found an apartment I could afford. Sixty dollars a month, a skylight studio, on the top floor of 215 West Thirteenth Street. Five flights up. A very large, high-ceilinged room, half of the ceiling an inclined skylight, the whole length of it, twelve windows in all. A small kitchen, with barely enough room for stove and icebox. A small bathroom. A door opening on a terrace about nine by twelve feet, overlooking back yards and the back of a factory, but one can smell the Hudson when there is a breeze.

I bought simple unpainted furniture, beds, large worktables. The previous tenants left a brown wall-to-wall carpet. I covered this with American Indian serapes.

Dorothy Norman will publish my essay "Woman in the Myth," inspired by all I wrote about Hélène in Paris.

I write every day. I wrote about the Rue Dolent, Pedrito, the clubfooted shoemaker who loved to watch people walking by his cellar shop. He could see only their feet. Pages on Paris life. Atmosphere. I do not know yet where they are leading me.

Henry said of Dali's work: "The River Styx, the river of neurosis that does not flow."

He also said that what I call "inhuman" is what he defines as "beyond the human."

Beautiful autumn days. I love the Village. I love the Italian shops selling homemade spaghetti and fresh cheese, the vegetable carts which sell small fruit, small vegetables, not the tasteless giant ones. Macdougal Street is colorful. The Mews, and Macdougal Alley, with beautiful small houses of another era, cobblestone streets and old street lamps. On Macdougal Street there are night clubs where they play a subtle, low-keyed jazz which occasionally explodes.

I sat on a bench in Washington Square and wrote the story of Artaud, a composite of real fragments from the diary and imaginary conversations.

Went to call for the condensed manuscript version of the diary. Charles Pearce, of Duell, Sloan and Pearce, said it was marvelous, but could only be published in a limited edition.

Caresse Crosby had a scheme. She wanted to bring the surrealists André Breton, Paul Éluard, Benjamin Peret, Pierre Mabille, *et al.*, to the United States. She thought of getting a boat herself. She went to Florida and found just what she needed, a secondhand boat, big enough to cross the ocean, to bring back all the artists who wanted to come! What a shipful that would have been!

When all the plans were made, and the surrealists had accepted, the boat sank while it was being launched.

The studio is A-shaped, and flooded with light. Next to my bed, I have a bookcase filled with books on one side, and on the other a table I bought in an antique shop. It is painted with scenes from Spanish history, and the top of it is like a tray with handles of wrought iron. Two lanterns are stuck at each end. Gonzalo tells me it is a feast table. On feast days it was carried to the entrances of churches and set up to sell refreshments. Candles were lighted inside the small lanterns.

It stands in the ascetic studio like a magical jewel in the plainest setting.

The first night I moved in there was a storm. A violent thunderstorm. I felt it was a bad omen. Is the war coming here, too? What is happening in the world is monstrous. Just as people are learning the use of gas masks, I feel I have to wear a mask of oxygen-giving dreams and work to keep alive the cells of creation as a defense against devastation. I do not want to become hard and callous as other people are doing around me. They shrug their shoulders and don another layer of indifference.

Henry is preparing to leave for his tour of America. People have not responded to his marvelous book on Greece [*The Colossus of Maroussi*].

Gonzalo tells me all the stories of the maltreated, the exploited, the enslaved, the persecuted.

Millicent tells me about Harlem. Her dignity, her bearing, her fine eyes, and face touch me. The very first day she came to me sent by my mother, and she sat sewing, the thread rolled to the floor and I picked it up for her. This gesture established the quality of our relationship. She has a total absence of servility, and she liked my attitude. I respect her and she is loyal and devoted.

I cannot reconcile the constant talk about democracy and sociology, with such harsh prejudices, and such dogmatic, puritanical narrow-mindedness.

Sometimes I think of Paris not as a city but as a home. Enclosed, curtained, sheltered, intimate. The sound of rain outside the window, the spirit and the body turned towards intimacy, to friendships and loves. One more enclosed and intimate day of friendship and love, an alcove. Paris intimate like a room. Everything designed for intimacy. Five to seven was the magic hour of the lovers' rendezvous. Here it is the cocktail hour.

New York is the very opposite of Paris. People's last concern is with intimacy. No attention is given to friendship and its development. Nothing is done to soften the harshness of life itself. There is much talk about the "world," about millions, groups, but no warmth between human beings. They persecute subjectivity, which is a sense of inner life; an individual's concern with growth and self-development is frowned upon.

Subjectivity seems to be in itself a defect. No praise or compliments are given, because praise is politeness and all politeness is hypocrisy. Americans are proud of telling you only the bad. The "never-talk-about-yourself" taboo is linked with the most candid, unabashed self-seeking, and selfishness.

If people knew more about psychology they would have recognized in Hitler a psychotic killer. Nations are neurotic, and leaders can be psychotic.

The ivory tower of the artist may be the only stronghold left for human values, cultural treasures, man's cult of beauty.

[October, 1940]

Henry has begun his odyssey of America.

Gonzalo has not been caught in the great machine of political ideologies which sacrifices individual lives for theories that pass, crumble, change, and are corrupt at the core.

Against hatred, power and fanaticism, systems and plans, I oppose love and creation, over and over again, in spite of the insanity of the world.

We live in an era of destruction. Destruction and creation are sometimes balanced: great wars, great cultures. But now destruction is predominant. People die for systems that are masks for personal power and gain. Against them I close the door of a small but loving world, cells of devotion, care, work, to fight the disease and madness of the world. A small world has sometimes defeated great systems born of delusions.

The forces of destruction and insanity are now spreading to Greece, bombarding Athens. Incredible nightmare.

Visited the Patchens. Something baffles me here which I never experienced before. I feel at times as if I were living in a Kafka nightmare of closed faces, silence, inexpressiveness. People do not reveal themselves, they do not seem even present. I miss the warmth and flowering which creates bridges. Patchen has nothing to say. His work, in spite of Henry's praise, seems to me like that of a sword swallower, swallowing itself, a hymn to destruction. He seems blind and deaf to others. His wife said to me: "You should not read Dostoevsky. He was a drunkard and a gambler, who beat his wife."

John Dudley arrived with Lafe Young. On my couch he spread his new drawings, and two hundred pages of writing; he talked about his birth, his faith, his strength. The mother of artists has given birth again. He wears a corduroy hat from Kenosha, he demands my presence to become an artist. He also demands five dollars for a quart of Scotch although I showed him that that was all the cash I had in my pocketbook and it was for buying food. I had just sent money to Henry, who was stranded in a small town with a punctured tire. Henry is traveling through America while Greece is being bombarded. How wonderful that he preserved his experience, his vision of Greece, from disaster.

Forty-five volumes of the Diary are lost. In Paris they were packed and expedited in a box, and the box disappeared en route to the ship.

The Communists accuse the capitalists of destroying the artist, but they are completing the job by their persecution of the imagination and the dream, which is the laboratory of the unconscious, where the psyche exists and breeds, and where man's inner nature is allowed to live and create.

By forcing the artist to become aware of his responsibilities as father, son, citizen, they take the same attitude as the *bourgeoisie* who insist that he share the burdens from which the artist sought to free himself, in order to perform another service, as impersonal, as necessary to the world as other services. The artist is tutoring the soul, civilizing the savage in us, necessary to a humane society. The artist may be obliged to reject the Communist pressure to use him in jobs for which he is not fitted.

When the artist is forced to enter the immediate present, he loses his own peculiar perspective which enables him to connect and relate past, present, and future.

There is a confusion here about the nature of the service he can render. To say that the artist is not serving humanity is monstrous. He has been the eyes, the ears, the voice of humanity. He was always the transcendentalist who X-rayed our true states of being.

His role in European culture is clear enough. Here he is given an inferior status, because he is not obviously and directly useful. His usefulness cannot be measured. The artist cannot serve directly. Proust made a deeper study of a servant, Françoise, than any dedicated proletarian writer. Mike Gold, in the *Daily Worker,* calls any poem born of revolutionary struggles great. Man is forbidden to concern himself with anything but the struggle for bread. If his capacity for dreaming, imagining, inventing, and experimenting is killed in the process, man will become a well-fed robot and die of spiritual malnutrition. The dream has its function and man cannot live without it.

What a writer must ask himself today is which of the two roles he is best equipped to fill. Is he a breadwinner and a revolutionary in the world of action, or a breadwinner and a revolutionary in the world of the spirit? The man of spirit is needed to re-create in terms of art a world erected by the materialists. If this alchemy is destroyed, then the *meaning* of everything we achieve will be destroyed, too, because it is the artist who gives the meaning, as well as the religious man.

Throughout the ages man has dreamt in order to create a larger world, and to dream he has to use language figuratively (which reveals the presence of meaning in otherwise empty acts); to dream he has to transcend reality and he cannot be drafted into action. He has to make his own detours (to gain philosophical and psychological perspective) or he becomes a reporter. If the artist cannot practice this transmutation, then no one can, and we become animals again. People forget that the artist deals in symbols, that is, reality illumined by the soul.

Cathedrals were created after Catholicism. A truly communistic literature will be born long after practical Communism. As soon as John Steinbeck wrote about the tragedy of the Okies, he was hailed as a great writer. What a confusion of values!

Literature, the ultimate gift for expressing the most subtle aspects of man's thought and feeling, may not survive persecution: first by religion, then by the *bourgeoisie,* then by Marxism, and now by commercialism.

The intellectuals are saying the moment is too tragic for literature, that this is the moment for action. If so, where, in which chambers of the brain will thought and interpretation, the guide to action, exist?

It may be this obscure instinct which has made renegades of the writers who were Marxists a few years ago. Writers can influence revolutions and evolutions only with their own weapons. Clichés never converted anyone but hysterical crowds.

John Dudley came to stay in New York, to take a studio, to work. He came expecting help from me, money, support, active devotion, inspiration. Anaïs, find me a studio. Anaïs, I need a painting teacher. Anaïs, take us to hear some jazz. Anaïs, find a backer for our magazine. Anaïs, help me to write, help me become an artist.

For the first time in my life I cleanly cut the umbilical cord. There are words I can no longer say, words I have said too many times. They die on my lips. I can no longer say to John: "Don't be afraid," when he trembles before a room full of people.

They sleep late. They drink all day. "We must find a cheap studio, but I am a child. I don't know how to go about it." I cut advertisements out of the paper and gave them to John. But John said: "I'll wait until you can come with us."

The same week Robert Duncan asked me for money. Henry telegraphed me asking for money for his return trip.

I believe the maternal in me, the mother, has been properly devoured, to the last bit, and she is dead.

Dinner at Dorothy Norman's. The same subdued, formal, arctic climate. But after dinner Luise Rainer arrived in a long, white, floating dress, her hair floating, her gestures light and graceful, flowing too, a mobile, fluid quality and radiance. Her face expressive, animated, showing as it did in her films a greater sadness than the role called for. She has a childlike impulsiveness, swinging between gentleness and sudden quick decisions.

Her face is small, her eyes dark and mischievous, her neck so slender one feels immediately protective. Her voice has a whispering quality, her laughter is tentative and subdued. Muted tones, yet eloquent, arresting.

She can reach extremes of feminine coquetry as in *Frou-Frou*, or extremes of self-sacrifice as in *The Great Waltz*. Even in this formal room she remained as exposed as she did in her acting, revealing tenderness, vulnerability, feminine provocativeness, devotion. In her acting she gives herself while remaining true to herself, and she was doing the same that evening. She wears no make-up, she repudiates the outer signs of her stardom as an actress. I always thought her one of the most moving figures in film acting. And here she was, soft, yielding, imperious, pliant, seeming deeper than anyone around her emotionally, making them all appear suddenly wooden, trapped in their clothes, unable to move. Her tragic face makes every role seem deeper, and now when she lifts her eyelids, the story is lost and there appears a woman with a sadness older than the world.

Her authoritarianism is that of a child, and I respond to it and loved her instantly.

Letter from Henry:

. . . The college at Black Mountain was in a superb Tibetan setting. When I'm driving I'm in a sort of trance. It's really superb and sufficient in itself, and apparently inexhaustible. It's only when we stop, when we hit the towns, the restaurants, the people, that everything pales. There are two worlds always—the day and the night. The country belongs to the Indians and the Negroes—that seems quite definite to me. The white man has brought only ugliness and misery to the picture. The postcards of Ducktown, Tennessee, give only a faint idea of the devastation which goes on. Imagine an area of fifty square miles so poisoned by the fumes of the copper plant that everything is killed off and the earth itself made to look like a convulsive red scar! Grand to see in a way, like a Doré illustration of the Inferno. But what a place for men to live in. . . .

Henry returns from his wanderings. He tells me about America. He reads me sections he has written. He has been looking for something to love. Nature, yes, that was extraordinary. He tells me about the stalactite cave, the wonders of it, and how they placed in it a radio because it was the best place for a receiving station! Henry is not impressed with size, power. He looks for a deeper America. He tells me about the ugly places and the beautiful places.

In order to extract the essence, I feel, one has to distill. American writers, Thomas Wolfe for instance, were overwhelmed by the bigness of America, and sought to render this by cataloguing its multitude of rivers, mountains, cities, its billion faces. What he described was quantity, gigantism, and not its *greatness*. The symbol was invented for just such a condensation. If a writer is overwhelmed by the physical vastness of what he has to cover, he can deal with it only by condensing it into a quality, not physical numbers. When I hear the loudest factory whistle in the world, hear the most raucous of all wailing ship sirens, see the enormity of the machines in factories, I am not impressed. It is material. The human adventure, human receptivity, has to find a way to make one *feel* power, force, but not by mathematics.

In Europe, enlightenment came from the few, and they led. Now the few are oppressed and the masses rule. The mass is not yet educated, and it is not led by the brains of the country but by the salesmen who are selling, not educating.

At this moment Henry is angry; it may be a personal account he has to settle with America. I am not angry but I seek desperately for the sensitive and human America. But I feel anger and violence in the air.

With Henry a wealth of talk, ideas, impressions, excitement in writing, descriptions, storytelling. He is always good-humored when he is not a reformer.

He looks fragile, but ageless, merely a little tired from big nights, harassed by invitations and people's dependence on him. Because here people turn to him for help. He has pushed Patchen. He read the *Journal of Albion Moonlight,* praised it, advertised it. He is asked to solve problems, to help, to write letters, to beg for others. The first volume of *The Rosy Crucifixion* lies on his desk. His life with June. We have dinner together at a Chinese restaurant.

He was still in a daze about his wanderings through America, trying to sort out his impressions.

It occurred to me that the radio receiving station at the bottom of the stalactite caves in Virginia was a marvelously symbolical scene. Another scene which seemed meaningful to me was one we saw in a vaudeville show. A man was singing, standing next to a phonograph. Suddenly something went wrong with the machine, and then one saw that the man had not been singing but making the motion of singing by moving his lips, and that all along the song came from the phonograph record. A voice came from the machine and said: "Now you're on your own." The man had no voice. I would have started the American journey book right there. We laughed.

Henry told me about the book collector. They sometimes have lunch together.

He bought a manuscript from Henry and then suggested that he write something for one of his old and wealthy clients. He could not tell much about his client except that he was interested in erotica.

Henry started out gaily, jokingly. He invented wild stories which we laughed over.

Henry entered into it as an experiment, and it seemed easy at first. But after a while it palled on him. He did not want to touch upon any of the material he planned to write about for his real work, so he was condemned to force his inventions and his mood.

Henry never received a word of acknowledgment from this strange patron. It could be natural that he would not want to disclose his identity. But Henry began to tease the collector. Did this patron really exist? Were these pages for the collector himself, to heighten his own melancholy life? Were they one and the same person?

Henry and I discussed this at length, puzzled and amused.

At this point, the collector announced that his client was coming to New York and that Henry would meet him. But somehow this meeting never took place.

The collector was lavish in his descriptions of how he sent the manuscripts by airmail, how much it cost, small details meant to add realism to the claims he made about his client's existence.

One day he wanted a copy of *Black Spring* with a dedication.

Henry said: "But I thought you told me he had all my books already, signed editions?"

"He lost his copy of *Black Spring*."

"Who should I dedicate it to?" said Henry innocently.

"Just say to a good friend, and sign your name."

Henry said, "He must be real."

A few weeks later Henry needed a copy of *Black Spring* and none could be found. He decided to borrow the collector's copy. He went to the office. The secretary told him to wait. Henry began to look over the books in the bookcase. He saw a copy of *Black Spring*. He pulled it out: It was the one he had dedicated to the "Good Friend."

When the collector came in, Henry told him about this, laughing. In equally good humor, he explained: "Oh, yes, the old man got so impatient that I sent him my own copy while I was waiting to get this one signed by you, intending to exchange them later when he comes to New York *again*."

Henry said to me when we met: "I'm more baffled than ever."

When Henry asked what the patron's reaction to his writing was, the collector said: "Oh, he likes everything. It is all wonderful. But he likes it better when it is a narrative, just storytelling, no analysis, no philosophy."

When Henry needed money for his travel expenses he suggested that I do some writing in the interim. I felt I did not want to give anything genuine, and decided to create a mixture of stories heard, inventions, pretending they were from the diary of a woman.

I never met the collector. He was to read my pages and to let me know what he thought.

Today I received a telephone call. "It is fine. But leave out the poetry and descriptions of anything but sex. Concentrate on sex."

When I gave sensuous or poetic-erotic descriptions, the client would complain, so I began to write tongue-in-cheek, to become outlandish, inventive, and so exaggerated that I thought he would realize I was caricaturing sexuality. But there was no protest.

I spent days in the library studying the *Kama Sutra*, listened to friends' most extreme adventures and wrote:

Bijou was enormously interested in psychic phenomena, in hypnotists and clairvoyants. She loved to have her fortune told. Her painted eyes, her heavily powdered face, her walk, her hoarse voice all proclaimed her profession, but when she entered the semilighted rooms of card readers, crystal-ball readers, etc., she felt innocent, and open to any romantic predictions.

She heard of an African from the Belgian Congo who was a famous soothsayer. All the women in her neighborhood had gone to visit him. The parlor in which she had to wait was ordinary, anonymous, all except for the big black Chinese curtain hanging in front of the magician's lair. It was covered with embroideries in gold thread of dragons spitting red fire and with eyes of green jade.

Each time the African lifted it he glanced at the people waiting, with green eyes which seemed to shine in the dark like the eyes of the dragon. He gave Bijou a heavy stare, and then vanished with the woman who had arrived before her.

Then came Bijou's turn. She found herself in a room which was dark except for the illumined globe in the center of the table. On the floor there were many pillows. The globe illumined his face and hands and nothing else. He wore a burnous.

Bijou explained that she wanted her fortune told but that she did not want to be hypnotized. The African told her she would get her wish but that first of all she must lie on the pillows and relax and close her eyes while he consulted the crystal ball. Bijou closed her eyes. He laid his hand on her forehead. It was warm and dry like sand. Then his voice came purring and warm:

"You are not happy, and when you are not happy you become very unfaithful."

"True," murmured Bijou.

"Rest," he ordered gently, "while I watch the crystal ball for signs about your future."

The softness of the pillows and of his voice lulled her.

"Sleep. You are drowsy, now, you keep your eyes closed, let the lids get heavier and heavier. Let your body get heavier and heavier, your legs, your shoulders, your head, your eyelids. Heavier and heavier."

Bijou felt heavy and drowsy but not unconscious. Her eyelids felt heavy, and she could not make the effort to open her eyes. But she felt her dress so lightly lifted that she could not be certain. It could have been a breeze. Lifted by a breeze. No human touch. The air was lifting her skirt it seemed, and exposing her silk-clad legs. Where the stockings ended she felt a light touch. As if a feather had been brushed against her skin. The touch was so light that it was as if the skin had a thousand tiny eyes and the touch had lifted their eyelids, and light and heat fell upon them, waves, currents, vibrations of response. Each tiny cell instead of contracting at the touch, expanded and became twice as sensitive. She never moved. Her deepest fear was that the hand should stop, grow timid, withdraw. She wanted to move, so as to place a leg a little more sideways, separate from the other so that the fingers could reach the inner skin which was more sensitive than the skin of the thighs.

The skin of her eyelids was invaded with a reddish sunset light. It was as if the skin cells had carried red wine, first to her eyes, and then through her neck down to her breasts. The tips of the breasts acknowledged the current of warmth. It could not be a man's hand. It must be silk, a feather, the hair of a soft animal like a rabbit. How slowly it worked its way upward, as if knowing it must wait for all the little cells to awaken, and follow, cumulatively aroused, and like rivulets, foaming towards the center, the edge of small waves of pleasure adding one to the other, increasing as the hand reached a softer and softer and softer skin. Sleep, said the voice, sleep, said the voice, and indeed all but the core and center of pleasure slept—an opium sleep filled with fleshly dreams, odorous, effervescent, humid and lush, this miniature jungle now entered by the finger, hair and pearly drops of woman's essence.

Woman's pearl was the center of this electrical storm, a hushed storm, whirling, wrapped in cotton but incandescent, streaks of lightning, the flesh become a lightning conductor, iridescent with light, striking gongs of pleasure; one, two, three.

Sleep, said the voice, but she had no desire to awaken to any fortune told but that of being a woman, who could feel in her body as keen a pleasure as a piercing beautiful piece of music, more pleasure than a sunrise or a sunset, more beauty than a lagoon spreading its iris surface, more intoxicating than the pistils of flowers and their pungent incense. . . .

"Less poetry," said the voice over the telephone. "Be specific."

But did anyone ever experience pleasure from reading a clinical description? Does not the old man know how words carry colors and sounds into the flesh?

A CABLE FROM PARIS. THE BOX OF DIARIES WAS TRACED AND FOUND LYING IN ONE OF THE SMALL FRENCH RAILROAD STATIONS. THE WAR HAD PASSED IT BY. IT WAS SHIPPED BACK TO THE BANK AND REPLACED IN THE VAULT.

Henry is experiencing for the first time being asked for help, to solve others' problems. He was amazed by the multiplication of the needs. When you help one, five more appear. For the first time I found Henry depressed because he had awakened suddenly to the needs of others. He was overwhelmed.

I said: "I have lived with this knowledge since I was a child."

"I can't bear it," said Henry.

Suddenly he was aware of his own situation, his problems unsolved. How was he living? He asked questions. He discovered that no sooner do I get my allowance than it is gone. The second day my pocket is empty. And then begin antics which wear out my energy. Borrowing, juggling, postponing, intrigue.

I confessed that I was growing physically unfit for the struggle. I am always short of money and in debt.

Henry was moved. I was sad to witness his awareness (his first moment of awareness came when he took care of his father); awareness brings sadness and heaviness. I would have preferred to keep Henry gay and insouciant.

The only time I ever asked him to accept coming to terms with commercial offers was with Doubleday. He was not pleased with the advance of five hundred dollars and had dreamt of more. He wanted to reject the entire effort and then I asked him to accept it because it would unburden me. Strange that as the mother dies of exhaustion, the children begin to awaken. Henry was not willfully selfish, but unconsciously so. And I did nothing to open his eyes. Henry's eyes were opened by the hardships endured by those who did not have anyone to lean on.

Edgar and Louise Varèse live on Sullivan Street, near Bleecker Street. Their house is built of red bricks. The back of it gives on a series of gardens belonging to houses of the same style and period. It looks European. The neighborhood is Italian. At number 188 I walk down a few steps and push a red door. Inside I ring two doorbells, one for Varèse's studio, which is on the level with the garden, and the other for the floor above, where the living room, dining room, and kitchen take on a green tint from the trees in the back yard. Sometimes Varèse opens the door to his studio, or I hear thunderous, Olympian sounds coming from there, and Louise appears at the top of the stairs to welcome me.

Varèse's glance has a lightning quality. His bushy eyebrows evoke a jungle growth. Louise Varèse is beautiful, with the beauty of the Anglo-American, lean, tall, blue-eyed, looking like the heroines of Edith Wharton and Henry James. A lady. A lady with a warm manner and a sense of humor. She is vigilant of Varèse's comfort and needs. She softens, without dimming it at all, Varèse's imposing, vivid appearance. He is tall, rough-hewn. He is fierce, revolutionary, and impressive with his intransigence, his wit, his cutting remarks on old-fashioned composers. His opinions are sharp, unwavering, his estimates final, absolute. His evaluations are what the surrealists called *une entreprise de démolition*. The demolition squad. The ground is leveled. He makes room for new music in no vague terms. He seeks new tones, new timbres. He does not believe in the traditional orchestra. He has created new sonorities. The sounds that issue from his laboratory are new. They seem to come from other planets.

When he takes you down the narrow turning stairway to his studio, it is a cave of sounds, coming from bells, recordings, gongs; and the music seems composed of fragments of music, cut and re-pasted like a collage. He is satiric, mocking, fiery, like a volcano in eruption, and what he played was deafening, as if I were inside a volcano itself. His power suits the scale of the modern world. He alone can play a music heard above the sound of traffic, machinery, factories. He alone has the proportion to hold his own in the vast continent of America. He has the vigor, the vision, and the power.

He is intimidating at first. He mocked my love of Proust. *"Ah, vous souffrez aussi de la Proustatite!"* Louise smiles tenderly, standing behind him, reassuring. He is no Visigoth, but he is one of the giants of music. He looks too big for the small house in the Village. The sounds he plays shake the old walls.

When I return to the parlor upstairs, Louise shows me her writing nook, her books. She translates from the French. She translated Rimbaud's *Illuminations.*

Kay Boyle persuaded her to do it for the Black Sun Press. But it was never published. Meanwhile, she talks about him as if the *Illuminations* had indeed illumined her, and I tell her that it was reading Rimbaud which made me break with realism, which propelled me into space and caused me to write *House of Incest.* The images I used were at first all taken out of actual dreams.

We also talked about Henri Michaux. She told me a story that is very little known about Michaux. He married a young, beautiful South American girl. One evening, her filmy nightgown caught fire and in a few seconds she was burned fatally.

Part of him died with her. But he would not expose his sorrow to the world.

From the *Journal of Albion Moonlight* by Kenneth Patchen.

I have forgotten my mask and my face was in it.

Man has been corrupted by his symbols. Language has killed the animal.

We permit no one to enter the web of flesh where we have our home . . . We retreat more deeply into ourselves; with each advancing moment the self retreats from us.

What horror can be greater than an army of monstrous dogs led by a human intelligence.

I say I hate the poor for the humility which keeps their faces pressed to the mud.

I have spent two years becoming a saint. It was not easy because always the man I was got in the way. This man's name was Albion Moonlight. He was puzzled by my behavior. I feel that he is nearly dead now.

Beware Albion Moonlight . . . They are beginning to suspect the truth.

He describes the nightmare of the war. The nightmare of the fragmented self. All the voices of the subconscious speaking simultaneously. "I propose to make the future and the present and the past happen at once."

"How is it possible to act if there be no result whatsoever but murder?"

Patchen does not exist in human life, human emotions. His figures are those of a nightmare, mutilated and incomplete. He is not in the dream either because if he were he would reach a world of cosmic unity, the collective unconscious. He is a man who reads newspapers and has nightmares. A blind man in the world of man.

What he describes is an animal awakened to fear and danger and hunger and murder. *Albion Moonlight* is chaos. If in Patchen there is a quest for insight and awareness it is the fumbling one of a blind man touching everything in darkness. His assertions seem like orders to force the self to be born, but the self is shattered, drifting, floating. Each time he begins anew. But the personage dissolves into nothingness. He begins again. He describes a hundred abortions of the self. Each day a birth, abortion, and murder. No flowering. A blind man caught up in the violence of action before he has found his soul, the metaphysical seeing-eye dog. He seeks the reality of other human beings, but must murder in order to approach it and possess it. Or he himself must be murdered. The dimension of feeling by which people truly possess each other never appears. The book is full of groans, cries, but they are all physical, animal. It is a drama of impotence and destruction. Albion Moonlight has a vision which dissolves him and he is born and dies many times but is never truly born or never truly dies. The figures are incomplete, maimed.

They are prompt to action and lacking in emotional dimensions.

There is a confusion of languages, gutter jargon, literary, colloquial, inflated to achieve rhetorical grandeur, a Tower of Babel creating only chaos. Albion is lost in mass murders. He is in limbo, the space before birth, when the eyes are not yet open. A child is weeping. He is possessed and haunted. There are all the preparations for birth, the preparation for the poem, for the novel; they are announced, about to be written, but never take form. Albion Moonlight carries an umbilical cord which was never severed. The amniotic fluid poisons its fetus. Every word is like floating debris, which does not coalesce into a thought.

An eye looked over his shoulder and made a cruel judgment.

There are always dogs waiting. They smell death and decay. There is a recurrent nightmare of martyrdom, persecution, and punishment. Albion is persecuted by soldiers, by gangsters, by his friends. He is always trapped.

Close the covers of this book and I will go on talking. You will be told that what I write is confused, without order, and I will tell you that my book is not concerned with the problems of art but with the problems of this world, with the problem of life itself, yes, of life itself.

I give them a look at the naked, snarling animal.

Albion writes a journal. Then he vanishes. A hand is writing a novel and seeking to capture Albion. Men embrace women. Men are murdered. Men appear in a setting of war that is not a war. Albion dies many times. But he is not born.

He utters cries of affirmation to create himself: "I am tender, I am strong, I am. I am."

It is a nightmare of violence. Every act of love or desire is an act of murder. Every act of sex remains strangely unconsummated, a murder takes the place of it. What I see in this book, what cries behind windows, haunting every scene, sightless, voiceless, throughout the drama of violent acts, what is murdered each time anew, what passes from one man to another, is a soul dispossessed by violence, crying to be born, *a soul not yet born.*

But where is the whole vision which will catalyze this chaos and guide it to its birth? Is this the American nightmare: violence, castration, fragmentation?

Is it Albion or Patchen who is blind and touches the letters of the writing as if they were Braille, the raised letters which must be touched but cannot be allowed to penetrate the blood directly through human vision? Chaos is born out of the great fissures which happen in the telling of the story. There are pauses. Silences. Mysteries. Fissures. It is a quest in the darkness, a stuttering. What is he hiding from? What crime has he committed? Is it a story of atonement, punishment? The self has to begin each day anew to reassert its existence. Every phrase is a contradiction of the other phrase. If language has killed the animal, then how is it only the animal is present in the book? When the animal repossesses man he goes mad. Murder takes the place of the sexual communion. Sightless, voiceless, wordless, howling animal Albion Moonlight.

Patchen comes sometimes without warning. He rings the bell. I know his ring because it is so heavy. He stands mute at the door. He does not utter a greeting. He sits down. Or he goes to the icebox to look for a drink. He sees that I am working. There is a half-finished page in the typewriter. He evinces no curiosity. His flesh is heavy.

I attend to his comfort. "Do you want coffee? Do you want a sandwich?" I attempt to create a conversation. "What do you hear from Henry?" I give him my notes on *Albion Moonlight*. He does not understand them. He turns on the radio. At first I thought there was a softness in his animal eyes. I talked to them. But they revolve unseeing. He is inert. He has the paleness of the sick. I understand Artaud's madness but not Patchen's. I understood Artaud because he *felt,* and was artistically articulate. But there is another reason. Artaud's was a torment of the spirit, and Patchen's is a hell from which all spirit is absent.

In his madness, Artaud never became a snarling animal. Artaud's concerns were with expression. With creation in the midst of his own nightmare. Patchen says only: "I need fifteen dollars for my gas bill." I explained the reduction of my income, the writing I was doing for the collector, and my last money order sent to Henry. There is no human understanding or response. Only silence and sullenness. No possible friendship there.

Tanguy said: "I used to walk through Paris by the hour. The streets nourished me. Every walk was an adventure. Every café meant a conversation. My life here is not nourishing. It is the country of silence and impersonality."

I thought of the heavy silence of Patchen, of his inarticulateness.

At Dorothy Norman's formal dinners I meet many important people, but the conversation is always an ideological argument. People do not give of themselves. It is all impersonal and social.

She is intelligent and educated, but nationalistic and insular.

I have an unfortunate weakness. I cannot bloom in the cold, the impersonal. So I withdraw. The only ones who are open-minded, curious, and who seek me out are the young. They want to hear about everything. Robert has read Saint-John Perse. They want to hear about Picasso, Tanguy, Max Ernst, about the artists, poets, writers I had known, about life in Paris.

Every morning after breakfast I sit down to write my allotment of erotica.

This morning I typed: "There was an Hungarian adventurer . . ." I gave him many advantages: beauty, elegance, grace, charm, the talents of an actor, knowledge of many tongues, a genius for intrigue, a genius for extricating himself from difficulties, and a genius for avoiding permanence and responsibility.

He traveled with two great Danes and such an air of authority that he was nicknamed the Baron by hotel managers and bellboys, who have an eye for typing human beings. He could please the most varied types of women. He was a vivacious dinner partner, a sensational dancer, he could sail a boat, drive any car, recite poetry. No woman could hold his interest very long.

When he needed money he married an heiress and discarded her so gently and with such charm that she always made him a parting gift.

66

On the stage of an Argentine burlesque show he saw Anita for the first time. [Are there any burlesque shows in Argentina?] She wore many petticoats of dazzling textiles, a tight bodice and a shawl.

As she removed the petticoats gradually, while singing and undulating her hips, her slanting eyes, which did not close like other women's by letting the lids fall over them but like a cat who lets both lower and upper lid meet not too tightly in a sign of supreme enjoyment, watching the world through a mere slit of jewel-like intensity, so her glance seemed to fall upon the part of her body she was offering, like a guideline.

After a while she closed them completely as if concerned only with the inner ecstasy her own gyrations brought to her, and the men in the audience felt they could stare at her avidly, she was not aware of them, she was hypnotized and offered to all men in the audience.

The undulations were so exact a replica of what a woman's body achieves in the sexual dance, horizontally, which she miraculously enacted in space, that the men followed every wave and ebb of her dance as if about to witness a sudden arrest and a cry which accompanies the stabs of extreme joy they were able to dispense.

Only as she left the stage, after this secret, intimate, closed-eyed abandon, did she open her eyes wide, and the specks of gold of which her eyes seemed made, fell directly upon the Hungarian adventurer.

He arose from his front row seat and went to her dressing room.

There were so many bouquets of flowers from admirers in the little room that she seemed to be changing costume in a garden which, like herself, had reached its maximum flowering. She was standing, and with one leg raised and the foot resting on the rim of a gold chair, she was busy powdering and rouging a second mouth. Her admirers were leaning over to catch a glimpse of this pistil more complex than the heart of a flower, and more fleshy than the mouth with which she smiled at them.

When the Baron walked in she merely lifted her head but did not change her pose. He caught a glimpse, above the heads of other visitors, of the tender-skinned, flushed, humid lips surrounded by glossy black hair. With a last puff of powder she left them all for the last performance for which she was famous.

The theater was filled with small dark boxes, heavily curtained, in which the men awaited her visit. Having requested her presence they waited. She arrived on a wave of perfume and rustling silk. She did not sit beside the man but kneeled. Her heavy breasts surged upward from the compressed bodice. She kneeled and bent over the ritual of deft caresses with jewelled hands and avid mouth. Her tongue found all the secret places her fingers had not reached.

But when the Hungarian leaned over and tried to make her stand so he could embrace her, she slipped from his grasp.

He could not forget her softness to his touch, her firmness, her changes of rhythm, her teasing.

He left for Rome. There he took a suite at the Grand Hotel. It happened to be next to that of the Spanish Ambassador, who was visiting Rome with his two daughters, one fourteen and one fifteen years old.

The Baron charmed them, too. They became such good friends that when the two girls had nothing to do they would rush into his room and awaken him. They would rush over to his bed with screams, teasings, laughter not allowed by their more pompous parents.

They were both beautiful, with huge soft black eyes and long silky hair which clung magnetically to his face and hands. They wore short white dresses, short white socks. Their skin was lightly suntanned and flawless. A childish down, not yet hair, soft as a newborn chick's feather would catch the sunlight. Almost every morning the Baron was awakened by the two girls running into his room, laughingly throwing themselves on his bed. Now the Baron awakened in the morning in a rather hyper-sensitive and vulnerable state.

Often he had been dreaming of Anita in the small, dark, curtained box of the theater, of her hands and mouth, and of her refusal to go to the very limit of their enjoyment. A foamy, light, full blue quilt concealed the prominence of his dream, and as the little girls did not mind how far their little skirts flew upward, and how tangled their legs became as they sat astride him, fell over him, pulled his hair, and began childish conversations with him while lying over his body, the Baron's delight in being so fondled and handled would grow into excruciating suspense. One of them was lying on his stomach, and all he had to do was to move slightly to reach his pleasure. He did this playfully, as if he meant to push her off the bed, saying: "I am sure you will fall off if I go on pushing this way." She said stubbornly: "I won't fall off," and, laughing, she held on tight to him as he rocked, as if he were a horse galloping while trying to shake off its rider, or a boat rolling over the high seas. He pushed her little body up and down as she lay prone and holding him firmly in order not to slide off. Her sister came to her help and sat astride to keep his motions from getting too violent, and now he had to move wildly fighting against their weight over him, and the thick blue quilt rose and fell, legs, panties, quilt all tangled with wave-like rhythms, laughter, and delight.

Suddenly they discovered what they believed to be one of his fingers held up for them to catch and they pursued this finger, which moved under the quilt, seeking to catch it, and he covered himself and played the trapped animal under the quilt, and they caught this finger at times tightly, at other times lost it, at other times hung on to it, and then he growled under the quilt, sought to bite them, any place at all, and they sought to escape, but always returned for more surprises, more attacks, more wrestling with the animal, until he came out panting, from fatigue they thought, and ready to surrender.

I sit at work every day. I send Henry an airmail letter. He has given the new, expensive briefcase the collector gave him, to an escaped convict, to help him on his way. I mail magazines to Henry's father, a carton of cigarettes. I have to go and get my passport stamped again to get permission to stay another six months as a temporary visitor.

At four I see Gonzalo and we discuss the *Daily Worker*'s review of Hemingway's work (another traitor to Communism, says Gonzalo). The drama of *Wuthering Heights*, too, is a result of bourgeois society. Society and capitalism are to blame for everything. Marxism gives Gonzalo a perfect alibi. Neither he nor Helba will confront their own share in their destiny. That is why he hates psychoanalysis so bitterly. It makes one face how much of one's destiny is one's own doing.

But for Gonzalo the solution to all problems lies outside. I go to the other extreme and blame myself for everything and never consider myself a victim of anything but my own weaknesses, my own flaws. This difference can never be bridged.

Has the hearing aid made a difference in Helba's life? Most of the time she turns it off to have quiet, so she does not hear the door, or the phone, and Gonzalo, when he forgets his key, has to climb up the fire escape.

A telephone call: "The old man is pleased. Concentrate on sex. Leave out the poetry."

This started an epidemic of erotic "journals." Everyone is writing up their sexual experiences. Invented, overheard, researched from Krafft-Ebing and medical books. We have comical conversations. We tell a story and the rest of us have to decide whether it is true or false. Or plausible. Is this plausible? Robert would offer to experiment, to test our inventions, to confirm or negate our fantasies.

All of us need money, so we pool our stories. I could not turn them out fast enough, so I inserted some of Robert's, some of Virginia's, some of George Barker's.

I decided to write a chapter on beds. The beds that inhibited and those that stimulated sensual adventure. I thought first of historic beds, beds from antique shops, beds in French castles, and Italian mansions. Those I had found not good to make love in, because as you lie in them you think of famous personages, of Napoleon, Du Barry, kings, queens, famous courtesans, actresses, aristocrats, titled names, great names, generals, their mistresses.

In any case, the historic pageantry affects one like a masquerade, one is entered into by a figure from the past, one lies down on the elbow of another personage, one is haunted, possessed, and begins to act like a ventriloquist. One is in rivalry with famous lovers. One cannot find one's own self.

Too much history affects you like a costume. At least, that was how I felt in a bed in a beautiful Italian castle, in which I never felt like myself but like a countess I had read about in one of Pierre-Jean Jouve's most beautiful novels. She took over my body and spirit. I was either trying to outshine her, or I, the novelist, was seeking the missing data on the particular ways of love-making of a woman born in embroidered, initialed sheets with lace edgings, on a bed which was perfumed with sandalwood sachets, and warmed beforehand by devoted servants. Somehow, it marred my personal style.

And as against that, I had found beds in strange hotel rooms occupied by anonymous lovers, bestirring my imagination. Unknown, I could enter into their heightened meetings.

A hotel room meant secret, dangerous, and heavily guilty assignations. The pale echo of a stain could be reconstructed as a sign of pleasure. The anonymity permitted me to create the love and be warmed by it. Anonymity enclosed me, too, included me, and I could give my maximum and feel it would remain a secret, not registered in the guest book. I could furnish the room with lovers of my own choice, glimpsed in the street, in the bus, in a garden. I could share in their delights.

Another bed which was an aphrodisiac was the Bohemian mattress on the floor. Escaping from the elevation seemed also to bring one closer to earth, to flesh, and there was no fear of rolling away from the bed, falling. It suggested a lair, closer to primitive life, Oriental life, closer to the senses, travel and camping in deserts, closer to human and animal nature. It reminded me of Fatima in Morocco, of harems, tents, of *A Thousand and One Nights.*

It was not good to sleep in beds occupied in childhood or adolescence, in guest rooms with family life woven around them. In proper and unwrinkled beds. In beds which had an aura of grandparents' armchairs, of the long illness of a parent, or those that resembled a bed in which one slept as a virgin. No, these were detrimental, they lowered the fever charts, they stilled the imagination which could draw energy and fire from other lovers.

Now Venice, the beds of Venice, they were saturated in legends of love. The lapping of the water made them seem to be floating barges, and the slow rhythm ensorcelled, and love-making was part of dreaming. The poets confused the oscillations of beds of desire with the gondolas.

Again Pierre-Jean Jouve; literature added to one's own personal experience, wove a rich tapestry of love scenes. I remembered the deep, downy quilted beds of Swiss peasants, the deep, many-layered peasant beds of France, the thin-mattressed copper beds of the south of Italy with the cold tile beneath one's feet, soundless beds receiving sighs, and creaking beds accenting certain elegant gymnastics.

The universal cosmic beds of pine needles, moss, dead leaves, wheat, wherever the beauty of a place, or its scents, or its rhythms, conducted an orchestration of the senses and inspired harmonious equivalents, musical and human counterpoints.

I am sure the old man knows nothing about the beatitudes, ecstasies, dazzling reverberations of sexual encounters. Cut out the poetry was his message. Clinical sex, deprived of all the warmth of love, the orchestration of all the senses—touch, hearing, sight, palate, all the euphoric accompaniments, background music, moods, atmosphere, variations—forced him to resort to literary aphrodisiacs.

We could have bottled better secrets to tell him, but such secrets he would be deaf to. But one day when he has reached saturation, I will tell him how he almost made us lose interest in passion by his obsession with the gestures empty of their emotions, and how we reviled him, because he almost caused us to take vows of chastity, because all that he wanted us to exclude was our own aphrodisiac—poetry.

Virginia tells me she is enriched and liberated by my writing and our talks. There is an interesting interplay between Virginia and her analyst, and his comments on my work and our talks. Life repeats itself, she becomes identified with me, repeating my imprisonment in bourgeois life, my liberation through Henry and June. My writing is talking for me, stirring people to live, arousing passion and life. Virginia suddenly realized she had never lived, loved, suffered or enjoyed.

She lives in a loft on Fourteenth Street. The first floor houses a shop, a hamburger bar, a shoe shop and a synthetic orange juice bar. I climb a bare wooden stairway painted a dusty grey. The place is cold, but the hallways and lofts are big and high-ceilinged and the only place possible and available to a painter. There is space for easels, canvases of any size. There is a lavatory outside, running water and washstand inside, and that is all. On weekends the heat is turned off. The enormous windows which give on the deafening traffic noise of Fourteenth Street have to be kept closed. There are nails on the wall for clothes, a Sterno burner for making coffee. We drink sour wine out of paper cups. There Virginia and Janet paint, study acting and dancing, type when they need money.

The setting is fit for *Crime and Punishment,* but the buoyancy of Virginia and Janet and their friends, lovers, is deceptive. It has the semblance of youth and gaiety. They are in their twenties. They joke, laugh, but this hides deep anxieties, deep fears, deep paralysis. At first I was taken in by the humorous and playful surface, but afterwards I remembered the words of D. H. Lawrence: "All rosy and healthy on the outside, but all ashes inside."

I started an epidemic of journals. Suddenly they had to look inside. The outside and the inside did not match at all. The analyst sends me thanks for facilitating his task.

A big talk with Gonzalo. I was waiting for a propitious moment to combat his prejudice against psychiatry and psychoanalysis. I pointed out how at a certain point it touches upon Marxism, how it is equally a struggle for a sense of realism, how it fights against the basic evils which cause distortions and deformations in our lives.

Gonzalo sees no value in psychology at all, rejects it all as mystical, metaphysical nonsense. I said: "What are you going to do with the hopelessly twisted ones whom Marxism cannot save?"

"Give them five hundred dollars and they will be cured of all their ills."

"The other day a rich society girl committed suicide. Psychoanalysis can dissolve delusions, worlds built on pathologic lies. It can dissolve false superstructures and re-establish life and a more sincere, more simple human base. Analysis can bring one face to face with the problems created by a bourgeois society and can lead the individual to achieve greater liberation and growth. It does not counsel revolution, but if enough people struggle against limitations of all kinds the world would be altered anyway, and changes made from the inside."

Gonzalo would only admit that there were many whom Marxism could not help. "Look at me, nothing has changed my life, nothing will cure my laziness. You with all your theories, have you changed me?"

Then spontaneously he said this terrible thing: "I am so depressed by my laziness that at times I want to kill myself. I think that is the reason why I almost killed myself on the porch the other day."

Gonzalo had been building an enclosure for my porch, out of

plywood, tar paper and plastic. Working on a little window he had made he leaned backwards, putting his whole weight on a very thin wooden railing which would have broken if I had not cried out in time. He would have fallen five stories to the pavement.

Afterwards he was stunned by his carelessness. Today he understood it.

"Gonzalo, now you see how destructive it can be not to become aware of what torments you. You never admitted your passivity was a torment. We must find something that you love to do to deliver you of this guilt for not acting in the world."

Gonzalo admitted a relation between this seeking of death and his guilt at not working. This was great progress as he always repudiated all connection between suffering and guilt.

When he admitted that Marxism could not help an already formed character, he asked me what could. I showed him that there was a developing interest in psychiatry in Russia. It could not be totally rejected. At first he said: "You want to help the putrid ones."

He has no horror of physical illness, but he is intolerant of neurosis. I said, "*neurotic,* not putrid."

He finally understood that I was talking about disease. He could see how the revolution could only carry along those capable of simple, direct action. He saw the swift current of political activity running ahead and he himself *incapable,* or *unable* to become a part of it. Unable to *act.*

Gonzalo does not understand my activity against destruction and death. He does not see that I tried to reverse the destructive current of his life.

He believes that any neurotic, given food and money, can be cured. That if Artaud had been given his theater to work with, he would not have gone mad. He thinks that I saved him and Helba with food and money, but not with spiritual gifts of love, faith, creativity. For the first time today I felt I was getting deeper into the sources of his self-destruction.

Finally, to relieve Gonzalo of an unbearable guilt I told him what I truly believe: "Not all of us were intended to be tied down to daily humdrum work. Some of us who rejected monotonous daily tasks developed a magnificent gift for living. You have a capacity to bloom in leisure, unknown to men at work, men in harness. You have a genius for friendship, for love, for human life. In others this becomes atrophied. You bring great gifts to living. You bring an openness to adventure, a poetry, fantasy, and imagination that spring from the habit of pursuing pleasure and freedom. No man in harness knows how to exploit the present until it yields up its intimate perfumes and riches, having no thought of tomorrow, or preserving himself for the next day's task. This channelizing of energy which does not run free produces atrophy in human life. The gratuitous pleasures, the habit of waiting for things to bloom, time and patience to cultivate the blooms of developing friendships to their greatest fruition, this is never attained by the disciplined worker. They become 'clocked' by patterns which crystallize, harden them.

"Every time a person keeps an appointment and sacrifices the present, this present is killed, aborted, and finally the self is living in a condition of perpetual abortions, postponements, denials, non-flowering."

Human flowering was Gonzalo's greatest gift to others. It was Henry's greatest quality. The goal was to live fully, not to construct. Gonzalo, a few days after settling in New York, knew all its streets, cafés, restaurants, out-of-the-way places, quarters, characters. He staked out first his exploration of the land, which no one at work has time to do.

Human life the goal. Laughter born of irresponsibility. Tolerance born of his own defects. Rich adventure born of leisure and independence. Talks at the bar by which he enters all kinds of realms, lives, experiences. Wisdom born of the streets.

And then regrets for not having built anything he can see, touch, be proud of. So I end by praising the laziness with which he was lashing himself!

Robert is writing a diary which reveals strange feelings and currents of life taking place in darkness, as yet inchoate, unfocused, which require great skill and attentiveness to bring out of their chaotic formlessness. I read his big, square handwriting.

Robert's diary could flow into this one and become a part of it because the quest is similar. We seek ultimate awareness by way of the symbolical meaning of our acts and dreams.

But what happens that the life in New York does not glow and glitter and expand for me? Why is it not as rich? Or does not seem as rich? Create, Anaïs, invent it. My houseboat story lies unfinished. Why? I am not fecundated or nourished by the present. I reread old diaries and everything is there. They are full, they are alive. It makes me want to go on writing. Surely the magic is accomplished. What I hated to lose is not lost. Henry is there forever. Louveciennes. Artaud. Allendy. Rank. War dispersed us. But I possess the fire of those days. Is it creation to make something live forever? It will live forever. It has not died.

What happened that life in New York does not expand for me? Do I ask for an impossible brilliancy, intensity, consuming fullness everyday? John Dudley's youthful fire was not that. Dorothy Norman's utterance may have been the key to the blight. "America errs on the side of health. Many European influences were unhealthy and we had to reject them." Health was also on Dudley's lips. The health they speak of is hygienic sterility. It rejects the experience of life, maturity, ripeness, risk. They refuse to evolve, ripen, alter, out of fear of death. They try to cheat time and remain young by standing still and remaining virgin. They think one remains young by not living, not loving, not erring, not giving or spending or wasting one's self.

It is a kind of artificial preservation.

The collector sends Henry a telegram:

Dear Henry, Very much impressed by Anaïs's writing. Have forwarded one hundred pages to my client making it clear that he is under no obligation to pay for this installment. I think he will be interested in others provided the material is similar. What do I do now? Greetings.

The symbolic interpretation is the only one which expands, enlarges the world, makes it boundless, illimitable. All others reduce it. Marxism is a reduction to the practical. Dreams, mysteries, myths, symbols, are as necessary as bread.

l was reading Dane Rudhyar when I received a letter from him about *Winter of Artifice*. "You have done there a striking work, so open, so rich with psychological content, so valuable." He is a Frenchman who was once a composer. He changed his name, and became a well-known astrologer in Hollywood.

I dream that somewhere in Morocco people are imprisoned in heat. They are inwardly consumed. They look burnt, ashy. They are forced to live underground. I cannot bear it.

I was copying an incident from earlier diaries and laughing at my own absurdity. It was during the early period of my acquaintance with René Allendy, when I still saw him as a magician, not a man. He was the wise man, a mythical figure.

He had expressed the desire to see my house at Louveciennes. I could not let him take a train like an ordinary man. He had to be *magically transported.* So I spent my month's allowance on renting a car with a chauffeur, which I said belonged to the Countess Nellie, to create more atmosphere, and he stepped into this car and was transported to Louveciennes. What childish nonsense! Today I see Allendy as others did, as a French doctor with a beard, who was handling as well as he could a power beyond his understanding. Today I feel compassion for the French doctor with a beard who was so much idealized, placed on a pedestal, treated as a magician. What an uncomfortable situation, how he must have hated this idealization (dehumanization) and how he must have thought that he had failed as an analyst if I were still capable of such mythmaking.

I ask myself where am I now? In a place that denies myths, and sees the world in flat, ordinary colors. Without colors, exaltation, ecstasy, or any of the heightened visionary elements.

Robert does not take the place of Carteret, he is too young. He is confused. He seeks the alchemy which makes life incandescent. He has it as a poet, but he seeks awareness, and Jean Carteret, even in the middle of his fantasies, could orient himself, could interpret, could clarify.

Where am I now? In human life. My imagination follows Henry

on his trip through America. Henry's essay on Balzac appeared in
Twice a Year, with my story of Hélène. I am sad. The earth is heavy
and opaque without dreams.

Reading old diaries makes me want to continue my adventures.
Flavors. Sensations. I even possess between the pages of the diary
the first contact I had with the erotic atmosphere of Paris, my first
awareness of it. It was the beautiful openness and naturalness of
the French exposing their caresses in the street, in cafés, which
make the erotic climate of Paris. It is a city impregnated with love
and lovers.

Early in my arrival in Paris, I was standing on a street corner. I
was waiting for a bus. I was wearing a light summer dress. I looked
up accidentally, and saw a couple leaning out of an open window.
They were embracing in the sunlight, half-hidden by pots of flowers
and the curtain which swung in and out of the window like a sail
swollen by the wind. Behind them one could see the big white bed,
unmade. I felt the echo, the vibrations of their caresses through my
body like a quivering breeze. It was not an image. It was a vibration, a shuddering from head to foot.

Naturalness of life in the streets of Paris, of Italy and Spain, is a
sharing of life.

I received one hundred dollars for my "erotica." Gonzalo needed
cash for the dentist, Helba needed a mirror for her dancing, and
Henry money for his trip.

Gonzalo told me the story of the Basque and Bijou and I wrote
it down for the collector.

The Basque was a painter in Paris who was given the nickname
because he never took off his beret even in bed. Bijou was the reigning
queen of the prostitutes and had a house of her own with a red light
over the door. One rainy night the Basque had enough francs in his
pocket and he felt very rich. People had said he was the best of the
primitive painters, and he never told anyone that he copied his subjects
from postcards. He was in a euphoric mood and wanted to celebrate.
He was looking for one of the red lights which signaled pleasure. An
ample, luxuriously padded woman opened the door. Everything about
her was larger than nature, her eyes, her breasts, her smile. But not in

an unpleasant way, merely expansive, more like a face seen in a film close-up, or on stage.

Her eyes traveled immediately to the man's shoes to judge how much he could afford for his pleasure. Then, for her own satisfaction, her smoky, heavy-lidded, black-rimmed eyes rested awhile on his trouser buttons. It was mechanical. Faces did not interest her. Her attention was spent exclusively on a certain region of a man's anatomy. Her burning eyes had a fanatical way of appraising a man's possessions. It was professional. She prided herself on pairing people according to the most subtle rules of the *Kama Sutra* and with more acumen than other women. She would suggest certain conjunctions. She was as expert as a glove fitter. There was no pleasure if the glove was too tight or too loose. Bijou felt that nowadays people did not give enough importance to proper fittings. People were growing careless. If a man found himself floating in too vast a garment he made the best of it, but according to Bijou he would miss the clutching embrace which annihilated loneliness. Or if one had to slip as if under a closed door, shrinking or suffocating or fearing to laugh heartily for fear of immediate displacement, that would also be inharmonious. People were losing the art of perfect conjunctions.

It was only after Bijou had completed her exploration that she recognized the Basque and smiled at him. He had made the mistake of changing his suit, for when he came with paint on his suit he was always allowed in, and could come and sit before a drink and sketch the girls, and talk with them. The artists often came just for company and rewarded them with sketches. Bijou knew he was difficult to please. He was a gourmet of women's jewel boxes and liked them velvet-lined, affectionate and clinging. Bijou gave the Basque a generous smile. She liked the Basque personally, and it was not for his short straight nose, his glossy black hair, his almond-shaped eyes, not for his red scarf or the roguish angle of his beret. It was for his royal amulet, and for its expansiveness.

She was the Basque's favorite, too. He knew Bijou's delectable flavor, the natural mossy humidity which needed no coaxing, the delicate sauces in which she knew how to wrap the shell-pink morsels she served him. The Basque liked Bijou's honeycombs and alcoves. And the Basque also liked that she did not require too many tributes, too many emollient compliments, too many suave words and prefaces, and introductions, and bell-ringings and aphrodisiacs. She came bathed in her own propitious atmosphere, marinated, salved, *à point*, creamed, perfumed, born not like Venus from a shell, or a wave, but from the very core of a bed already warmed, from the petaled chaos of sheets, of feathers, mattresses, out of uneven, undulating surfaces, already imprinted with bodies, from under a tent of flesh and accumulating delights. There was no need of tuning up, nor to be careful of stains, for Bijou loved the stains of love-making like those of some melted mineral, dropped like a tear by the woman or sprayed by the man as from an atomizer.

What Bijou would have liked was to have been Catherine the Great inspecting her private regiment, an army standing at attention, presenting the only arm which could conquer her. She saw them in her reveries. She would be the general decorating the most silky ones, the most rigid ones, the most leaping ones. She would reward them with a kiss on the tip merely to draw the first tear of pleasure. She would reward insolence, impertinence, revolt, indiscretion, anything but inertia or lethargy. From her dreams at night her flesh was always tender as if it had been simmered all day under a delicate fire.

Bijou also knew the collector's art. She had found contrasts between her girls, the one who fell asleep and delivered men of guilt, the one who was cold and incited violence.

When the painters discovered Bijou they felt they had found the woman who possessed all the attributes of the prostitute. It was as if this constant living in a climate of sensuality had grown a particular kind of body, produced a phenomenon. Bathed in eroticism, this quality pervaded her body, her gestures, and was as apparent on the exterior, on the surface, as a species of fruit or flower one could recognize among hundreds of others.

This constant living in the eyes, molded by the hands and desire of man, had given her eyes, skin, and motions a singular quality, one which could only be described as the dark and secret womb turned inside out for all to see. Her hair seemed as alive and electric as an animal's, of a texture as lively, as pungent as if it had been dipped in sex. It was the most sensual hair, heavy, coiling and uncoiled, warm, musky, strong. It bristled when caressed, like the hair of an animal. When someone caressed it, she could lie absolutely still, quiet, languid. And as if there were some delicate nerve connection between her long hair and the Venusian hair guarding the center of her sensuality, when her hair was caressed her hand went naturally to the hair between her legs in synchronized movements, to smooth and enchant its tendrils simultaneously.

Her skin, too, had a glow which was erotic, not alone the living glow of it, the transparency which revealed the pale turquoise veins, but the almost imperceptible vibrancy of nerves and blood under caresses. The satin surface registered the flow of blood, the palpitations of desire. The contraction of the muscles responded to the hand as a cat does; one expected to hear a purring. Her skin was warm and dry like desert sand when she first lay in bed, but later it would become moist and feverish when the tides of pleasure washed over her.

The Basque had sought many times to describe her eyes. "Eyes of the orgasm," he once murmured. "That which other women keep secret happens right in your eyes, in the open." With her eyes alone she could give this erotic response, a code language, one quick flicker of its iris, a leaping flame when the contact was made. She was the queen of the prostitutes, Bijou. Her mouth had not been designed to speak words, to eat. The way it moved, prepared itself to open, seemed more like a prelude to a kiss. There was an expectancy, a slight swelling of the lips. Like the mouth of sex itself, moving to take you in, carrying no words to the ear, no human sound, but undulating in preparation to kiss, hold, caress. Like a wave about to curl around you. The nostrils expanded, to breathe the presence of the lover. To meet her in a public place was like making love in public, for every word she uttered then, every greeting, every gesture she made was like an exposed love scene. She kept nothing for the alcove, for the night. Even in restaurants, eating, or playing cards, or waiting before a drink, she did not sit as other women do, as if for a moment they had forgotten their body, to concentrate on cards or food. No, Bijou's body participated in every act of life. Her breasts were pressed against the table, and vibrated when she laughed. If she laughed it was the sexual laughter of a satisfied woman, the laugh she will have after an orgasm, a laughter of a body enjoying itself through every cell and pore.

In the street, walking behind her when she did not know the Basque was following her, he could see even urchins following her, who had not yet seen her face. It was as if she left a trail of animal perfume, an animal scent behind her. Before they had seen her face men followed her. Strange how the women around her seemed suddenly disguised, camouflaged, as if to distract men away from their desire rather than openly challenging it. The Basque loved this Bijou, who walked nakedly sexual through the city of Paris. . . .

Robert wrote in his diary:

I want to tell you about the hurt feeling that I have in me. I am suffering because you do not love Kenneth Patchen.

What happened was that Patchen was begging money from everyone, and I had none to give. So he appealed to Henry, who sent him money only to turn around and ask more of me, so that when Patchen asked me for Henry's address while he was traveling I would not give it to him. Henry reproached Dorothy Norman for not helping Patchen. Dorothy Norman complained to me. I told Robert what she had told me and he told Patchen. When Patchen wrote to Dorothy Norman she naturally denied having refused to help him or having been offended by Miller's request.

Robert had divided himself between identification with me (his feminine self) and identification with Patchen (his masculine self). He felt that if I loved Patchen the two sides of himself would be in harmony. He felt that I would reduce his guilt if I helped Patchen. We would form a close triangle. But aside from the fact that I was overburdened (and Robert knew just how much) I did not believe in Patchen nor in his work. This disturbed Robert.

Robert felt that we should all be sacrificed to Patchen.

"I am giving enough," I said to Robert.

He felt guilty even for the fact that any time he had no money he could come and eat with me. But he knew all the time that I was in debt and I could not understand his insistence that I should be responsible for Patchen.

Robert stands nearest to me at the moment, and the clearest. At first I did not entirely hear him. When I first met him at the Cooneys his eyes did not seem to focus, and neither did his words. He was wrapped in a nebula of chaos. But he moved in the same world as Jean Carteret, without the luminous precision and cohesion. But we would talk. The miraculous understanding came with his diary. His diary was a complete emotional revelation.

He came at first as *l'enfant terrible,* perverse and knowing. But in the diary he grew larger, stronger, firmer. He is physically beautiful. He talks as if he were in a trance. He talks flowingly, like a medium. His voice remains on one tone, as that of a somnambulistic monologue. At such times he does not hear anyone. At other times he is open, absorbing, aware.

In his diary there was a human warmth which he did not show in life. By an exchange of diaries we entered each other's private life as we could never have without them, for he goes from me to young men and our love is purely fraternal. He has great charm, seduction. His features are delicate, he has a slender Egyptian body, the shoulders very straight, the waist narrow, the hands stylized.

With me he is firm, definite, boyish. He never shows me his feminine side. This I can see only in public, in the presence of men. Then he becomes pliant, undulant, flexible. He deploys coquetries, oblique smiles and oblique phrases. I see the body soften, become woman right under my eyes.

When he talks about his consuming hunger, his "children" (those he protects), his renunciations, his quest for the father, his need of love, I hear my own words. At night, after writing in his diary in my studio, writing poems at the same table at which I work, he goes to friends. He always returns still hungry for something they do not give him. He lives penniless. He gives whatever he has. There is a demon in him, a poet seeking tension and intensity. He does not stay in the paradise offered to him by his lovers as they are offered to a woman. He seeks violence, and fire, and renewal. When he seduces someone he has a gleeful expression, as a woman might. He is vain of his power, triumphant, celebrating his power. His feminine ruses, tantalizing advances, elusive retreats. Games.

In our talks he is completely free, open and flowing, recounting his life, love scenes, dreams, analysis, memories, future poems.

He lives close to woman. He does not seem to have any hostility or revengefulness towards woman.

The night I read his diary on Patchen I was unhappy at what he had misunderstood, and unhappy that he had not taken my side or wished to protect me.

His interpretation was that I wanted to stay in the *House of Incest*, to protect an artificial paradise. But *House of Incest*, I said, was not a paradise, and I had long ago abandoned paradise by way of Henry and June. That was not my quest at all.

He wrote:

You have chosen not to include Patchen, not to understand him. Why do I feel this guilt towards Patchen? This morning I sat with you in the flood of warmth, of roots which we seem to share together. Do we have a right to this, to be as plants, have you a right to be so fragile, so beautifully bewitching, for you are enchanted and enchanting. Is it your state of enchantment which I reflect when I am with you, or am I writing your book? Do you shut out the monsters, the demons, the nightmares of Patchen? You and I have failed to help Patchen. Let me tell you about me. How I have wished to help, wanted him helped. I am so confused as I walk around in this Patchen purgatory. It is my own guilt, not yours, and if I had wanted you to deliver me from it I should discuss my guilt, whereas I am using such subterfuges, such deceits, transferring it to you.

[January, 1941]

The collector accepted another hundred pages. I received another hundred dollars, which paid for doctors' bills for Helba, and for Henry's trip. But the old man asked for an expansion of the sexual scenes.

Henry left yesterday. He seems frail. He has lost the joy he found in Greece. He is not happy in New York. He is forcing himself to travel, to write.

I feel mysteriously exhausted, deep down.

I work on erotica for the collector.

Robert understands at last that *House of Incest* is the crystal born of dreams (the poem), but that my life is not, that it is human. His own language: consuming, movement towards, dance, flow, transgressions, are some of my favorite words. It is as if we had extracted the same words from the dictionary. For out of the dictionary each one of us chooses a particular vocabulary, with insistent, repeated words which are the key to our psychic life. He likes to describe people in terms of bodily attitudes, as if they were paintings or statues.

Robert's birthday is January seventh, the same as June's.

Robert came with a recording by Edgar Varèse. He danced for us. It was a creation. He invented a nonhuman, abstract dance, a war of elements, torn, resoldered, percussion gestures to the percussion sounds of Varèse. His face was like a mask. He was removed and stylized.

I love his humor, his trickeries, and language. It is the fecund labyrinth again, with so many rooms, cells, vibrations, percussions, repercussions. Strange that for others we seem to alter, change, and they do not follow our quick gyrations, they are almost mistrustful of our quick-change artistry in life, our transformations, fluidity. But for each other this multiplicity of selves is merely a rich spectacle, a game which we enjoy and are not baffled by. Even when he dances and his eyes are glazed, expressionless, as in an Egyptian fresco, or even when he plays the idiot and no longer recognizes me, or the beast towering over me with grimaces and lines out of Saint-John Perse, or Cocteau, we laugh.

He is quite clear to me in all his metamorphoses. I am also clear to him, and when I choose suddenly, in the midst of my Bohemian life, to dress up and play the chic and snobbish lady going into a chic and snobbish world, he laughs and knows it to be a masquerade.

Kenneth Patchen stands outside like a great inarticulate, ungracious animal, dreaming as animals do, with grunts and spasms, barely awakened. He is afraid of my world. He stands before me awkward and heavy, opaque. This would not matter so much, but *what he does not understand he seeks to destroy.*

When Gonzalo comes I try to lure him out of his depression by playing Varèse's *Ionization.* It comes from other planets, from the steel on Mars, russet tearing notes, knives, saws, the sound of falling planets, fragments whistling through cyclones, tearing space. Vibrations from places we have not yet seen.

Gonzalo's darkness is like the darkness of earth itself. He is unshaved, bitter. A sheaf of black hair runs wild behind his ear, the high cheekbones make him seem to be laughing even when he is sad. The black bushy eyebrows are like bat wings, his eyelashes as black and smoky as those of Arabian women with their kohl-painted eyes. The eyes as black and bottomless as volcanic lakes, no specks of sun or moon in them, the black of rain forests and caves.

I try to tell him we cannot live forever only in the actual and the present, or we stifle. The realm of the literal is a prison.

Gonzalo thinks that symbolism is an outworn form, which has died with romanticism, but he cannot understand that it is the key to a vaster universe, our unconscious, and to trap doors in the infinite. And that it is a modern man of science, Freud, who established once and for all its inseparable part in our existence. Gonzalo has closed the door on this vast world, which we enter by way of the dream.

When you are trapped in destruction, open a door to creation. Read Gerald Heard on dilated consciousness. Walk out of the house of death which is war, which is the virulently contagious madness of war.

From Robert's diary:

Who more than I can understand this hunger Anaïs describes for abandon, the terrible meaning that we place upon sexual contact, because for us it is more than personal, it is contact with the unknown. There is an orgasm of the soul itself, a terrible rushing upward, reaching beyond the body. The body represents the only barrier to completion and we go back again to the body of the beloved to renew this ascension. It is seldom achieved for me. With Ned, I had to be touched to reassure myself that the ascension could be made once more.

I wrote in Robert's diary:

Why do you care so much what Patchen will think of your diary? Do you know that it is more moving than Patchen's, that it reaches deeper, it is more human?

Robert writes:

I have a horrible suspicion that beneath all this articulateness lies something which I have forgotten. Our greatest betrayal is our infinite gentleness. We exist in all the delirious countries of the sexual world back of the act. Another magnificent afternoon with Anaïs. She draws me into the marvelous, into clairvoyance. Shall I pretend she is not to read this? No. All that takes place in these meetings is open. These afternoons shall be cut away: islands. They are my confessions in the inner room of the *House of Incest*. Anaïs, with her painted eyes, created the mesmerist's chamber and her smile keeps the flow of mystery.

When one is uprooted, transplanted, there is a temporary withering. I always panic at this and think it permanent. I thought my life was shrinking. The failure of friendship with Patchen, his total lack of understanding of me frightened me, but the flow with Robert restored my confidence, and I began to sprout new leaves.

Someone gave me an organ-grinder's monkey they had seen in a pet shop and which had appeared on the stage. He was about a foot and a half tall. As soon as he arrived he went berserk. He leaped from curtain to curtain, balanced on electric wires, spilled a bottle of perfume, pulled clothes down from the hangers, scattered the sea shells, and when everyone rushed to catch him he ran to me for refuge and in this way won my protection.

It was impossible to put him back in the cage. He was so rebellious that I gave up and I locked him up in the bathroom when I went out that evening, thinking there was little he could upset in a bathroom. But when I returned he had opened the medicine chest, opened every bottle, spilled their contents in the washbowl, opened the toothpaste tubes and squeezed the paste all over the bathroom, opened the talcum and face powder and powdered everything, unwound all the toilet paper and scattered it like serpentines all over bathtub and toilet, scattered the Kleenex. He had smeared his face with toothpaste, emptied the laundry basket, and when I arrived was banging on the door with the hairbrush. When I opened the door he looked up at me innocently, climbed on my shoulder, bared his teeth as if he were laughing, and began to look for fleas in my hair.

I tried to lure him into his cage by placing grapes at the bottom of it, as he is very fond of grapes. He looked at me mockingly, slipped his long arm through the bars, picked up the grapes without getting inside. I had underestimated his reasoning power and the length of his arms.

He insisted that I stand by while he ate. He picked up his rice with his fingers with great delicacy, cupping them around it. His nails are lacquered black as if covered by nail polish. I tried caresses and cajoling words to calm him before slipping him into his cage. He responded, but with equally coaxing gestures, pleadings, ruses. He finally let me place him inside, but cried when I left. When I returned from the street he received me deliriously. He uttered little cries like a bird.

He had a genius for destruction and for comedy. Someone gave him a few sips of beer. He threw himself back with laughter and slapped his stomach. He took sudden likes and dislikes to visitors and expressed them plainly. He would take up their glass and spill it, or go up to them and slap them.

Sunday, when I cooked pancakes and gave him a banana, he

looked puzzled. He fetched the telephone book, opened it, peeled the banana, placed it between the pages and closed it. After a while he opened the book and showed me the flattened banana, his pancake.

No matter how restless he is, if I take him into my arms he cuddles tenderly and goes to sleep. But the apartment is a shambles. He opens books, pretends to read, and then throws them on the floor. He scatters my papers, he scatters the food on my plate, he opens all the closets, he falls asleep on my dresses and also urinates on them. He tore the bathroom shower curtain, destroyed all the packages of cigarettes, scratched Virginia.

He dominates the entire household. When I gave him a teaspoon of beer he pretended to walk unevenly, to fall off his cage. His grin is irresistible. Everyone has to laugh constantly.

One evening I left him in the cage, but not tightly locked. He got out and pulled down every inch of electric wiring in the studio. He sat on a tangle of wires, very pleased with his achievement. My typing was covered with the smoky marks of his toes on my carbon paper. He tore apart my costume jewelry, ate the flowers in the flowerpots, hung from the transom cord until he opened it and escaped to the roof.

We ached from laughing, but I could not keep him. I could not work, go out, or cook without his finding something to do to divert my attention.

It was so difficult to give him up that I asked someone to take him back to the pet shop while I was out. I had become attached to him. When I came home he was gone. I went into the bathroom. There on the white wall were smoky imprints of his dirty paws, five clearly marked fingers, like a farewell message. I wept.

Robert writes in his diary:

The discovery of God comes with the confession of impotence. My love for others becomes confused with the hunger for God, for the annihilation of self, and the whole relationship slides into a terrifying chaos. It is not in contact with another human being that impotence is so terrifying, but because the ascension is not made then, because I know that it is only by exploding my self that I can reach union with God.

That is why I seek dynamite in the one I love, I am miserable when there is no war only because then there is no tension, no motion. I crave strength. I am starved for strength. Not for someone who would give me strength, no one can do that, but for someone who can open up my own strength. What are these many things I am? So many other levels of being, the animal, the divine, the animistic, the elemental. The battle is within me, and at the end I will know explosion, the final fusion, union with God. Yet I stand now trying to prevent anything from happening, paralyzing my movement towards Paul because I fear catastrophe.

Robert insists that I accept Patchen. Deep down, I cannot, neither as a writer nor as a human being.

I made a Freudian slip. Speaking about Patchen's a-sexual aura, I said: "What Patchen knows about sex would fit in a thimble!"

Henry writes from "The Shadows," Weeks Hall's residence in New Iberia, Louisiana:

The place is beautiful. House of the best old style, far better than Caresse's—with magnificent formal French gardens, statues, pools, ponds loaded with azaleas, camellias, roses, etc. Trees full of moss—frighteningly beautiful. Place is in the heart of old France—people still talking old French. River passes back yard—magical dreamy river. Don't know what's what yet. Only arrived last night. But rather expect to be back in New Orleans Monday. [Abe] Rattner goes back to New York next week—can't continue any longer.

At the first opportunity I have to sit down and write that Don Juan story for the collector, I will. Then I'll feel done with him. I don't want to do that work any more for anything, and urge you not to do a stroke more than you feel like. . . .

Paul came. I saw Robert change before my eyes, become woman, seductive, tantalizing, coquettish. I saw Robert's body dilate with desire. It was like being admitted into the secret chamber of homosexual love, and seeing a Robert who would otherwise be concealed from me.

Paul said: "You two resemble each other."

"Robert is more truthful," I said.

"He loves less, he is narcissistic," said Paul.

Warmth in the air. We are sitting in the Spanish restaurant Jai Alai. There is the smell of saffron and the vivid Spanish voices. The taboo which exists between Robert and myself and which makes us behave so abstractedly, almost somnambulistically, towards each other is annihilated for a moment.

I could look with Paul's eyes at Robert's finely designed body, at his narrow waist. But his face expressed dissolution and was so open that it was like an act of exhibitionism. Everything he felt was suddenly revealed to the naked eye because of the presence of man.

Gonzalo cannot do political work because he cannot discipline himself. What else can he do?

Is his guilt towards Helba a proof of his love for her or its opposite? At times it seems like the demonstrations of a dead love and Gonzalo seeking to atone for the death of love by offering a sacrifice in its place. At times he is aware of his self-destructiveness. Helba supplies him with an alibi for not working, and this is an important role for her. He needs her.

Robert writes:

Anaïs, we exist in a great world of fire and sea. Patchen is outside of our world. It is because he is locked out of our world and is trying to get back into it that we must understand him, accept him. He is the saint atoning for his acts. He atones for the murders committed by the human race. You and I were never separated from the human. I am more separated by my hermaphroditism.

About Paul I feel another thing. He seemed at first like a gracious creature, but then I felt a vicarious activity, an invasion of my creativity. I felt that he stopped my creativity, halted it, in order to examine it. I have to stop and explain. He does not understand me intuitively as you do, and I am forced to explain. He stops the smallest thought to examine it. There is no explanation for the meaning of soaring, for a lyrical state. One has to be inside of it. He is outside.

I knew he had not given Paul his true self. He acted like a caricature of woman. He broke away with cruelty. He went off and made love to a girl, and even though he did not have an orgasm he acquitted himself well enough so that she asked him: "You must have done this before."

Robert answered: "No, I am just well-read."

But after that he stopped reading my diary, saying he did not want to become engulfed in my life and start living my life, not his. I learned from his diary of a drama which does not exist in the love of man for a woman.

Paul treated Robert as a woman, and Robert sensed the danger in this, for in woman's abandon, in her yieldingness there is a fulfillment of her feminine role, whereas when the man yields in this way he is condemned to passivity which destroys the active side of him, cripples him, and may produce that caricature of the woman which the homosexual knows to be a symptom that his masculinity has been conquered.

In Robert, to lie passive and be treated like a woman in bed is not a fulfillment of his deepest nature but a destruction of one side of his hermaphroditic body for the sake of another, a partial crippling. So what is left is the feeble half-woman only with a woman's weakness, the defeated woman still flaunting her seductions superficially as the prostitute does, a pretense, not a deep experience.

Robert would not allow this to happen. He had begun to assert his masculinity through his work. What I reinforced in Robert was his active, masculine side.

He saw then, how I looked at the softening of his body, the swaying of his hips. His face became that of the coquette, receiving flowers with a flutter of the eyelashes, oblique glances like the upturned corner of a coverlet, the edge of a petticoat, the stage bird's sharp turn of the head, the little dance of alertness, the petulance of the mouth pursed for small kisses that do not shatter the being, the flutter and perk of femininity, all adornment and change, a mockery of the evanescent, mysterious fluidities of woman, a mockery of her invitations, a burlesque of her gestures of alarm or promise.

The woman without the womb in which child and creation coil and erupt, the woman without the womb in which awesome mysteries take place. In place of the full woman, this travesty of the woman, never leading to any magnificent fusions.

I watched Robert and he must have felt my eyes watching this disguise, this masquerade, because it ceased as abruptly as it had come.

Robert leaves his diary on my table saying: "At first with you and me it was the myth. But now I feel it is human."

Patterns, interweavings, repetitions. Echoes of other lives. Virginia and Robert imitate my life at times but with all the cruelties I never practiced. I try to tell them cruelty comes from impotence, that it is only those who cannot make love who kill. They betray each other and take pleasure in doing so.

Robert writes a "Trial" in his diary in which he asks himself: "Why did you seduce P. knowing it will injure V.? Did you really want him or were you testing your power against a woman's? Why did you seduce C.? Did you want his protection, his maturity, his knowledge, or did you desire him?"

Years ago Henry said: "Your only weakness is your incapacity to destroy." Am I going to learn this from those who surround me now, or am I being pushed into rebellion because I refuse to be sacrificed again to a Dudley or a Patchen? Patchen was repeating the inertia of Gonzalo and Helba, the criminal attitude: Society owes me care, food, and I will revenge myself for what it does not give me.

Patchen asked me several times for help but in a cold, impersonal way, without troubling to create first of all a bond of friendship, a bond of fraternity entitling him to demand all of me.

I cook. Millicent comes to clean only once a week. And meanwhile Patchen tells me he will not allow his wife to work for him. She is half my age and twice as strong as I am.

I evolved a plan to ask everyone I knew to contribute a small sum every month. Patchen took no part in this activity. He could not get up in the morning in time to telephone Dorothy Norman. I took his manuscript to Scribner's. He telephones me: "Would you send me ten dollars?"

I said I couldn't. I had just telegraphed Henry all I had. I wrote him a long and stormy letter. I told him we all knew the artist should be taken care of, but he had no right to demand this of

other writers like himself who were not wealthy. As it was, everyone came to my studio to eat, as if it were a cafeteria. I was doing nothing but serving coffee and sandwiches. My work was stopped.
I finally gave up answering the bell. I worked on the story of Moricand. On Jean Carteret's story. On the houseboat story.
Robert finally accepted my rebellion against Patchen's cold use of me. "Now I know you are a human being."

Robert and I sat at the same table working. He is reliving his early life. When he came to his description of his love for a young friend he wept. He said: "Art cannot carry me through all this."
When Robert was not desired every day he believed it was the end of the love. He had to prove the existence of this love through constant incarnations. Over and over again. Nothing permanent, nothing enduring seemed to be created for him except through passion.

Henry sends me the genealogical history of my family in New Orleans.

On getting back from New Iberia I called on Dr. Marion Souchon, the seventy-year-old surgeon and painter (a Creole), whom I had asked to investigate the Anaïs Bourdin family.
To my surprise he handed me the enclosed document which he had gathered in my absence—a big job which I could never have been able to undertake alone. He was on the point of giving up the search, finding no record of Anaïs Bourdin at the City Hall, when another Creole overheard his secretary telephoning and volunteered to help.
The real data comes from the church records. Note that Anaïs Bourdin was Catherine! Later, when she married, she called herself and signed herself C. Anaïs Bourdin. But this is the one. She was born in February 1815, not 16, if you notice. I could not get the hour though I asked for it. But there is quite a history given here, I think. They even knew your mother was in Paris in 1935. The names of the Bourdin children are interesting, eh—Numa, Herzenide, etc. Notice too that there was originally some German blood—Andres Flack. The will of Bernard Bourdin is also of peculiar interest, don't you think? I understand that the present Alfred Remeche is interested in genealogical matters. Hope I can meet him and tell you more. Your great-aunt Emily is Blanche Vaurigaud—an

old maid of seventy-seven or eighty. I've kept a copy of the data in case I meet these people. Later I'll turn over the copies to you.

Last night I had dinner at the Feiblemans' home—the most modern home in New Orleans. Something quite sumptuous. Was offered a beautiful room to stay in but refused. Need privacy. See too many people. This is the friendliest place I have struck in America . . . Anaïs, you should try to get hold of a book by Charles Fort called *The Book of the Damned*. It is a very queer book—you will see. Read it thoroughly—contains startling data and still more startling beliefs. . . . Queer names to places down here. One town called "Slaughter."

Look at the map of the state if you can. The mouth of the Mississippi sounds romantic but isn't. Only to the hunter and trapper. It's bleak, desolate, forlorn—despite the oranges and bananas, etc. Wherever the palmetto grows it's dreary. I still stick to it. . . . About Patchen. I have no doubt that all you say is true.

Henry sends me a letter he received from his father:

I am writing this to you so that Mother won't know about same and please don't mention anything about this note in your next letter. I am on my last carton of cigarettes as I gave some to Mr. Woolf for his birthday the other day, that was the least I could do for him as he has been good to me in taking me to the doctor and if this reaches you in time would you mind making that carton to be Julep, the mint-covered cooled cigarette. I like to use them in combination with the others. A carton of those would last me a long time. After those send me the usual Pall Mall and for which I would thank you. Incidentally if you could spare just $1 and put the bill in the letter when you write to us it will be O.K. Mother won't keep it on me but please don't send any more than the above amount. Again, thanking you and mum is the word, with love, Father.

Robert's dream written the day after he was cruel to Paul.

People are talking about me. They are looking for me. I have committed some crime. Now I can hear them beating about the bushes. I am hiding in a little socket. Now I find a little eye here. It is alive. It is a place where the earth looks out at the birds. I realize now that the voices are those of birds that are nesting inside of my head back of each ear. I put a little glass cup over the earth's eye so that it will not feel the cold.

Robert comes in the morning. We write, and talk just enough to keep the writing flowing. I sometimes read what he writes while he is writing it. He flows amazingly in talk and writing. It is a torrent of new words and images.

He says: "Declare your treacheries."

I say: "No, protect those you love."

When I see Gonzalo he is cornered by his inertia. He is ill. He has a toothache.

I say: "Go to the dentist." He answers: "It does not hurt now!"

I say: "It will hurt later during the night and keep you from sleeping." He says: "It does not hurt now. I cannot think of what will happen later."

Henry telegraphs me:

My father is dying. Send me thirty dollars for the plane.

I had just mailed another carton of cigarettes to the humble, gentle German tailor.

Letter from Henry, from New Orleans:

. . . Tomorrow I'll tell you all about my stay at New Iberia. It's a book in itself. Greek book still unsold. Also never a line from the collector. New Iberia—marvelous setting but the man (Weeks Hall) is a talker. I wrote you one letter from there—that was about the only free time he gave me. I would have gone nuts if I had stayed any longer.

The old Dr. Souchon is very friendly and eager to cultivate me. Have given his secretary the dope on Anaïs Bourdin and hope she will have the information for me tomorrow when I call on Dr. Souchon. This is a miniature France, with an accent as of N.Y. when it is not old French.

I wrote Faulkner, asking if I could call on him—at Oxford, Miss. But I haven't had a reply—and rather doubt that I ever will. Spent last evening talking about Tibet with a hunter and trapper friend of Weeks Hall. This world is somewhat like Faulkner's books. Completely introverted and decadent and isolated. Well, I'll expand on it tomorrow. Don't kill yourself. I picture you bent over the machine all day.

Henry's father died. Henry arrived two hours late. Henry was resigned, mystical, quiet. He talked about New Orleans, his trip, what he had seen. We did not talk about his father. He was going back to his family. He had to attend the vigil of his father.

"It is like a deep sleep. It did not hurt me to see him. He was so cold to the touch. That frightened me. He did not suffer. It was good that he died. The doctor said if he had lived he would have suffered."

Robert is emerging as a poet. His talks are like bonfires. His hair falls over his eyes as he writes as if he were an eager child drawing. His fingers are always stained with carbon paper or type-writer ribbon and he leaves his fingertips on my pages, as the monkey left paw marks on my bathroom walls.

Early diaries re-create a state like opium smoking, where one little incident, one caress, one scene, one word produced enormous elation, diffusion, expansion, heightened sensations.

The actual life comes in small pieces, but it creates great echoes. I was like an opium dreamer and the focus was not clear, actuality and reality half-veiled. That may have been the cause of the exaltation. But after that the writing and the vision became clearer and sharper. I focused on the human drama, movement, action. Less on the marvelous heightened sensations they caused. The writing grew tighter, more economical. The focus on life. In the last diaries, there is at last a fusion of life, fantasy, reverie, action, and they flow together. I dream, I carry out the dream, I live, I dream about what I live, and this nourishes the next step, which is the story.

Robert writes in his diary:

I have a great hunger as I read these diaries. It is the male creative hunger to devour, take all and digest it. You, the woman, do not have this impulse. The very process of the diary is that of life itself, not devouring but nourishing, not transformed by art but passing through your body, your senses.

There is not in you the same urge. Writing is part of living, part of the life function. The diary is the great river in progress, down from the mountains of childhood come the tributaries, through the beginning places, broader and broader. Now we have gone into a new country. The writing of the girlhood is gone, and the diary speaks a new language. The mountains from where it started have become very small in the distance. Everything is new. The face of the father, the face of the mother, Joaquin, Anaïs. The river flows swiftly. Sometimes it floods. Mists rise at the conjunctions with fire. Mists like clouds of sulphur rise from the burning fires within the currents of the water itself. We cannot see. Out of the mist blindly an island, a rock, a tree will loom, obscurely transformed into a cloud. Then we meet it. Suddenly we surround its form. We feel it is a real form. In Joyce's *Finnegans Wake* all life flows within the river, the woman Anna Livia Plurabelle. And all life is indestructible, gigantic. Joyce has made the man's creation, the moment that flows, it is a perpetual river that runs into itself again, built upon the circles of life and death, birth and rebirth. The wake which is both the crossing into the death and the waking from the dream into life. In this diary you may achieve the woman's creation, the flow, the river which becomes monumental. It will be the form which is within life itself, the woman's creation which is generation. It is your life itself which will become monumental. The writing is only a record, a vicarious record of that creation as a photograph would be a vicarious record of physical form. For a man it is the book itself, the geometric problems, the gigantic pillar, the pillage, the city which becomes monumental. These are polar essences.

The telephone bill unpaid. The net of economic difficulties closing in on me. Everyone around me irresponsible, unconscious of the shipwreck. I did thirty pages of erotica.

I could ask as Patchen does: Why does no one help me? Robert brings all his friends in need. I feed them.

Letter from Moricand, still in his small hotel room, cold, hungry. The needs of people will drive me insane. I know some of these needs are created by themselves, acts of self-destruction. Why do they all act self-destructively and then turn towards me for help? Why are they so willing to burden me? Why don't they wish to free me or protect me? Because I give with love and understanding? Because they feel that I will respond? I get ill when I have to reject a burden.

A young man called Fair. A thin, consumed young man, skeletonic. He was brought to me. Dudley and Lafe were there that night. I felt he was utterly dislocated and I did not want to see him again. I felt he was about to fall apart right there before our eyes. I eluded him. One night I was so ill and in such pain that Dr. Jacobson had to give me a morphine injection. Fair telephoned me at four in the morning. It was like a symbol. I was ill at the pain of having to reject new burdens (Dudley and Lafe) and the voice of Fair, who cannot sleep, who drugs himself, calls me when I am fighting off new burdens. Fair invited me to dinner. I would not go alone. Finally he wrote me a last appeal: He was leaving for Ecuador. Could he say farewell? I let him come. The next day he rang the bell at two A.M. He was drugged. I sent him away. The next morning I received a letter! "I need you as the one luminous point in my madness."

I cannot escape the role assigned to me. A struggle to get my writing done. I am rebelling against my destiny because I am being stifled, submerged. Physically I am not equal to it. I shall be devoured.

Awakened to the consciousness of being without a cent. Telephoned the collector. Had he heard from his rich client about the last manuscript I sent? No, he had not, but he would take the one I had just finished and pay me for it. Henry must see a doctor. Gonzalo needs glasses. Robert came with B. and asked me for money to go to the movies. The soot from the transom window falls on my typing paper and on my work. Robert comes and takes away my box of typing paper.

Isn't the old man tired of pornography? Won't a miracle take place? I begin to imagine him saying: "Give me everything she writes, I want it all, I like all of it. I will send her a big present, a big check for all the writing she has done."

Anaïs is being murdered by her children.

Robert says that Patchen put a curse on me. Because I told him I feel so low physically and asked him not to come for a few days he is offended, hurt. When I do not answer the bell he climbs up through the fire escape, leaps from the fire escape onto the porch, and then climbs up through the transom. When I come out of the kitchen, I find him sitting at my desk.

My typewriter is broken.

With a hundred dollars in my pocket I recovered my optimism. I said to Henry: "The collector is contradicting himself. He says he likes simple, unintellectual women—but he invites me to dinner."

Henry sees Dr. Jacobson, who says he can cure him but that the medicine will cost thirty-eight dollars.

Henry cannot break his contract with Doubleday, he must continue traveling even if the advance was so small.

Gonzalo and I walk the streets, trying to find work he could do. I try to relieve his guilt by telling him there is an ugliness in being paid for work one does not like, because I feel the ugliness of working for the old man. There is a purity in those who do not work, like the purity of the child.

One of my children stole my fountain pen!

Robert is worried about the draft. He joined his friend Jeff hitchhiking through the country.

"Under a Glass Bell" story was accepted by a little magazine. No pay.

Robert is back. He discovered that his journeys were to be made by writing. So the two typewriters are clicking in unison again.

I have a feeling that Pandora's box is the mysteries of woman's sensuality, so different from man's and for which man's language is inadequate. The language of sex has yet to be invented. The language of the senses is yet to be explored. D. H. Lawrence began to give instinct a language, he tried to escape the clinical, the scientific which does not capture what the body feels.

I write another erotic story.

Gonzalo had a friend, Manuel, who indulged in a special form of enjoyment. His family had repudiated him and he lived in Montparnasse. When not obsessed with erotic exigencies, he was an entertaining talker, a witty café companion, and very learned.

His favorite theater of denudation was the Bibliothèque Nationale. He loved the quiet, the peace, the old scholars studying, the occasional handsome young woman student doing research. He loved the labyrinth of bookcases, of files, in which one could get lost. He would peruse the books, until he reached the vision of some young woman bending over a book, taking notes. Tired of the pose, she might raise her head, and there stood Manuel, exhibiting his prize possession in his hand. The shock, the flush, the reaction delighted him. It was more dangerous, more exhilarating than when he exposed himself at parties, for the artists laughed at him, and half the time no one was impressed.

The paradox was the contrast between his ascetic face, the monk-like leanness of the body, the dreamy poetic eyes, the austere features even, and all this in such dissonance with his exhibition.

If his audience ran away from him he experienced no pleasure. If the victim stayed and stared at him then he fell into a trance of pleasure, his face would become ecstatic.

Women usually tended to run away from him. He had to resort to trickeries. He posed as a model in the art schools but as he revealed his responsiveness to the stare of the students he was thrown out of class.

If he was invited to a party he would seek empty rooms, or a balcony, or a deserted terrace where couples came to kiss, and then put on his performance.

Often he stood at the corner of the street, naked under his coat, and if a woman passed he would open his coat.

It took many years for Manuel to find a mate to his obsession. It happened when he was taking a train to the south of France. He was alone in the compartment and had already stretched out for a comfortable sleep when a woman came in. She was quite attractive, dressed with piquancy. She wore a tight tailored skirt, a fluffy blouse. She took off her hat, loosened her hair, kicked off her shoes, and lay down on the opposite side.

Before falling asleep she gave him an elusive smile. At first she lay stretched out, moving only slightly with the motion of the train. She had such long eyelashes he could not tell if she were completely asleep or not. It seemed to him that a sliver of iridescence showed through the closed eyelids. Just in case she should open her eyes, he deftly and quietly unbuttoned his trousers. He wore no underwear, and the flesh of his manhood showed, shell-pink and clear-toned, at rest. The woman raised one leg, as if to rest from the stretched-flat position. As her skirt was tight this gave Manuel a vista up her thighs not quite to where his eyes would have liked to wander. After a moment she raised her other leg. A small shuddering ripple passed through the sexual baton of Manuel.

She was naked. Manuel could see the pubic hair, the flowerlike vulva. She opened her eyes. They smiled at each other.

He could see the pearly moisture of pleasure appearing on her skin.

They were married in the south of France.

Pierre Mabille,* writer, physician, writes in *Miroir du Merveilleux:*

He who wishes to attain the profoundly marvelous must free images from their conventional associations, associations always dominated by utilitarian judgments; must learn to see the man behind the social function, break the scale of so-called normal values, replacing it by that of sensitive values, surmount taboos, the weight of ancestral prohibitions, cease to connect the object with profit one can get out of it, with the price it has in society, with the action it commands. This liberation begins when by some means the voluntary censorship of the bad conscience is lifted, when the mechanism of the dream is no longer impeded. Magic ceremonies, psychic exercises leading to concentration and ecstasy, the liberation of mental automatism, are so many means capable of

* Author of *Thérèse de Lisieux, La Conscience Lumineuse, Egregores, La Vie des Civilizations.*

refining vision through the tensions they induce. It is a means to enlarge normal facilities; they are a way of approach to the realm of the marvelous.

Dream: I am visiting a royal family in a castle. I have no legs. I walk supported by my crinoline. Occasionally people carry me. There is a feast. I feel beautiful, although legless, graceful and light. The king himself carries me. He is stirred by my nearness. He takes me on his knees and kisses me and says he wants to marry me. But there is a revolution.

The masses fight the black-shirted men. I run away. I hide behind a tree. A woman is watching me from behind the window of a house. I decide to ask her for refuge. As I enter I say with great confidence and sense of power: "I am the Princess."

She hides me in the attic, from where I can see the fighting. Then the woman's three sons come in and say: "We have won." I am not sure who has won. I look at them carefully and conclude they are dressed like royal subjects, not revolutionaries. They help me to leave and return to the castle. There is an atmosphere of aristocracy and pleasure.

On my birthday, February twenty-first, Gonzalo said: "I just remembered that today is my mother's birthday."

This did not surprise me.

Gonzalo deceived me at first because of his bigness, because of his physical power, because he could knock a man down, and drink all night without need of sleep, because his angers were like cyclones. So at first I did not detect the child in him. He claimed from me indulgence, the love his mother did not give him. I protected the child through years of drunkenness, through ineffectual revolutions, through so many failures and defeats and dangers, through his moments of blindness and selfishness. That is why he burdened me with all his problems. He expected no fatigue or rebellion from me.

When his mother's love died because of his anarchy and because he ran away with Helba, I was assigned to replace her and to grant all the demands his real mother denied him.

I have such a long-suppressed desire for frivolity, for insouciance, freedom! But now I must write to keep my small world together.

The collector says: "You can start working on another volume."

Gonzalo's opium consists in childhood memories, in returning to the place where he was born.

"In the jungle there is a huge, giant flower called the 'rose of the selva.' Its leaves are so big and so thick that the Indians cut them down to make canoes, and on these they can float down the rivers.

"There is an animal who seeks out women and while they sleep he tries to place his beak inside their sex. He crawls up their legs and inserts his beak and the women die of fright and horror. He was called a *chinchilito*.

"Once I heard about a man who had to deliver a coffin. He took it by bus, but as there was no room inside the crowded bus he was sent to the top with the coffin. During the journey it began to rain hard. The man was getting soaked. He decided to get into the coffin and cover himself. More people came. They sat with their backs against the coffin. The man inside the coffin listened to their conversations, got bored, lifted the lid and asked: 'Is it still raining?' The Indians panicked, threw themselves off the bus, one of them broke his leg."

Letters from Henry:

I met a pleasant couple through [Ben] Abramson [in Chicago], who is a good friend of theirs, a friendship that ripened through books. Found all my books here allocated in a complete library of erotica, one of the finest I've ever seen. The man and the wife are intelligent, have lived in Europe and Mexico, widely read, interested in painting and music, extremely sympathetic, hospitable, etc. . . . They have a tremendous library, including photos and films—locked in a big vault hidden behind a secret bookcase. Very interesting. I think I have now seen about every kind of erotic film ever made—including animals and machines. I'm glutted. . . .

Abramson is practically sure of publishing *World of Sex*. He may also publish the other two stories, but I am not certain yet. . . . They would be sold out rather quickly, he thinks—because he has a special list who waits for these things. He may also sell the original typescripts at the same times and get more money thus. I can't get any advance on them. . . .

I'm leaving at five today for Des Moines to stay with Lafe until Thursday, I believe, when I will go on to St. Louis and Memphis to Natchez. Reason: I want to complete the impressions I accumulated at Dudley's. The "Letter to Lafayette," which he is really writing now in fine pencil hand in a fat ledger, is an amazing work. He has marvelous themes —bigger and more symbolic than Patchen's—and I like the way he is doing it. I am going to write about Lafe and Dudley, and this Letter, in my book. I also want to see his father (Dudley's), who is a character—and little Joe the drummer. I have a stack of good notes on the subject.

Unfortunately, since I left Detroit I haven't added a line—too much to soak in. But I expect to resume at Lafe's place and from then on, when I will be quite alone again. I haven't any fear now of not having the material for the book. I'm loaded, overwhelmed with material. And I can write any time I isolate myself. . . .

[April, 1941]

Caresse Crosby came. Canada Lee is starring in *Native Son*. We went to the play together. Then to Harlem, where Canada Lee runs a night club. We talked. Drank. Listened to jazz. Some jazz flamboyant, some creating tensions not by increased loudness but by the subtlety of its gradations. Some jazz is like velvet, some like silk, some like electric shocks, some like seduction, some like a drug.

How could one not love the people who created such a music, in which the rhythm of the heart and of the body is so human and the voice so warm, emotions so deep. Charlie Parker, Fats Waller, Duke Ellington, Benny Goodman, Cootie Williams, Benny Carter, Teddy Hill, Chick Webb, Mary Lou Williams, Count Basie, Lionel Hampton.

And Canada Lee with his eye injured in boxing, the only profession besides music in which the Negro can shine, is allowed to shine, as the poor boys of Spain were allowed only the possibility of demonstrating valor and quality in bullfights. Canada Lee, with his warm, orange-toned voice, his one unclouded eye glowing with tenderness and joy, his stance loose-limbed, natural; in life relaxed, in music and acting tense, alert, swift, and as accurate as a hunter.

The place is a cloud of smoke, the faces very near, the hypnosis of jazz all-enveloping and, even at its most screaming moments, dissolving the heart and throbbing with life.

Caresse and Canada have been friends for a long time.

Caresse is one of those who are concerned about our lives becoming less meaningful than in Europe, less vital, less sparkling and warm. We talked about this with Canada. The only authentic life of emotion and warmth seemed to be right there, at that moment, with the jazz, and the soft voices and the constant sense of touch between them. We feel more restrictions, less freedom, less tolerance, less intimacy with other human beings. Except here in Harlem.

Henry writes:

Have been through some great country since I left Little Rock Sunday morning. Went through country roads into the mountains—dirt roads, the dust almost choking me. The whole terrain like a giant washbowl—full of great buckles—like a scenic railway. Today even more wonderful country. Taos may be better—the Navajos—over near Arizona border. Free, nomadic Indians, raising sheep and horses. Practice polygamy. Are multiplying so rapidly that by 2040 they will be 1,000,000—perhaps the dominating race-group of America. So an Indian authority says.

The Negroes too are rapidly increasing—and we are practically stationary, you know. It would be a fine ironic piece of justice if the next century saw the land revert to the Negroes and Indians, eh? Not altogether improbable, either.

I don't care a hoot for Santa Fe itself—tho' when you walk out of town and look at the mountains it's grand—very much like Greece. But the natives here (Spanish and mixed bloods) are not nearly as interesting as the Greeks. There's something monkeyish about them—no character and backbone of their own. Imitators. And these wretched Indians wandering around in a coma trying to sell blankets and jewelry—remind you of the Arabs in the Paris cafés. On the reservations I imagine it is quite different. But it's not easy, even when you have permission to penetrate this country. Not accessible by car. Roads terrible and no shelter. It's cold as the devil tonight—winter.

This morning beautiful and crisp, the snow dripping from the trees, the sky very blue, icy blue. I'm wondering if I can stand the altitude. Feel fine, look fine, except for the most violent headaches. Took six aspirins today and then couldn't drive it away. . . . It's a batty, goofy place—seedy. Big difference between the Arkansas people and those out here. Difference comes from rootedness. The floating types are no damned good, I find, our best types are our backward people who stayed put (most of the South, for example). They developed character. The most wonderful people are found in the paradisiacal places. Because they are looking for an escape from all struggle. That's terribly obvious. Hits you in the eye. Lawrence was terribly right when he said in that book about Italy "the whistlers go to America."

Caresse took me to visit Colette, a beautiful opera singer, living in luxury, protected by a famous banker. She has a castle in France, she is free to come and go. Having just finished reading "The

Dreamers" by Isak Dinesen I associated her with Pellegrina. Under the externals of beauty, fame, luxury, runs a streak of tragedy. She loved a Spanish pianist who did not love her, and she slashed her wrists for him. She seemed to be the most fulfilled and pampered woman in the world, and yet her face bore marks of sorrow.

We sat looking down at New York City from the top of the Waldorf Towers, surrounded by crystal, silver, deep carpets, tapestries, silk, brocade, damask, paintings, waited on by quiet, suave servants so well trained they seemed almost invisible.

My wine-colored suit came from Lerner's and cost seven dollars. Caresse gave me a grey silk blouse. My cape is cut out of my worn-out caracal fur coat and the hat I wear is the same I sported on the Champs Élysées years ago. But Colette said: "You look dashing."

I did not want to be Colette, living in ostentatious luxury. But I did wish I had a castle in France and the means to move about when a place or event was painful. With the power to move away from one role in life into another.

Letter from Henry:

. . . When I asked a mechanic today when the climbing would end he said, "Not for several hundred miles—not till you hit the Great Divide." I am halfway across the continent now—imagine that. Ahead of me lie cactus, sagebrush, desert, Indian ruins, tremendous mountain ranges—up to 14,000 feet. At Albuquerque I'll come to the Rio Grande. In Arizona the great Colorado River. In Washington the Columbia River. The best part of the trip lies before me—I am just on the threshold.

The great distance to cover had me buffaloed. I can only travel about two hundred miles a day in this jalopy. If I had a better car I could do three hundred and fifty miles easily. But my tires are worn smooth and I can't take any risks. I need three new shoes before I dare to do any difficult driving in the Rocky Mountains.

It seems to me these western men are very gentle, tho' outwardly rough. Almost girlish. Certainly childish. It's tremendously empty here. The horizon is always fifty miles off. The towns are seventy-five or a hundred miles apart. God help me if I get stuck between places. Tho' I've got that figured in advance. I'll just leave the car and get someone to haul me to the next town with my luggage. Then find someone to come back for it.

There are lots of roamers now on the road west. Floaters. I don't dare pick them up—they might slug you for a dime.

At home I discard my elegance (!) to match my other friends' working clothes—corduroy, leather jacket—and walk down Broadway with Gonzalo to see a jungle film. Gonzalo tells me stories of Peruvian adventures for my erotica.

Henry's adventures through America seem to be irritating rather than inspiring. His letters are often angry.

I went to a party at Mercedes Matter's, the daughter of the painter Arthur Carles. I met musicians, painters, a whole roomful of well-known people. I danced with John Nelson, an imaginative architect. He told me about his project to design a house of many moods, on many levels, with a roof which would slide away and let you see the sun or stars. Rooms for intimacy and rooms for formal occasions. He described sliding panels, variations in space and height, and I told him I had once dreamed of a house like that which I called the dream of the Chinese boxes. Sliding panels and mysteries.

Danced with Pierre Matisse, the son of the painter, who owns a gallery in New York. With Harvey Breit, the poet, who has sea-green eyes, a husky voice, and skin which looks tanned by a setting sun, tinged with copper. I talked with Isamu Noguchi, the sculptor, slender, stylized, with such delicate features. He invited me to his studio to see his works. Luis Buñuel was there, with his thyroid eyes, the moles on his chin which I remember from so long ago when we first saw the surrealist films in the Cinémathèque, in an attic room, cold but crowded, where the films were introduced by a pale-faced Henri Langlois, and as he talked I remember thinking that his paleness was most appropriate for someone who spent his life in dark projection rooms. This was the first club of experimental films, separate from commercial movie houses. Buñuel and Dali were there. Buñuel now works alone. He has a fierce sharp humor, a bitter sarcasm, and at the same time towards women a gentle, special smile.

Saw Mme. Pierre Chareau, the wife of the architect, who was my neighbor in Louveciennes. He was the first architect to build a glass house in Paris. She kept a decorator-furniture shop to help him. I did not make friends with them at the time because I heard her voice over the hedge, telling the gardener or the maid what to do, and it was so loud and strong and authoritative that I shied away from her invitations. For me, at the time, she became another plump, forceful, domineering mother. I was very ashamed of my aloofness when she wrote me the first fan letter I had ever received on the publication of my book on Lawrence.

Now, at this party, she appeared quite different, a very brave woman who sent Pierre away from France at a time when he might have been put in a concentration camp as a Jew. "He was the valuable one to save," she said. "The one who could not be replaced. And he is helpless in life, so I stayed to dispose of our belongings and raise a little money for the trip. I am giving French lessons, if you know anyone who is interested."

Saw a play (*My Heart's in the Highlands*) by Saroyan, the American Maeterlinck. His poetry lacks strength, it is sentimental, but his humanity and humor touch me. The words evaporate, leave no memory, but the feeling of sweetness remains.

A strange night at the Tavern on Macdougal Street. A basement room. Two Negro musicians, one at the piano and the other playing bass. The piano seemed frivolous, a rippling waterfall, but the bass stirred a deep pulse. The piano hung sonorous festive garlands. The bass was a giant heartbeat.

Paul was awaiting a homosexual adventure. The rhythms of the music which gave me pleasure, caused him anguish, for they seemed to announce a joy, and each time the door opened I saw that he expected some marvelous person to enter. The suspense created by the jazz was a preparation for joy, which I would find for certain but not Paul. For him, as no one appeared at the door, no one he could desire, it would be another night without love.

Paul's eyes are riveted to the door. His blood will flow back to its source unspent, his love will flow back and everything that flows back is like poison. For Paul a sexual encounter is monotonous, because it is merely sexual. He says: "It is always the same."

I say: "For love it is never the same. What goes on inside is never the same, just like this music which changes every instant. For love there are a million variations, a million nights, a million days, contrasts in moods, in textures, whims, a million gestures colored by emotion, by sorrow, joy, fear, courage, triumph, by revelations which deepen the groove, creations which expand its dimensions, sharpen its penetrations. Love is vast enough to include a phrase read in a book, the shape of a neck seen and desired in a crowd, a face loved and desired, seen in the window of a passing subway, vast enough to include a past love, a future love, a film, a voyage, a scene in a dream, an hallucination, a vision. Love-making on a winter night is different from love-making on a summer night, under a tent, or under a tree, with or without a cover, under a shower, in darkness or in light, in heat or cold."

The bass had a steady rhythm, sex sex sex sex sex, but the flights of the piano were never the same, and the piano spoke of love, as emotion, mood, heat, climaxes, ascensions, variations, variations.

For Paul, sex did not appear at the door of the Tavern and at midnight he said sadly: "Let's go."

I bought paint that can be used on glass, and we painted all the windows like modern stained-glass windows, fourteen windows in all. The studio looks like a pagan cathedral. Each one of us painted one windowpane.

Then Robert began to paint the plain wood furniture with colored crayons which gave a waxy surface to the plain wood. He made beautiful designs on the wooden chests, on the benches, on the chairs. Tangled forests of flowers, leaves, mandalas, lace patterns, monsters out of nightmares, exotic birds, cosmic wheels, clowns, waves, eyes, oceans, clouds, sand, earth, fire.

While he painted he monologued on Henry Miller, Patchen, Bob and Virginia.

"In *Tropic of Cancer* there is no passion between people, only lust. Miller never falls in love, the characters are unrelated until June comes. At first I couldn't read Miller because of the absence of love. In Dostoevsky there is a constant passion between people."

He was writing abundantly, acting, dancing, talking, shining, burning, a fountain of inventions. He was reaching a peak of joy, of radiance, and then: ORDER TO REPORT FOR INDUCTION.

Robert is gone.
He left me a beautiful gift: *Seven Gothic Tales,* by Isak Dinesen. The story of "The Dreamers":

> If I come to think very much of what happens to that one woman, why I shall go away, at once, and be someone else. There are many that I can be. I will be many persons from now on. Never again will I have my heart and my whole life bound up with one woman, to suffer so much. You must from now on, be more than one, many people, as many as you can think of. . . .

This story affected me deeply. It seemed to offer a solution to the difficulties of my own life. I went out for a walk, to calm the agitation and exaltation it produced in me. After reading it, I felt as if my own wings were growing out again, as if I could soar again, and as if I could recover my powers of magical transpositions and disguises.

I had been struck with Noguchi's beauty. A Japanese body, trim, stylized, held erect, but unexpectedly green eyes and an ambiguous smile, speech which does not reveal, words which are oblique, erasable, which dissolve and leave no trace. The pure small nose and tender mouth speak one message and the modern artist another. I did not know then that he has Scottish blood. He is the son of a Japanese poet. I see the Japanese sensitivity but it is secret. He lives in one of the exquisite houses in Macdougal Alley, one of the few, rare streets left in New York, in which the two- and three-story houses are unified in architecture, like those of a European village. It is closed to cars, and has old lanterns at the corners. It has trees, interesting, odd-shaped windows, and an atmosphere of other countries.
Noguchi took me to his house in his sports car. The enormous sculptures he makes were not there, but I saw a large table filled with miniature replicas of his work, models two or three inches high. Placed all together like this they made a city of the future, a new world, a universe of forms I did not at first perceive.

When I came home I happened to be looking up some information in the Encyclopaedia Britannica and opened the page on mathematics and geometry. There was a whole page of clay models, models of mathematical abstractions, illustrating advanced mathematical concepts of geometrical abstractions. And they resembled the sculptures of Noguchi. I began to see the new forms born of a scientific era. My first inkling of this had been at the Museum of Natural History. In one room I found magnified models of blood cells. Before I knew what they were, I thought they were the most beautifully designed, the most aesthetic forms I had seen, and I wondered whether our art concepts were born from some mysterious source such as the designs of our blood cells.

At the party, I had also talked with Edgar Varèse. He feels that America does not want his music. He has a sense of frustration and rebellion. He wants to explode in some revolutionary way, to assert the music no one wants to hear. He told me of a nightmare he had. He was brought before the guillotine. He stood in front of it. He was undressed. His head was cut off.

As he mocks psychology, I did not dare offer an interpretation. But I told him my dream of him as a lightning conductor who became the conductor of lightning.

As they admire my *House of Incest,* he and Louise, I confessed to him that I felt the same way, I felt America did not want my writing.

The poets are confused about their roles. They set themselves up as philosophers or men of action. I do not think the poet should preach, seek to convert, philosophize or moralize. Henry, Saroyan, Robert. If you live as a poet the poet's duty is to maintain his power to create the marvelous *by contagion.* If the poet maintains himself inside a dream and is able to communicate this capacity to others by osmosis, well and good. But he should not step out of this dream to preach, to meddle with political and practical constructions. Let him remain a poet and reveal magic coincidences and magic possibilities. The one who has the vision is not necessarily the one who knows how to actualize or embody this vision. The old communities understood this. Each one had his role allotted to him.

The poet to supply his visions, his song, his inspiration (from within) and the others to hunt, fish, build, and the wise men to interpret events, omens, the future. The poet's business is exaltation and how to impart it.

I feel the poet is losing this power because he is joining the prosaic, the contingent, the mediocre everyday details, the mechanism. Saroyan has moments of pure poetry. When one brother plays the piano and hears three thousand miles away his brother who left him, playing the cornet, that is a moment of poetry. When Agnes protects the mice and the brother protects Agnes's legend from which she draws sustenance, that is a moment of poetry. But when Saroyan steps out to moralize, to generalize, to preach, he destroys his poetic power.

At midnight Joaquin telephoned me that Mother fell out of the car, was not gravely hurt, but bruised. I left for Williamstown. I took care of her, braided her hair, made her bed, cheered her, loved her. There was no danger.

Going to bed that night in their simple, almost monastic house, I asked myself when did my mother's love for me die. It was when I married, when I left her house, when I ceased to be her child. Her sickness mitigated the martial qualities which usually rebuff tenderness. As she sat there, trying to work at her bookbinding again, I saw her for the first time in my life, tender, innocent, small. Her body seemed smaller, her hair more delicate. Her great commanding air gone. Her fierceness gone. For a moment I could express my love. *La grande batailleuse.* As she waved to me from the window as I left, she was once more healthy, the mother lioness again who made her children feel like children forever.

Letter to Robert:

You refuse to free yourself from serving in the Army by declaring your homosexuality. And by this you will live a double lie, for you are also against war. At the same time you feel burdened with guilt. Our only prison is that of guilt. Guilt is the negative aspect of religion. We lost our religion but we kept the guilt. We all have guilt. Even Henry has it, who seems the freest of all. Only domestic animals have guilt. We train them so. Animals in the jungle do not have it.

Everything negative should die. Jealousy as the negative form of love, fear the negative form of life.

You speak of suffering, of withdrawal, retreat. Face this suffering, for all the real suffering can save us from unreality. Real pain is human and deepening. Without real pain you will remain the child forever. The legend of Ondine tells of how she acquired a human soul the day she wept over a human love. You were caught in a web of unreality. You chose suffering in order to be awakened from your dreams, as I did. You are no longer the sleeping prince of neurosis. Don't run away from it now. If you run away from it without conquering it (I say accept the homosexuality, live it out proudly, declare it), then you will remain asleep and enchanted in a lifeless neurosis.

An evening with the Tanguys and the Varèses. I wanted to forget the rejection by American publishers. But Varèse's rebellion awakened my own feelings of frustration. In being deprived of publication I am deprived of existence, forced back into solitude, disconnected from life. Being published would have been a bridge between myself and American life. Without it, it means a shrunken life, a small world, less expansion and contact with the world. Louise Varèse said: "You look like a *princesse lointaine.*"

I answered: "But I don't want to be one. I do not feel remote. I am a human being."

Kay Tanguy wanted to help me meet more publishers. All the time, inside my head, like a tune one cannot get rid of, the world saying, Anaïs, your work is not necessary to others, the world does not want you, you cannot talk with others as Henry does, you are condemned to a void.

Henry and Varèse can talk. I cannot talk. I can only talk through my writing. I am mute in life. I must write. In writing I talk with others, I touch them. Let me be published. By not publishing me you seal my lips, you entomb me, you deny my existence. I love the world, and you throw me back into my small personal world.

Strange feelings, among friends, and loving friends. That night I felt unable to live if deprived of expression as a writer. The bridge. It was my first bridge. To reach my father. To reach Europe.

To keep the people I loved from vanishing. Writing against loss, against uprooting, against destruction. Writing against erasing. Time erases. Writing against the flaws of memory, the distortions of memory. Writing against death, separation. And now silenced. Books created my world. How will I create worlds without them? Without them my world is small and silent. Enclosed. Remote.

That night after the party I had a dream. I dreamt that writing on paper was false, that to tell the truth one must write on a strand of hair which comes directly from the brain, long phrases inscribed on the hair like Chinese characters, wonderful phrases I could not remember. This dream came also after John Slocum, literary agent, told me he could not do anything for my writing.

I read the *Microbe Hunters*. With Gonzalo I walked through the Lower East Side ghetto, an incredible place. Some shops, some old people, some of the street scenes are a direct transplant from Europe. Men with wide-brimmed black hats and long beards. Women in black dresses. Exotic foods and billboards in other languages. Special restaurants, coffee houses, German beer gardens, bookshops.

On Fourteenth Street I see Russian movies. The sincerity of the acting, the emotional beauty of the voices, the emotional range of the faces make other films seem vulgar and inane.

Virginia Woolf walked into the sea. This is her suicide note to her husband:

I have the feeling that I shall go mad and cannot go on any longer in these terrible times. I hear voices and cannot concentrate on my work. I have fought against it and cannot fight any more. I owe all my happiness to you. You have been so perfectly good. I cannot go on and spoil your life.

Amazing directness and simplicity from a writer who explored all the ambiguities of the English language, whose writing was so abstract and mysterious and labyrinthian. Simple, direct, as all true suffering. It was the first time she spoke as a human being.

Today I wrote fifteen pages for the old man.
In Hollywood, Henry is having cocktails with Miriam Hopkins.

Citizen Kane, a film that magnifies a thousand times the drama of emptiness. It is an emptiness I never experienced in Europe. In Europe one is bathed in history, in a rich past, in an atmosphere of spiritual enrichment, of significance.

It was symbolical that the castle and the art objects became absolutely devoid of meaning except as possessions of material value. It was symbolical that space could not be diminished by any tenderness or warmth.

This was my first encounter with the drama of emptiness. Massive, external objects, possessions, which Orson Welles depicts well. Giant stones, giant scale which in Europe is either a historical castle or a church, a cathedral or a monument, here became a monument to emptiness, impotence. Kane was the very symbol of inhumanity, absence of capacity to love, of sentimentality and greed, a total failure as a man. Orson Welles, fascinated as he is with the physical world, could cope with such scale, such an accumulation of meaningless matter. He has the camera-eye which could take in all of Kane's vast, empty, cliché, grandiose void. The symbols were vulgar, as they should be, crossword puzzles, rosebud to build on, a gate. Pulp writing was suited to the subject.

What is appalling is the scenic grandeur, the overpowering masses, noise, exaggerations to signify impotence. Power and powerlessness to obtain human happiness. I was reminded of the fish that swells up to frighten its enemies. Gigantism, monstrous, either physical or psychological, a disease. A tragedy of powerlessness, a Frankenstein monster of a new sort. What kind of soil, system, place can nurture such a monster? Loveless, sexless, mindless, all nonhuman, like some abnormal growth of a gland in a bottle. A man with only one obsession. Is Welles aware of the monumental ugliness of *Citizen Kane?* Is he a part of the camera-eye which sees only the externals? Was there something we did not know that would make Kane a human being? Greatness and bigness confused. Anything big is great. Is the camera as empty in its vision as its subject?

Dorothy Norman will publish sections of the childhood diary. She is the only one, with the Cooneys, who believes in my writing.

Henry writes from Hollywood:

So many things have happened. This is the vital spot (for people like us) in America. It is quite inexhaustible. The people I've met are workers, not lounge lizards. Just to recapitulate a few of my engagements recently—

1. The evening with the movie director and his wife, Jarmila. The picture of Tibet, the very scenes used in *Shangri-La* and *Yamaluru,* which is the real Shangri-La.

2. Evening with Larry Powell (whom I met in Dijon) librarian now at university here. Showed me your books. A saintly man—utterly out of the Hollywood picture. We became great friends. He is the friend and biographer of [Robinson] Jeffers, whom I see next week.

3. Visit to Peter Krasnov, probably the best sculptor living. A forest of musical creations in utter poverty. Another saint and utterly unknown here in Hollywood.

4. Visit with Luise Rainer. This I must tell you in detail later. It was wonderful. One comes away feeling sorry for her—she's a tragic figure. And awfully like you in some respects. Showed me her horoscope just done by some cheap American woman. Her caustic descriptions of Hollywood and the movie people unforgettable. Five "air" signs and a Gemini. Same birthday as my mother. Really intelligent, direct, and no more of the actress in life than on the screen—herself all the time. She's going to New York, 28 East Seventy-third Street, if you want to see her.

5. Evening at Willie Fung's saloon where the Desert Rat was playing the piano. Wonderful. I recognized the Chinaman immediately—from the screen. Something so unlike anything you would connect with Hollywood. In a dirty little hole with just a group of us for clients.

6. [Hilaire] Hiler's new home—his new piano, new paintings. Colossal work he did in San Francisco—the Aquatic Park decorations—his magnum opus. And of course his new girl, an imitation of Laurette.

7. Barrymore and John Decker I told you about, no? That too was immense. Living in his "Chinese tenement house," rooms denuded, looted by his ex-wife, the young girl of the newspapers. The most real and natural person I ever met.

And now I am going to Joseph von Sternberg's home for the afternoon. A friend of his telephoned me to say he has read everything I wrote and bought copies of my books for all his friends—"the man he wants to meet most in this world!" Now then—I had heard of his erotica collection—$100,000 worth. The other man I have in mind is Walter Arensberg, a very great person here—a millionaire with the finest collection of modern paintings in America. Saw it twice. He likes me. Likes my work. Said he knew I was "pure" and "innocent." A very good friend of Marcel Duchamp's, whom he is bringing to America. There I met all sorts of interesting people.

At any rate, I'll be in Carmel sometime during this week. May make side trips to visit Steinbeck and Krishnamurti and the Rosicrucian Center. Am going to the most interesting part of California—the wild, rocky, fogbound coast between Carmel and Frisco. The point is, Anaïs, that it is only out here that I have begun to get something out of America. If I had known I'd have cut a good deal of my itinerary. The good and the bad are mixed. You hit all levels here. But the good is good. I am so filled up with things to write now. Yesterday I met a waitress and had a wonderful talk. Place was empty. She talked like Balzac's Seraphita about love with a capital L. Most amazing. What happens here is that being isolated from the rest of the country, being in a favorable climate, the sun, water, mountains, life easy and cheap, people broaden out in sympathies, become genuinely goodhearted. It can sound cheap and sickly, sentimental, or quite noble, according to the person. But just as America is less envious, more generous than France, so out here there is a difference between East and West—the tendency being to develop the heart and the soul. You may think I am getting slushy. No, I mean it. I haven't lost my perspective. Something has happened here which may flower hundreds of years later. It won't on the Atlantic coast. That seems dead to me now. Especially New York—like a prehistoric city. The cordiality and hospitality here are immense. And people do lead their own lives. Especially those from Europe who have settled here to earn a living.

I have seen *Citizen Kane* a second time last night. And it seemed even better than the first time. Do see it! The part that concerns Marion Davies is very wonderful—cruel, terrible in its implications. And tell me what you think "Rosebud" means. I have a good clue myself.

The greatest person I have met here is the Swami. That's the high spot of my trip. Judge from that.

Have become aware that America is rejecting all European influence like children who reject their parental influence. Nothing must come from Europe. They are busy trying to find their own style, their own art. But they borrow and imitate as we did when we were young, only we were grateful to our influences, we loved those we learned from, we openly acknowledged our roots, our origins in literature, our ancestors. Here I feel a kind of shamefaced stealing from the European artists and a quick turnabout to deny any such influence. None give thanks or acknowledge that none of us were born spontaneously without a past. I can understand wanting to be born anew, a new type of man or artist. But I cannot understand prejudice or hostility. I cannot understand when the publisher says that no one will read a novel that takes place in Europe. There is an atmosphere of separatism. The foreigner is an outsider. There is no fraternizing. The art patrons invite all the foreign artists together, as if they should be kept together. I seek to mingle with American life but I feel a suspicion, a mistrust, an indifference.

I gave a dinner for Dorothy Norman and her husband. He is tense and detached. He tells me he does not know what to do when his business leaves him two or three hours of leisure. He flicks crumbs off his suit as he talks. He looks unhappy. Dorothy Norman shrinks from life, from deep experience. She is honest and says: "But I am ashamed of my turning away. All destruction estranges me. Hatred too. I hate Patchen now, and I can't bear to hate or to be hated."

We need money for taxes. I owe Dr. Jacobson money, Helba needs new tests. So I write erotica. I have done in all five hundred pages. Eighty pages in one week.

Robert declared his homosexuality and is on his way back.

The Village streets. A soft evening. Open bars, the blast of jazz music. Confused voices, laughter. A feeling of leisure as you might have in an old European village. Flower vendors on the streets, and on Bleecker Street the most colorful vegetable carts, fruit carts, as in Italy, and women in black, shopping.

[June, 1941]

Luis Buñuel gives a program at the Museum of Modern Art. He walks up and down the aisles, rubbing his hands, saying: "It is a slightly morbid program." Morbid! A Spanish village dying of goiter. A film taken inside Bellevue. An island where people are dying of leprosy. Flesh disintegrating, rotting before actual death. People began to leave. At the end the hall was almost empty. Buñuel loves to shock, to frighten, to horrify. Buñuel with his popping eyes and a mole on the tip of his nose, reveling in showing a leper praying with his stump, or a leper without lips playing a flute.

Henry writes:

I've had graphic descriptions given me by the most successful script writers of what they are asked to do—it's frightful! It would drive me mad in a week—and besides I do not have the talent for it. They are all ashamed of themselves and the money does them no good.

We are all seeking to live in the present, to find our life in the present. We have forbidden each other to talk about the past or to live in the past. But Tanguy talks about Breton and the cafés in Paris, Gonzalo constantly recalls Montparnasse. The freedom. Carteret is in the south of France, demobilized for ill health. He met Dr. René Allendy there, who was dying and keeping a diary record of his death for medical data. Such Spartan objectivity seemed consistent with his whole life.

Tanguy complains: "I used to live in the streets. Here I never want to go out." Henry, too, complains that he does not like to walk the streets as he did in Paris.

The tragedy is that just as we were about to enjoy our maturity in Europe, which loves and appreciates maturity, we were all uprooted and placed in a country which loves only youth and immaturity. It makes us feel ill at ease. I am always sought by the young and we meet on an ageless plateau. I do not make them feel the difference. But I feel it. The mature here are tough intellectuals, harsh, rigid, and as D. H. Lawrence would say "all up in the head." Ideologies only, words, no feelings and no experience of life. They are only interested in ideas, politics, science, not in art or aesthetics or life.

I am watching Henry age, and Gonzalo age, and I feel the weight of their aging.

Dorothy Norman invited me to her summer house in Woods Hole for the weekend. A beautiful large house by the sea. I met Luise Rainer there. Nothing fascinates me more than the actress who makes visible, expressive, every mood and feeling, whose every gesture reveals, communicates, fascinates one. Luise's walk, with her swinging hair, her voice, her impetuous gestures, a constantly varied spectacle. Her voice ranges from a whisper to a shout, her face changes every moment, quicker than the lights and shadows of the day, sun, shade, evening or morning light. Even when she reaches for the jam, or leaps up to go for a swim, there is something to watch. I was in my room combing my hair when she shouted imperiously under my window. "Anaïs! COME DOWN!"

She was waiting in her red open sports car. She wanted to drive to the ocean. There was a fine mist, and the wind blew through our hair. We stopped at the edge of the ocean. Luise said, "Across this vast ocean is Europe."

Europe!

What was she remembering? She was born in Düsseldorf. Her father was a banker. She had a comfortable childhood. She wanted to be an actress. She had the whims of a child, the sudden impulses, the leaping quality, and a wistfulness so deep that one did not dare question the cause of it.

We stood on the beach, looking out to sea, yearning for Europe. Then suddenly we laughed at ourselves. I told her how among ourselves we had sworn never to mention the past again and each time one of us did it we would say: "White Russians!" Paris was full of White Russians who had once lived luxurious lives. It became a cliché, like the hard-luck stories of prostitutes. One knew that every taxi driver was in the past a Russian prince who had lived in a palace and had chauffeurs of his own. They ran all the night clubs, they wore their sumptuous uniforms while performing doormen's duties. They wept and told such stories so frequently that one ceased to believe in them.

I had met an authentic White Russian. She was a quiet, well-bred woman who sewed for a living. When she came to get work from me, she asked if instead of taking it home she might stay and sew in my home, just to breathe again some beauty and grace she had once known in her own home.

Letter from Henry:

The thought of New York seems horrible after the splendid country I see out here. This last trip was marvelous. I almost got the feeling I had in Greece—except that here nothing is *sacred*. Maybe that Mexican bookseller Misarachi can be induced to bring out the abridged version of the diary. You think you will like Provincetown? I always heard it was very arty. Dos Passos lives there.

I met a disciple of Varèse's—John Cage of San Francisco—very fine young man! Was interested in Buñuel, oddly enough.

The West gave me a temporary hopeful feeling—maybe delusory. At bottom America kills everything—but between the East and West there is a great difference. I have a feeling that Doubleday will not take my book—a hunch. That gives me an uneasy feeling. And Decatur Street again! Every time I break away I feel completely divorced from that past —and then it comes back at me again, like a trap. But I do want to be back to see *you*. I was in hopes of bigger things, that's all. A real break with old problems.

I had disapproved of Moricand's talking incessantly about Max Jacob and Blaise Cendrars. I thought it was because he was fifty. I thought he was more intent on resuscitating the past than in observing Henry, Carteret, or myself. He indulged in obsessional, minute descriptions which were interesting the first time but which he repeated not for our pleasure but for his own desire to situate himself once more in that period of his life. Even later, when we became close friends, we were more often a public for stories demonstrating Max Jacob's wit and brilliance, Cendrars' savagery and incredible vocabulary. Cendrars was a fascinating paradox. His adventures were physical, realistic, tough and rough, but the language in which he described them was so refined, ambiguous, lyrical, and surrealistic that the man in the street could not read him and it was his sorrow that anyone could read Miller but only the most sophisticated literary readers could read Cendrars.

When Moricand finally became interested in Henry, Carteret, or me, it was because he found some analogies, some parallels, some affinities between his new and his old friends. Anyway, we caricatured him, and we caricatured the White Russians, and now we were in danger of sitting at the edge of the ocean and sighing: Europe!

I have new friends. Do I see them clearly? Am I interested in them? Dorothy does not interest me because she is rigid and bourgeois, she is not a poet, she is not in life, she is not generous. Luise is an echo of Europe, so she is part of the past.

Luise is destroying herself somehow, she is without protection, alone and fragile. The expression on her face which overrules all the others is one of pleading. Pleading. FEEL. FEEL. All her acting demands feel, feel. Because she is vulnerable she is constantly hurt. "My life is always getting shattered."

By day, in shorts, with her hair hanging straight down, she is an adolescent girl. She has the smallest neck imaginable, a small head. She eats voraciously, as children do, impatiently, as if eager to go and do something else rather than sit around a table. What she acts she is. She is Frou-Frou, the essence of femininity, pliant, clinging, supple, but if one is drawn into this softness as by the softness of a child one encounters suddenly, as in children, a steely will.

Dorothy is a spectator. When all the men followed Luise Rainer, who wanted to swim at midnight, Dorothy would not go and she asked me to stay with her. She sat quietly sewing, talking objectively and slowly, detachedly. I wanted to be with the others. Their cries and laughter reached me. The indifference of Dorothy to pleasure and nature, her static attitude. A maternal, a dutiful attitude. Luise had to seduce everyone there, be the center of attention, demanded mine and I gave it willingly because I love the actress who can reveal herself, I love the full expressiveness, the giving to others of what most of us cannot manifest. I hate my own timidity which snuffs out my performances except to a circle of intimate loves. Exteriorization is a relief to my own subterranean worlds. For me it was not Dorothy the intellectual, analytical, observing one who attracted me but impulsive Luise, expressing her need of love, admiration, pleasure, and illuminating the bottomless black shafts of my psychic coal mines!

Even when Dorothy admitted honestly, "I am ashamed of all that repels me, so much repels me that I cannot experience," I could not admire such recoil from life.

Robert escaped serving in the Army; he came back to New York seeking a nest. There was no room for him at Virginia's because he had made love to her Bob. No room in my studio for him. He ended up at Marjorie's, who had an extra room. Either the experience had been a shock, or I had not noticed before that he does not feel for or with others. Living in intimacy with his diary I assumed he reacted with feeling. But when I said: "You hurt Virginia," he showed no feeling.

Life shrinks or expands in proportion to one's courage.

The world outside is too horrible to contemplate. The news is one long endless horror story. War between Germany and Russia. Outside, it is all brutality, sadism, carnage, madness, and treachery. At least the personal world contains a few moments of union, tenderness, creation. The savagery of the world outside is too great for me to bear. We all feel a part of what is being destroyed. Every bomb falls on a house we lived in, on a human being we love. And what can one do?

Are we needed in this new world, can we create a new world here?

In Paris I did not know William Hayter except as a friend of Gonzalo's. But when I saw him at parties, at cafés, or exhibitions, it was his intensity which was overwhelming. He was like a stretched bow or a coiled spring every minute, witty, swift, ebullient, sarcastic. He was a famous engraver and teacher of engraving. And his face seemed engraved rather than sculptured in flesh. As if every line he had engraved on his copper plates he had at the same time engraved on his face. The jaw was tense, the smile as if pulled by taut wires, his chin jutted like a perpetual affirmation, his eyes dilated to yield the maximum focus. To me he was a wire sculpture, a man of nerves. When his studio in Paris was filled with wounded refugees from Spain, he was active, boiling with either compassion, anger or inspiration, always at boiling fever point.

If ever an artist seemed made of the elements he liked to use, Hayter was one. Steel, sharp edges, sharpened instruments, acids, presses. But in his painting he showed the opposite side, he painted with diffuse colors, floating tones, and often an overlay of scrambled lines, like tangled wires, tangled cords, scratching out of the whole thing, as if asserting and then scrambling.

In New York he set up his famous Atelier 17 at which many well-known painters had worked at one time or another. The place was enticing to me, with piles of paper, inks, the presses, the vats with acid, the copper being worked upon. The miraculous lines appearing from the presses, the colored inks, the sharpened burins. The group working with him absorbed, intent, bent over under strong naked bulbs. He always moved about between the students, cyclonic, making Joycean puns, a caricature, a joke. He was always in motion. I wondered how he had ever spent hours bent over copper plates, delicate, demanding, exacting work. His lines were like projectiles thrown in space, sometimes tangled like antennae caught in a windstorm. I never saw him at low ebb or passive, and even pain, which he was known to have, seemed to inspire only a more desperate aliveness, alertness. A volcanic personality.

We all need a rest. We are leaving for Provincetown. A New England village with a Portuguese fishermen population. Sand dunes. A stark, colorful mixture, no foliage; grasses and sand and a sea which defied the summer colors, remained of lead. Many of the small cottages built on stilts or on docks, once used to store fishing nets and boats and now rented to summer visitors. In mine, all of wood, the nets are still stored over the beams, with jars of tar, and I can hear the ocean roll under the floor at incoming tide.

On the wooden pier, fishermen catch squid, which the Portuguese know how to cook.

The main street is filled with stores, coffee shops. More beautiful houses are built farther back from the town, in the sand dunes. New England puritanism closes the bars at midnight so the town is quiet then. An open hall attracts everyone for bingo games. The sand dunes are so white they seem at times like ski slopes. Some night clubs are on the beach. The tables are set on terraces and jazz floats over the beach. Couples lie in the fishing boats. The lights flicker from candles set in old beer or wine bottles.

The Flagship is the most beautiful place for dancing. The lanterns are red. Each table has a red candle. The hostesses are pretty girls, many of them art students and models. They wear flowers in their hair, and one of them a small Japanese umbrella. We all use bicycles to go back and forth from the beach.

We eat in Portuguese restaurants. The Portuguese are handsome. We walk along the boardwalk. We walk through the dunes. We visit Eugene O'Neill's house in the middle of the dunes. A tall, grey, wooden house, with narrow windows, a somber, grey, weather-beaten house. Something unutterably barren and sad, isolated. Like a perpetually abandoned, neglected house in the middle of the desert. A thirsty house, without greenery or water. Without shade or gentleness. Severe. The tall, narrow windows give me an uneasy feeling.

I wear my Saint-Tropez sarong dress, sea-shell necklace and earrings, the sea-shell comb. But this is not Saint-Tropez. What is missing are fraternity and warmth, spontaneous exchanges, friendliness.

At the beach people sit looking out to sea, pretending not to notice each other. There is no vibration or curiosity. No open joy, or community pleasure, as in Saint-Tropez. Groups stay by themselves. We were always so curious about each other, so observant. Here I get a feeling of invisibility. You walk by and everyone either does not see or pretends not to see. There was always a flurry of talk, of reactions, in Saint-Tropez, currents, crosscurrents, messages of eyes, transmissions, human telegraphic code messages of interest. Warmth. A magnetic warmth passing between people. Here they have cut off the currents between human beings.

Gonzalo and Helba have an apartment over a shop, on the beach. Virginia and Bob have a studio inland, a loft with very thin walls. They quarreled over Robert one night, for several hours. Suddenly the voice of a neighbor said: "I have been listening to you. I have been weighing all your arguments. I think that Virginia is absolutely fair and right, and the behavior of Bob and Robert treacherous and ugly."

Bob was completely shocked that anyone should have heard his homosexual confession and passed judgment on him. He had to know who it was, who now knew so much about him and had judged him. He did not recognize the voice. He rushed out into the hall. He knocked on the studio next to his. No answer. The studio was shared by three painters so he would never know which one had been there that night to hear his quarrel with Virginia. He rushed out to the town. He sat at bars. If anyone looked at him too intently, he felt it might be the one. He wanted to talk with him, explain himself, justify himself. Every face he saw now he imagined was the face of his accuser, of his judge. "That is the man who heard my confession to Virginia, that is the man who knows all about my secret life." The idea was unbearable to him. He walked with his shoulders bowed. He was silent. He looked haunted.

To cheer them I took them to dinner at the Flagship. Bob never tired of hearing how Picasso looked, how when I once met him in the street with Hélène, I did not guess him to be Picasso. He seemed short, stocky, and ordinary except for beautiful fiery large eyes, but all Spaniards have beautiful eyes. Bob wanted to hear about life in Paris. Ever since I had come to New York I realized even more the value and beauty of café life. The home and the studio were private. No one visited during the day. The day was preserved for work. Very often we did not even know where an artist lived or worked. But one was sure never to be lonely, for in the evening, after work, one could always walk into certain cafés and find friends gathered there. There was an element of surprise. One never knew who would be there, or who would come with a new friend, a visitor or a disciple. If there was a party somewhere, one would hear about it at the café, and would go in a group. Or if a need of intimate talk was felt, one left the group and walked to some small, unknown café. It was unplanned, free, casual. It was not difficult to meet an artist one admired. One sat at the café with a group of friends. Sooner or later someone would introduce one to the other and groups would mingle.

Gonzalo knew all the Spanish artists, the South Americans, the Cubans. Suddenly while I was re-creating the atmosphere, the talks, the appearance of each artist, Virginia stopped me with a prim tone of voice. "I'm not interested in the unfamiliar. I like the familiar."

After this I kept away from them.

I won ninety-five dollars at the Beano game.

We went to the Flagship to celebrate.

At the bar stood a man so magnificently handsome, so arrogantly handsome that I made fun of him to Gonzalo. I said: "There goes the *gallo,* the cock, such wonderful Don Juan plumage."

The next morning he walked in front of us at the beach. He took long steps, he expanded his chest, he seemed in a state of physical euphoria. He carried a Spanish leather hunter's bag, with a net pocket for game. In this net he carried oranges which he ate with delight. I was still mocking his obvious magnificence, but as he passed before us smiling to his companion it was a smile so brilliant, so wild, so sensual, that I ceased making fun of his overwhelming beauty. There was something proud and royal about him, some quality other than his physical appearance. There was joyousness, a lyrical joyousness.

When I sat at the beach alone, reading, he smiled at me. Walking home, as I reached my place, I saw him enter a cottage across the street where they rented rooms. The next day his red sports car almost collided with my bicycle.

He jumped out of his car and apologized. He had a foreign accent. He introduced himself. "I knew you were a European," he said. He was born in the Italian mountains, now part of Austria.

Later I sat having dinner at the Flagship.

The Austrian came in alone. He walked up to my table and said: "Please rescue me from a girl who has been pursuing me for two days. Say you are an old friend, that we had a date. May I sit down?"

A young girl came up to us and greeted him. He rose and introduced me. "An old friend of mine from Europe. She's a French
actress; doesn't speak any English. Please excuse us." The girl was
convinced it would be no pleasure to sit with people talking in a
foreign language. She left us. We had a gay dinner, in which he
tried to make me feel pity. "Women never leave me alone. They
insist I look like a Don Juan and must play the part. I am not always in the mood. I feel hunted."

"Any time you need protection from your Don Juan role you
can rely on me," I said playfully. He pretended we had known
each other intimately and for a long time. He is a singer and preparing his debut in America at the Metropolitan in *Siegfried*. I
laughingly dubbed him Siegfried.

He lived always in a musical world. Toscanini brought him to the
United States.

We ended the evening at the White Whale cabaret.

By now all Provincetown knew that we were two Europeans who
had known each other in Europe and we used each other to get
out of invitations or pursuits we did not care about. Once he was
invited to a masquerade party. He disappeared for two days. He
came back looking worn-out, and I could not help laughing.

It is difficult to feel compassion for a Don Juan who is too much
sought after, too much loved! Nevertheless, he wanted sympathy.
"Women are never satisfied. They keep the strictest accounts. This
girl compared notes with her roommate." He took off his blue
sweater. He offered me an orange.

We were sitting at the top of a sand dune. Looking down the
perfect white slope he remembered he was once an Olympic skier.
He also remembered the first girl he was in love with because he
had met her while skiing. She was the daughter of an English peer,
and he could not persuade her to marry him. He was dreaming of
how they skied down the slopes together.

Returning from the beach I found Dorothy Norman and Luise
Rainer waiting for me. They had spent the morning searching for
me. We all went together to the Flagship. Luise and Siegfried had
many friends in common. It was strange to have made friends with
him intuitively and then to discover we had lived in the same world

and could have met a hundred times at the houses of friends. He is only thirty-two, he confessed to Luise, but he is very polished and mature, and playful. His mother came from Málaga.

Luise said to me: "My dreams? All my dreams are dreams of fear." In the street everyone recognized her and asked for her autograph. Someone asked: "Are you sisters?"

When we parted in front of my door, Siegfried thundered after me, amplifying his voice: *"El Barón de la Mantequilla saluda a la Condesa de la Santa Burra,"* rolling his words as if he were announcing the Duchess of Guermantes. We laugh. He is exuberant, gay, poised, joyous. All the homosexuals tried to interest him.

Pouring rain today. No beach. The summer will soon be over. Siegfried leaves for Nantucket, for a house party.

We went together for drinks at Peter Hunt's. After cocktails, we had dinner. Siegfried grew more and more talkative, telling me fantastic stories.

"My father was born in Samoa. He did not leave Samoa until he was sixteen. When he took the ship home it snowed. He had never seen snow. He thought the snowflakes were butterflies, and he tried to catch them. He was amazed when they melted in his hand. He later became a general."

He calls Gonzalo "the motorized Inca." He jokes about the change of guards at Buckingham Palace when I say I am leaving him to meet Gonzalo. He salutes with rigid military stance. He is also Rabelaisian.

His Rabelaisian moods are paradoxical, like my father's. If only I could stay on the surface dimension of pleasure and lightness, on the key of humor. He has never known the caverns of obsession, desolation, homesickness, or little deaths. His only problem is that women have marked him as a stallion. He can never be tired, sleepy, indifferent. They disregard his moods, his needs, his fatigues, his moments of revulsion, everything but the phallus.

So he eludes the women, comes to the beach, waits for me. He sheds all his masks and roles. He talks about his voice, his studies, his work. He was sick of women. "You are more than a woman, you are a friend," he said. Everyone was jealous of the time he spent with me. Our afternoons were so sincere, mellow, tender, and trusting that the poor persecuted Don Juan said, at the end of one long walk, "This evening I have to go to a birthday party," in such a lugubrious tone that I laughed.

"Will I see you in New York?"

He does not think this should vanish like the summer. As I bicycle, the autumn leaves fly under the wheels. I hear the autumnal wind rushing through the old trees.

The book to read at the seashore is Proust. The undulant wavelike rhythm of his phrases are like the waves of the sea. I could follow their furl and unfurling as one watches a wave rise, roll, curve, fall and renew its breathing to swell and roll and fall again. The sea-sound of Proust's phrases rolling infinitely and ebbing. Proust the only one who knew that love could be a disease, could obsess one, devour one, destroy one.

Robert came and brought a friend. He tells me that this friend writes the most beautiful short stories. His name is Tennessee Williams. We sat under the overhanging fishing nets and I cooked lunch. Tennessee was inarticulate and his eyes never met mine fully. It is my misfortune that I cannot open up before an inexpressive face or silence. I felt again the terrible timidity which I can only overcome when the atmosphere is warm and smiling. I need warmth to bring me out. Tennessee was closed. He faded from my memory.

Siegfried asked me to come and say good-bye to him. He was driving away with friends. When I entered the small wooden cottage, the prim and narrow New England parlor, he had not yet arrived. His valise lay open on one of the small tables. It was fitted with a complete silver toilet set marked with his initials. The silver comb, brush, mirror, soap box, silver shoe horn, silver clothesbrush, silver cologne bottle all exactly like my father's. The resemblance between his love life and my father's struck me. The resemblance between their lives. Then he arrived and it was like seeing merely a larger, taller, blonder, more Nordic duplicate of my father; the same impeccable grooming, the fresh-blooming charm, dewy, radiant, the desire to please, entertain, amuse, delight. His head almost touched the ceiling. The little New England rocking chair protested at his weight, groaned. The flowered wallpaper, the dainty lace doilies, the artificial flowers seemed like a doll house in which a Viking had been trapped. With one note of his full-throated voice he could have brought the whole little cottage down.

One more radiant smile, one more playful fantasy, one more push to speed my bicycle, and Siegfried is gone.

No more music or laughter. I hear only the autumn wind blowing the leaves. More leaves fell on the library steps, but not from me. I had stopped my own autumnal shedding! Siegfried had restored glitter and sparkle to my life. The autumnal mood which was weighing me down before the summer had been caused by the young. They had made me feel less young. But Siegfried's maturity had uncovered the deeper sources of youthfulness to lie in laughter, imagination, enthusiasm, enjoyment, experience.

The record that was played all summer, the musical motif of Provincetown, was called "Intermezzo." It was in part stolen from *Tristan und Isolde*. Before I came, I was going to write a volume about our aging; seeing it happening to Henry, to Gonzalo first, and observing the first grey hair and the fine lines around the eyes when I smile, but now the theme dissolved in the sun and the sea.

The summer and Siegfried liberated me from the world of love and pain in which I trap myself, and opened vistas and intimations of pleasure.

The sea-sound of Proust's phrases echo through the marvelous eternal edifice of his lucidities. He painted only the sorrows.

Over and over again I had navigated towards joy. It was never in the same room with me, always across the way, always near me, but unreachable. Like those rooms full of gaiety one sees from the street, or the gaiety in the street one watches from a window. It eludes me. Will I ever reach it permanently? It hides behind the whirling merry-go-round of the traveling circus. As soon as I appear it is not joy. The manipulator of the spectacle takes off his mask for me: it is a tragic face. Joy is a foam, an illumination.

When I am dancing it seems to lie outside in an illusory garden.

When I am in the garden it explodes from the house. When I am traveling it settles like an aurora borealis over the land I am leaving. When I stand on the shore I see it bloom on the flag of a departing ship. Joy is in the street fair, but when I arrive it folds its tent, tidies its costumes, starts its motor. Have I ever possessed it? At moments, a joy which came in the form of ecstasy, ecstasy in lovemaking, a soaring, a lyrical flight, joy at beauty, at desire, at creation. But it is rare and fleeting. I want a joy that takes simple colors, street organs, ribbons, flags, not a joy that takes one's breath away and throws one into space. Not a joy like the mystic's ecstasies or the poet's ecstasies which lift one into an atmosphere others cannot breathe with you. There are so many joys, and I have only known the ones that come like a miracle and touch ordinary life with light. I wanted a simple one, the playfulness of Siegfried. His joy in biting an orange—and when the juice spurted out, he dipped his finger tip in the orange juice and touched the lobes of my ears as women do with perfume. His warrior shouts as he ran down the beach to challenge the waves of the sea.

Just as Montparnasse was for me a different Montparnasse than for other people, and just as the Village is not the same Village for me as for others, so Provincetown was no ordinary fishing town for summer tourists. It became the landscape of rebirth, a bridge from the withering effects of uprooting to the gold-dust sand dunes painted by so many artists, the place where I shed my fear of autumnal life, the autumn which has once more passed me by, not marking my soul, my faith, or my capacity for love. I came back with its sand of crushed glass, some of the whiteness of its beacons, the fever of its sun, reshaped, remolded by the waves, resoldered by its heat.

From a Montparnasse of my own I brought back deep and rich experiences; the Village is the backdrop of genuine artists and genuine relationships, and Provincetown deposited in me not its ordinary gifts, antiques, shells, fish, sailors' lanterns, nets, glass bowls, paintings, but a supply of summer to last through the winter.

[September, 1941]

In New York again. Telegram from Henry asking for money to return to New York. Telephoned to John Slocum to borrow money for a few days. Visited Frances Steloff of the Gotham Book Mart to discuss problems. Henry's *World of Sex* is selling well. My books were in great demand but now all out of print. Visited Henry Volkening, who told me Doubleday was dissatisfied with Henry's book on America, that it was unacceptable.

Talked with Luise over the telephone. She has serious anemia.

Invited to Mr. and Mrs. Bernard Reis's for dinner. A beautiful, luxurious apartment on Central Park West, filled with modern paintings and sculptures. André Breton, Yves Tanguy and his wife, Charles Henri Ford, who started a surrealist magazine *View*, Jacques Lipchitz, Lucia Cristofanetti, and others. People from the museums, art critics. I go there often now. They offer a warm, loving hospitality to interesting people.

Caresse takes me to Harlem and I meet friends of Canada Lee's.

Evening with Luise. A fragile Luise lying in her ivory-white satin bed, among mirrors and rows of outsize bottles of perfume. Her body and face so expressive that they do not seem made of flesh but of trembling antennae, a breath, a nerve, a vibration. She, the exhausted one, runs downstairs to spare her servant a trip. She lies back like a tired child in a sophisticated white fluffy nightgown which does not seem made for her. Her voice vanishes to a whisper as if she herself were going to vanish, and I hold my breath to hear her. Her head seems completely free of her body, like the Balinese dancers. Her hands are separately eloquent, as if they were puppets pulled by wise and accurate strings, two small puppets depicting a drama of their own.

She was destroyed by her marriage to Clifford Odets. It seemed at first such a romantic marriage. She had just won a top acting prize, and he a prize for the best playwright on Broadway. He was a Brooklyn boy, who had never traveled, and was harsh and narrow.

They fell in love and married. A disastrous marriage. Heaven and hell, more often hell. He lacked all emotional quality, he was tactless and crude. He mocked her emotionalism. She could not share his ambition and practicality. The differences caused immediate clashes. "We're both at the top of our careers, let's take a trip around the world and enjoy our love."

He answered: "This is the time to cash in. We risk being forgotten." Luise felt this was a surface alibi. Deep down, she felt, he was a dead-end kid, ill at ease in any world but his own. Europe and the rest of the world were the unknown, the unfamiliar, and therefore to be shunned. He had no desire for adventure, to explore or expand. He was going to remain on his own little piece of familiar ground, among his old friends. He hated romanticism. He hated foreigners. He was provincial and practical. Why did he marry Luise? An impossible marriage. And yet there was a sexual attraction. His very earthiness had awakened her as a woman. She was using her strength then to defy Hollywood rules. She turned down roles she felt unsuited to her. Odets took *their* side. She was punished, ostracized, deprived of work.

While we were talking, he came in merely to inquire about her health. He slapped the neat and elegant backside, made light of her sickness and promised to return the next day. He had a pencil-sharp nose, and spoke with a twangy Brooklyn accent. I could not understand what had attracted her.

After he left she told me the story of the birthday present. For his birthday she bought him a beautiful silver tobacco box. But to add a touch of poetry à la Vienna, she filled it with rose petals. He promptly emptied the box into the scrap basket saying: "Let's get rid of this junk."

Henry is slowly traveling back.

I fixed up the studio. Repainted, renovated, refreshed.

Siegfried came to see me. He arrived in such a small sports car that while he visited me the neighborhood kids lifted it onto the sidewalk. He had to fold himself up to get into it! During his visit he admired the studio. "It's beautiful here. I love the painted windows and the painted benches. You are a real artist. What am I doing here with only a few vocal cords to my name!"

Went to see Luise act in Barrie's *A Kiss for Cinderella*.
How to describe the transfiguration of Luise in her acting? Her voice has a wide range, and many shadings. Her expression is so intense it is like a mystic's trance. Her eyes shine almost unbearably. She dissolves and becomes ecstatic. It is more than the role calls for. Artaud would have loved her. She could become a flame and burn before your eyes. Her vulnerability is completely exposed. It is a shock to see a soul so naked. She makes the play appear inadequate and puny. She would make a fantastic Joan of Arc.

Acting throws her into an exalted state. I was amazed when she joined me that she expressed doubts, that she was unsure, unaware of what she had done. She felt empty and filled with doubts. She does not know her own power. In her, acting fuses with feeling and she consumes herself as she does it. It produces a miracle. I felt that she was not acting but dreaming out her own life. If she feels anxiety afterwards it must be to have revealed so much of her own emotions.

In the car, riding home, she kept her hand in mine and I kept telling her what I felt about her acting. I had brought her an appropriate gift, my Cinderella gold slippers, the last poetic gift I bought in Paris, the first transparent plastic, with gold heels.

She used the word exhibitionism in connection with acting. I contradicted her. "You want to make acting a magic ceremony. The public seemed terrifyingly opaque, heavy, inert. They do not think of acting in this way, as a ritual in which you must participate. It is because they did not participate that you felt exhibited. You had dreamt of being one with the public."

I brushed away from her small nose one of the artificial snowflakes which had stayed there all through the performance. When she left the car for a moment there remained on the seat a very tiny pocketbook like a child's, a bag of plums which she had been munching avidly as children do when they are eager to join the games. She is unconscious of her tangled hair, likes her face washed of make-up, has no desire to present to the world off stage the mask of the actress, the false eyelashes, the redesigned mouth. She will not be an actress in life.

"Write a play for me, Anaïs. Odets always promised that he would write a play for me, and he never did."

I do see a drama in Luise's life, but it is not one which would make a play. I see a conflict between the woman and the actress. She wants to act out projections of her self, to be herself on stage, and not become other women. She seeks extensions of herself. On the other hand, she repudiates the actress which brings an enhanced, heightened vision of life and character. She denies what the actress might bring into her life. It is a quest for her personal integration rather than the quest of an actress. As if acting would free her of her confused and uncertain self, help her find her core through the roles.

Proust and Dostoevsky are at opposite poles in the study of love. Proust studied its fragmentations, analyzed its disintegrations, the malady of doubt and jealousy. Dostoevsky studied the exaltations of instinct and impulses, the dangers of emotional passions. In Proust duality, in Dostoevsky an effort to dissolve dualities and conflict by a Christian self-annihilation, loss of self in the ecstasies of sacrifice. In Proust disintegration by analysis. In Dostoevsky through passionate instinctive blind impulses, masochism, the chaos of nature. In Proust the tragedy of lucidity, in Dostoevsky the tragedy of blind emotions, obscurantism, mysticism, contradictions.

Luise drove me to Cold Springs, to have lunch in a restaurant overlooking the water, a gentle peaceful place. Later, we sat on the edge of the water, took our dresses off and sunbathed in our panties and bras. We talked about our lives, confided.

I had thought she and Siegfried might love each other. But her impression of him was shallow. She only noted the singer's self-confidence, the on-stage charms. I was trying to tell her what lay hidden behind this appearance. When people think he is superficial, then he acts superficially. It offends his pride and he refuses then to reveal himself. But Luise thinks I am inventing Siegfried.

Luise said, "I feel in you the woman who can give herself, lose herself, but also a power of understanding beyond that. You can analyze and rescue yourself. I don't have this. I get confused. I am trapped and shattered. My first love died tragically. His plane crashed into a mountain in Tanganyika."

When she drives she seems to be scarcely touching the wheel. A miraculous airiness. She makes me so aware of her imponderability that I find it more and more difficult to describe her tangibly. Her eyes are dark and glowing, almost as though there were tears in them. Her skin is slightly tanned. Her hair is long and dark. While she was talking of her life with Odets, I realized we can never understand why people love each other, because to the lover they show a side we do not know. It is the lover who operates a transformation and it is to this lover we give our fullest self, our fullest gifts. We outsiders never see the enlarged human being who appears in the spotlight of an intense love.

I cannot see the Odets Luise loved. We give to our friends only a small part of ourselves. In the climate of love another being emerges. Possibly Odets never existed except in the light of Luise's love, invisible to me because I do not love him. I could see why Odets might love Luise. The actor allows us such intimate glimpses of human beings in a state of love and openness. An actress's way of making love on the stage or on film, we feel, is derived from her way of making love in life. The actress shares this moment with us. I could see from having seen her act, how her voice would sound in a moment of love. I could see how her smile would offer such open tenderness. On the stage you are taken into the secret being of another and witness the exposure of a human being usually only uncovered in moments of love. That may be why we fall in love with actors. They offer us those very special gestures, special tonalities of the voice by which we are enchanted and drawn to the one we love. This openness is the miraculous openness which takes place in love and it creates a current of love between audience and actor as between lover and beloved. The greater the richness of an actor, the more loved he is by many.

But in life, we cannot always obtain from the lover a full image or revelation of what he sees in his loved one. It remains hidden from our eyes. Because love not only can detect a potential, an unborn personality, a buried one, a disguised one, but also bring it into reality. So that all reality appears to me each day more and more subjective, dependent on the eyes of the lover, the eye of the camera, the eye of the painter, even as a room can appear one day glowing with color and the next day grey, according to our mood.

Luise is always saying that the Luise on the screen is not she. It is an image born of lighting, of artifice, enhanced by acting. She did not recognize or love the actress. Luise's image of herself and the image on the screen do not match. The woman on the screen is a stranger to her. She repudiated the worship, the flowers, the love letters addressed to her, as if the person on the screen were a fraud. She could not understand how I related them, how they fed each other, how together they did represent a complete Luise, one freed by acting, the other bound, one confident, the other filled with doubt.

It was strange, when I watched her dress once, opening closets full of movie-star clothes, movie-star hats on stands, movie-star shoes, movie-star furs and bags, she reached for a tiny skull cap with two inches of veil over the eyes, for the simplest beige dress, the simplest shoes, the ones least likely to appear glamorous.

In her very large, very spacious movie-star bed she did not sleep well, except when she covered her head as she did when she was a child and was frightened by a nightmare. The nightmare here seemed to be what this apartment, these clothes, these people, these film scripts and plays demanded and expected of her.

Valeska and Bravig Imbs.

An apartment in one of the old Washington Square houses. Two high-ceilinged rooms, with tall windows, a fireplace. All painted white, which adds to the airiness. Bravig in a Joycean play on words could stand for brave in Nordic languages and Imbs (limbs) would be a name applicable to his slender stylized body. He is blond, classically handsome. One places him on a ski slope. He is a designer. He painted a mural on the wall that separates the two rooms, columns, birds, and clouds, which made the place float in space and reminded me of Chirico, only more feminine. Valeska is

Russian. She has the big sensuous Saint Anne blue eyes, with a depth which draws you in, while his are like icicles. She carries one leg inert from polio, but limps with *élan*, with an upward sweep, a gallant overcoming of the weight, not at all like a weighed-down cripple, more like a dancer struggling out of a heavy costume, emerging with elegance and bravura. They both have style. Everything is casual, but the effect has style. We sat on garden furniture of iron and glass. The chairs are painted white.

I met Leo Lerman, who talks like Oscar Wilde, but has a warmth in his glittering dark eyes. Behind his constant game of wanting to amuse, I sense a sorrowful human being. But the door is closed to this aspect of himself. He parries with quick repartee, he is the man of the world who practices a magician's tour de force in conversation, a skillful social performance, a weather vane, a mask, a pirouette, and all you remember is the fantasy, the tale, the laughter.

Valeska is preparing a fashion show of dresses from Paris. I met her children, who were already in bed. I think of the evening like a water color by Dufy.

[October, 1941]

My brother Thorvald at the hospital. He was flying in South America. Among the passengers was an old guard with a madman, who was being taken to an insane asylum. In the middle of the trip he went berserk, started to attack the passengers. Thorvald knocked him out but broke a finger. The finger was badly set. It festered. It had to be amputated.

What a shock to see the bandage over the half-finger left to him. A greater shock to some maternal groove in me because I had to take care of them, Joaquin and Thorvald, and I can never consider them as strong, mature men to whom dangerous things can happen, and who can fight back, but only as children, perpetually in danger.

We only meet at crises like this, and then he is off again into his dangerous life, bargaining with natives in jungle forests for trees to be cut down for his plywood factory. He had to teach himself forestry, geology, medicine, archeology and languages. He had to go to work so young he could not go to college. He should have been the eldest, so he could fulfill his need to dominate. Or he should have been the youngest to be spoiled. Caught in the middle, he felt deprived of both roles. His way to relate to others is mostly by teasing, by disparaging, by fault-finding. For me he continued the fault-finding of my father and completed the loss of my confidence. Whatever praise I seek is to balance the first twenty years of no-praise.

When I returned from the hospital, depressed and exhausted, Luise called me up in her smallest voice: "May I come up for a little while? I want to see you. I had a very bad day."

We walked out in a fine drizzle. She wanted to talk about her three problems: Her acting—should she accept an offer from Hollywood? Odets—should she separate from him definitely? Her health —she is aware that she maltreats her body, eats erratically at any hour, capriciously, whimsically. I listened.

Luise said: "I have something at home I want you to hear."

She drove me to her apartment. There is a curved staircase which leads from the living room to the bedroom. Halfway up there is a large window of quartz which sheds a diamond-splintered light. Luise put a record on the record player, turned off the light, and we sat on the stairs. While we listened to the music the telephone rang several times. Luise did not answer it. She whispered: "It is Odets, and I don't want to see him." It was as if she thought the music and I would help her not to yield again. At one moment in the music we heard a subtle melody interwoven with a loud, pretentious, inflated trombone. Luise said: "Odets!" We laughed.

We sat at the top of the stairs, as if to escape from Odets's power, listening to the trombone overwhelming the delicacy of the violin.

The telephone rang four times. Then it stopped. Luise felt she had won a great victory. Every time she yields to him she experiences more pain. It seems like a hopeless relationship.

"When you are too busy," said Luise, "you must not see me. I do not want to be a burden."

"But Luise, we are like sisters. We need each other."

"You always remind me that everything that happens is really a marvelous story. I begin to look at everything that happens as a fascinating drama, a tale happening to someone else."

I gave her Dinesen's "The Dreamers" to read. The light from the glass window, the spiral staircase, the music ascending to reach us, all seemed like a tower built against the pain of human relationships. Even that phone ringing, insistent, demanding, and each time it rang Luise climbed another flight away from it.

Luise broke with Dorothy Norman. Dorothy asked me, "Luise says that I am hard. Do you think that is true?"

"It is true that you do not live by your feelings as Luise and I do. It is true that you live by your mind. You would never give up an engagement to console Luise at a difficult moment. You would not go walking with her when exhausted. She needs such proofs of devotion."

Dorothy has no empathy. Luise and I permit a friendship or a love to possess us completely, to rule our life, and others' needs must be answered immediately. If I should say to Dorothy: "I must see you. I need to see you," she would answer calmly, "Let me look at my engagement book. How about a week from today?"

She lives by rigid conventions, protected by her wealth.

I lost Robert because I could not feed him. It was the second time I refused to take on a burden. And so I lost him. "For us," wrote Robert, "there is no country more strange than tranquillity."

André Breton came. We talked about hypnosis, and all the writers we believed clairvoyant or prophetic. I still feel at times that he is more of a scientist of the unconscious when he talks than a poet, that he analyzes more often than feels, but he is penetrating, lucid and inventive in every word he utters. Certainly, when he writes he is a poet, and a most powerful one. It may be that being pushed into theorizing, teaching, and defining a group and works he had to become dogmatic. I feel surrealism has a wider meaning, more encompassing than he gives it.

Nothing could be more surrealistic than André Breton himself, with all the dignity and royal bearing he genuinely possesses, with his long hair brushed away from his leonine face, his large eyes and bold features, leaning over my hand to kiss it on top of a Fifth Avenue bus.

At night I dreamed that he and his wife embarked on my houseboat, and that a huge transatlantic ocean liner brushed by and set it heaving and rearing like a wild horse, breaking its moorings. Then my houseboat started to whirl madly, eddying vertiginously among icebergs. Mme. Breton was very angry with me. I felt we would soon be shattered to bits. We collided with an iceberg. On this iceberg stood two masons quietly mixing cement. I asked them to help us. They suggested a coat of cement at the bottom of the houseboat, to give it stability. I watched the operation with sadness. It seemed to me that the cement would make it heavy and that it would never float again.

Worked intensely on the Jean Carteret story. Decided to call it "The All-Seeing."

Luise feels that the actress Luise is more attractive on the stage than the woman Luise off stage. She is jealous of that heightened self. Off stage she is concerned with being too small. She believes only Luise the actress is seductive and enchanting, and that she is an illusion. That when people love the actress they love an illusion, and that if a man knew her well, intimately, he would be disillusioned. If someone tells her she needs powder on her nose it distresses her, as if they had detected a flaw. She feels the actress is a pretender. The exalted figure on the stage is the woman she becomes in moments of self-confidence, confidence in the actress, but this confidence deserts her when she falls back into her personal life. She needs the costume, lights, decor, challenge of another personality. "On the stage I am more attractive, but if I charm someone that way I feel it is a fraud."

"But only because you insist on making such distinctions between them. You exalt the stage personality and in daily life you seek its opposite, you dress negligently, you wear no make-up, you do not paint your nails, you choose neutral colors, you make yourself less attractive. As if to underline the difference. You split the two women when they could be unified. I say they are the same, but you create the difference between them. Don't forget, some of the acting comes from the unconscious, and this same impulse which gives you confidence or assertion on stage could be drawn from in life. You create the difference or contradiction between them."

"Because I don't want anyone falling in love with that other woman, I want them to love me for myself, not that heightened image."

At the same time, when I find her reading scripts and plays, I see that she is looking for a character that she feels identified with, some affinity, some role which might be an extension of herself. The acting is simultaneously a dramatization of a divided self, and at the same time she seeks through it the magic unification, two women made one through a role.

When I came home I copied some of the passages from the diary for her and sent them with this note:

DEAR LUISE, I will be your mirror. I have portrayed all your charms in the diary. I offer this mirror to you. Any time you feel unsure, every time you doubt yourself, every time you feel you have no power to inspire deep love, every time you doubt your beauty and charm, the mirror is here for you to use.

Siegfried telephones from a mysterious, tangled life of rehearsals, trips, social life, the feted singer idol (my father receiving applause and flowers from women offered to the figure on the stage, where the illusion we need for love is already prepared). In the love we have for those who are not on the stage, the illusion has to be created by the love itself. The people who fall in love with performers are those who fall in love with magicians, they are the ones who cannot create the illusion of magic with love alone. Luise may be right to suspect the love given to the actress. The *mise en scène*, the producer, the music, the role, will dress the personage in the robes of the myth needed by lovers. Is Siegfried one of them?

He has great agility in escaping the caverns of deep love's tortures. He is free of the obsession of jealousy. He flies at a safe distance from the planet Venus. But Luise enters the infernos of love deeply. She said: "Such a madness of jealousy that once when I saw a very beautiful little girl of ten I suffered at the sight of her, thinking, In ten years she will grow up. Odets may see her and fall in love with her."

Luise was upset the other night to see me in an old Schiaparelli suit given to me, which I cut to my size. She realized what I gave up for my children. I now have to turn down invitations because I have nothing appropriate to wear at Dorothy's formal dinners or other functions.

I do rebel at times, but it accomplishes nothing. Henry hated to return to New York, to face the rejection of his book, to face his mother again, to face the association of New York with his childhood, early adolescence and first marriage.

When he came he made several contradictory statements. That he could live on nothing, that he felt so good he could even take a job, that his integrity prevented him from writing scenarios in

Hollywood. At the last I said: "And what of my integrity, doing erotica for money?"

Henry laughed, admitted the paradox, the contradictions, laughed and dismissed the subject. But he is attracted to the life in California, which is an escape from his past and resembles a little more what he loved in Greece.

The joke on me is that France had a tradition of literary erotic writing, in fine elegant style, written by the best writers. When I first began to write for the collector I thought there was a similar tradition here, but found none at all. All I have seen is badly written, shoddy, and by second-rate writers. No fine writer seems ever to have tried his hand at erotica.

Caresse came to see me. The five flights of stairs are not very good for her heart, and she entered gasping for air, saying, "Your friends must really love you a lot to walk these five flights!"

She had a wonderful story to tell.

A hundred years ago there was a gold rush in Virginia City. People made huge fortunes. The gold mines seemed inexhaustible. They built fancy houses, fancy night clubs. They sent for crystal chandeliers from France, red brocades, rugs, paintings. The bars were built of the finest woods and marble. The town was in full bloom, big houses, theaters, hotels, vaudeville. Then the gold mines were exhausted and the town was completely deserted.

Today they had discovered an acid chemical with which to treat the leavings. Thus, the discards could be utilized. Caresse bought a house there for a hundred dollars. In the cellar of the house all one had to do was dig not too deep for the leavings, treat them, process them. For five hundred dollars she bought a gold mine which will yield ten dollars a day for at least several years. On Saturday nights one can gamble it all away or increase it at roulette tables or card games, as in the old days. Caresse was fascinated by the life, the atmosphere, the landscape, the vestiges of past splendors and extravagances. She thought it would be a good life and invited Kay Boyle and me to join her. We could write all day and earn enough to live by in short shifts at the mine. The crystal bar was beautiful, hung with red brocade, with white marble-top tables, the biggest crystal chandelier ever seen, and hundreds of mirrors and red plush settees. For a few days we contemplated this scheme of living, and were tempted, but finally Caresse was the only one willing to live it out.*

Luise had an attack of scrupulousness and because I have only mentioned what I like, love or admire (which is a natural tendency in me, because I enjoy loving more than hating) she insisted that I do not see the bad in her. I admitted that for my friends I had only one eye, and could never see the other side of them, and I playfully covered one of my eyes with a black patch and said: "I can't see anything bad about you. Anxiety is not a flaw." But she would not be playful. She insisted she must warn me, that she destroyed everyone she came in contact with, that all her relationships ended badly.

"Luise, it's not that I don't see the demon in you, we all have one. It's that I believe it can be defeated, tamed, sublimated, used for creation. Do you remember when you told me how you overcame your fear of snakes? You told me that you achieved this by studying the snake scientifically, you studied its anatomy, you went to school and learned to dissect one. Well, our demon can be equally defeated by being studied, and sometimes the best way to study it is to have a relationship in which it is disregarded, in which it has no place, as in ours. This way you can track down its reason for being. You and I have excluded it, to see how a relationship is possible without a destructive side to it. I am concerned with your demon because it hurts you more than it hurts others. I exclude it from our friend-ship not out of blindness but because I want to detect and track down what causes its interference. I wanted you to see it can be excluded, to prove that you have the power to hold it in check."

We were invited to a celebration for one of Luise's films, which had won a prize. It took place in a cafeteria! Women in evening

---

* Unfortunately, soon after she moved out there, the government stepped in and, as part of the war effort, appropriated the mines, which contained some other mineral necessary to war industry.—A.N.

dresses, women in silks, chiffons, capes, and lovely hair-dos, sat at those ugly tables, with paper cups, and took food out of cubbyholes with dimes and nickels, food which seemed made of papier-mâché. Weak coffee, ersatz chocolate, dry cake, trays without covers, paper napkins, self-service. Champagne in paper cups! Crude hospital lights, and the music harsh and strident against the tile floor, plastic furniture, plastic tables, chromium.

Everyone else thought it was amusing, an acceptance of modern life, smiled at the incongruity, but Siegfried and I made faces as if we heard one loud dissonance, a symphony of broken plates. He stood tall and detached, humorous, but out of place. He called my attention to the inflated boastings of actors, agents, producers, and said to me: "Shoot me instantly if I should ever talk like a dramatic tenor."

His cigarette case has a music-box mechanism, but in this bedlam it could not be heard unless you held it against your ear. I could not leave quickly enough. What made it worse was that it was also a benefit for the International Red Cross, with beautiful foreign costumes, saris, Chinese dresses, Hindu and African costumes.

Luise took me to hear *Porgy and Bess*. After the performance, backstage, she told the Negro actors: "We have a lot to learn from you. You are the best."

Siege of Leningrad. Gonzalo watches the suffering that takes place far away. His vision is telescopic. Mine is a microscope. I pay attention to the suffering right around me. Millicent. Helba. Among my friends. Or even those I know slightly. The tailor, the delivery boy. An old lady on the bus. I can alleviate what is near me, not the far. Men always use telescopes. Gonzalo overlooks the suffering of those near him.

Yet he thinks I am an escapist. Because I do not listen to the radio all day or read every word of the newspapers. Finally, after much needling I answered him. "I have a kind of courage you do not understand. I am far from blind, far from indifferent, but I will not indulge in impotent, passive despair. I will not add to the despair of the world. I am working on counterpoisons. If I knew what to do politically, I would act. But being helpless in that direction, I create a space in which people can breathe, restore their faith and strength to live. I prefer to worry over the fate of Millicent, of her children, her friends, of other Negroes. Prejudice seeks to crush them. I love their humanity and sincerity. I feel a power in them, and that behind the prejudice lies jealousy and fear."

Luise tells me about Odets: "He was always abandoning me, always leaving me. He used to leave at night after we made love, when I wanted him to sleep with me. When I was in Hollywood, he would come from New York with a small valise and I would look first of all at the small valise and think, He is already planning not to stay long. And I felt deserted as soon as he arrived."

George Barker comes, with his dilated Celtic blue eyes, his brilliance and accuracy of mind, vivid talk, electric and fertile. He places *House of Incest* beside Djuna Barnes's *Nightwood*, praises us both as poets. But objects to poetic prose as such. We should be writing poems in the form of a poem. He feels that poetic heightening, exaltation injected into prose, gives it artificiality. What an absurd attitude. "Prose," I said, "is dying of flatness, and poetry is dying of metered artificial patterns and formations. They need cross-pollination. Besides, poetry is a miniature, gives us moods and profiles, never a complete human being, character, time expansion. It is not revelation. There is more poetry in Proust than in the poets of his time, and more poetry in Djuna Barnes than in Dylan Thomas. You are taken in by a lot of typographical surface designs into thinking you are always reading poetry, but often a piece of poetic prose is *more* poetic."

He also confuses mystic and poet. The mystic aims at union with God, the poet at union with whatever he loves. The mystic must renounce the physical world. The poet is the lover, singing about what he loves.

We talk about guilt. He wants to return to Catholicism. I said: "It gave us more guilt than absolution, more crucifixions than resurrections."

"That was not the religion's fault."

"With Catholicism we repeat the crucifixion over and over again, increasing the load of guilt and the cult of sacrifice. We cannot ever free ourselves of the load of guilt."

"If we repeat it, it is because we did not accomplish it totally, wholly. It was incomplete."

"It has created masochism."

George Barker diagnosed my illumination, after the stillbirth in Paris, as suspect. He thinks it was too ecstatic for a real mystic, it resembled far more the love ecstasies of Saint Teresa. Suspect! Sensual! With intimations of pleasure!

"Only because you think of mysticism as an abstraction. Saint Teresa lived with her body, her senses, experienced her religious fervors as lovers experience sensual love, and then, of course, you cry like a good Catholic, that is sensuality, not mysticism."

George Barker is now living in the Bowery, in the most leprous, festering part of New York, a street lined with Gorki flophouses, with sour-smelling bars, with doorways in which sodden and decrepit alcoholics lie asleep, as eroded and distorted as the lepers of the Moroccan ghettos. His wife is ill with tuberculosis. He looks at moments like a fine trapped animal trying to scale the wall of his cage.

I told him the story of our erotica. How Caresse, Robert, Virginia, and others were writing. It appealed to his sense of humor. The idea of my being the madam of this literary, snobbish house of prostitution-writing, from which vulgarity was excluded.

Laughing, I said: "I supply paper and carbon, I deliver the manuscript anonymously, I protect everyone's anonymity."

George Barker felt this was much more humorous and inspiring than begging, borrowing or cajoling meals out of friends.

"Will you also lend me an advance for my memoirs of a sex maniac, so I may eat and warm myself while I write?"

Luise was ill with sorrow. She had paid a surprise visit to Odets, and had found his apartment empty, but all the vestiges of an orgy having taken place. Champagne glasses, bottles, a rumpled bed, combs, a nightgown.

She cannot achieve detachment from Odets.

Only one small lamp was lit by her bed. We sat in the shadows. Luise asked me, almost in a whisper: "Anaïs, do you think I am a ma-so-chist?"

"If you cling to a love which is no longer there, yes."

"What shall I do?"

"Come with me. Talk to a woman who understands women and has written books about woman's difficulty in separating, in detachment, in relinquishing attachments. She is a doctor, Esther Harding. Friendship is only a palliative. I can console you. I am not sure what Odets means to you. Come, get dressed."

I went to telephone Dr. Harding. She agreed to see Luise. I took her to the door of Dr. Harding's office. Just before she rang the bell, she turned back to look at me, and suddenly all anguish left her face. She made such a mischievous, childlike, mocking face that I knew at that moment that Dr. Harding would not be able to help her. She was armed to defeat analysis, so that I would have to continue to help her with love and sweet, useless word-potions.

The next day, when I called Luise she was triumphant. She had her victory.

"What happened?"

"She said the wrong thing right at the beginning. When I introduced myself she said, 'Yes, I know who you are, I saw you act in *Frou-Frou* and you were so feminine I wanted to beat you!'"

I will never believe that Dr. Harding said this, but if that is what Luise heard, it was what she wanted to hear.

Luise told me about the morning after she and Odets were married. She ran to the beach with elation and joy. He felt sleepy and promised to join her later. When he finally arrived she ran towards him, intending to leap into his arms. He drew away and let her fall. He was frightened by her impetus.

"Thinking about it now, I realize that this was a symbol of our whole marriage. He was never there when I needed him, or when I longed for closeness."

The story about Artaud appeared in *Experimental Review,* edited by Robert Duncan.

Henry said: "Now I have no need of returning to the past, to the story of June. It is all dead. I may write a book completely detached from the ego, the personal, the autobiographical."

Luise is disappointed because I cannot write a play for her. She had expected that of Odets. He promised and never fulfilled his promise. But he was a playwright, and I am a novelist. I try to tell Luise I cannot write a play.

She was hurt that I took her to a doctor. "Why didn't you advise me to save myself by my work, as you save yourself?"

"But I did submit to psychoanalysis first, and *now* I know how to rescue myself."

"I can save myself by work."

I could not say that I felt her neurosis had also interfered with her work. She is not reading plays as plays, but as roles which might deliver her from her own dramas.

"Luise, if you can work, choose a play, save yourself that way. There are only two ways out of neurosis, one by creation, the other by objectivity, which is psychoanalysis. Your personal life at the moment interferes with your acting. That was why I chose the second way for you, so your energy would not be wasted on mourning Odets."

"I want to get away from the ego, the personal. Analysis is yielding to interest in the self."

"When the self is troubled it demands attention, as a fever does. You will not be able to forget yourself while the self is in distress. Analysis is not an indulgence, it is a cruel discipline, it is a harsh confrontation. To pretend one can forget the self is playing the ostrich game."

"I am doing that in my own way. I have set myself tasks, I am studying singing, body movement, languages."

"That is only an escape from the self, not a confrontation, which you need, or else you will fall in love with another Odets, duplicate the experience."

"The mistake you made, Anaïs, is that when I felt a shock at the unfaithfulness of Odets, you took me to a doctor."

"That was not the reason I took you to a doctor. I took you there after a talk we had in which you seemed caught in a vicious circle. You could neither move away from Odets, love someone else, nor work. It was a moment of paralysis."

"I am strong, stronger than the other people you have helped."

"Don't confuse pride with strength. At this moment the greatest strength would be to yield, to permit yourself to be guided. You told me none of the plays you read meant anything to you. You asked me to write a play in which you could act yourself, in which you could be YOU. That means that you thought you would find through a play, through me as a writer, the meaning of your individual drama, its resolution. You sought clarification that way."

The next day Luise had found a way to wound me. "I am reading what you wrote about June. I feel like June, *and I took her side against you.*"

Was this her revenge for my trying to substitute a doctor for care and help which she wanted from me directly?

We did not see each other for several days. I had begun to withdraw from a friendship which was destructive for me, for we now shared only her anguish and no pleasures together. She called me. A different duel began. She asked me to revise a play someone else had written. It was so alien to my thought and style that I could not do it. "The patches would show," I said lightly.

"Then write a play for me."

"I thought I had already done that writing about June and Henry."

"But June has to win."

"In love nobody wins, Luise."

Where before she showed me only her softness, now she seemed intent on proving the power of her will. She had warned me that I did not see the other side of her. Now I could see the patterns of her relationships. First total abandon, empathy, symbiosis. Then a demand for the total giving of one's self, an impossible absolute. If what she needed was not forthcoming, then the relationship had to be destroyed. I could not give her all the time and care she wanted.

Robert is here again. When he asked me for two dollars to take Alvin to the movies I had to say *no*. To say *no* makes me ill. I cannot bear to deny anyone a wish. Robert had once said, "I will teach you how to say *no*." But he did not think I would use this knowledge against him.

Went to visit Varèse this afternoon. Again impressed with both the artist and the man. To recognize the unique value of a man and an artist, most people wait for the perspective of distance and time. But knowing Varèse, one has a more immediate clue to his true stature and unique place in the history of music. His personality and his music match each other, and give instantly the impression of greatness. He is a man who lives in a vast universe, and because of the height of his antenna he can encompass past, present, and future.

I can feel this each time I ring the bell of his home and he opens the door. He receives me with the warmth he shows to all his friends. At the same time I can hear all around him, and flowing out of the house, an ocean of sound not created for one person, one room, one house, one street, one city or one country, but for the cosmos. His large, vivid blue-green eyes flash not only with the pleasure of recognition but with a signal welcoming me into a universe of new vibrations, new tones, new effects, new ranges, in which he himself is completely immersed. He leads me into his workroom. The piano takes most of the space, and gongs, bells, instruments of other countries.

On the music stand there is always a piece of musical notations. They are in a state of revision, resembling a collage: all fragments, which he arranges, rearranges, displaces, cuts, glues, reglues, pins, and clips until they achieve a towering construction. I always look at these fragments, which are also tacked on a board above his worktable and on the walls, because they express the essence of his work and character. They are in a state of flux, mobility, flexibility, always ready to fly into a new metamorphosis, free, obeying no monotonous sequence or order, except his own.

The record player is always set at highest volume for open spaces. He wants one possessed, absorbed into its oceanic waves and rhythms. Varèse demonstrates a new bell, a new object capable of giving forth a new tonality, new nuance. He is in love with his materials, with an indefatigable curiosity. In his room one becomes another instrument, a container, a giant ear, enclosed in his flights into sound.

When we climb the stairway to the living room to join other friends, greeted by the gentle, gracious Louise, Varèse the composer becomes Varèse the conversationalist. He radiates in company, he is eloquent, satirical, and witty. There is a harmony between his talk and his work. He has a contempt for the cliché in music or in thought. His revolt against the cliché never ceases. He uses vivid, pungent language. He has retained the revolutionary boldness of youth, but always directed by his intelligence and discrimination, never blind or inaccurate. He never destroys anything but mediocrity, hypocrisy and false values. He attacks only what deserves to be attacked, never in personal, petty, blind anger. Speaking once of an unsavory political character he said: *"A faire vomir une boîte a ordure."*

This volume opens on a cool wintry morning, and a pale sun shines on a copy of *Twice a Year,* with seven pages out of the manuscript of the first diary volume, translated by me from the French.

Robert and I danced in Harlem last night. We read Harvey Breit's poetry, George Barker's poetry.

Henry is finishing his American book, Luise is reading a play on the French actress Rachel, and Veronica Jennings, of the *Saturday Review of Literature,* says my diary has "no universal quality."

Stieglitz is dying.

Dorothy Norman receives Henry in her office and does not give him a copy of *Twice a Year.* She is always concerned about selling it, about its commercial success, subscriptions. Wealthy as she is, she cannot forget finances, she pays her writers the minimum of one cent per word.

Edgar Varèse starts a choral society, the New Chorus. Paul Rosenfeld is writing that we should listen to Varèse.

Moscow makes a heroic defense. Gonzalo listens all day and all night to the radio.

Joaquin, a professor at Williams College, is reading in *Twice a Year:* "I will now make a portrait of my little brother Joaquin. He is six years old. He has long light brown hair, a small straight nose, big eyes, a small mouth. He is immensely intelligent, his nature is turbulent, but he is not bad. When he hurts me or I cry, he kisses me, he begs forgiveness. I always forgive him, he is so cute, he is a little anemic, like me, but he is very strong. I have forgotten to say he loves to destroy his toys and I have never seen one of his toys whole."

I gather poets around me and we all write beautiful erotica. As we have to suppress poetry, lyrical flights, and are condemned to focus only on sensuality, we have violent explosions of poetry. Writing erotica becomes a road to sainthood rather than to debauchery.

Harvey Breit, Robert Duncan, George Barker, Caresse Crosby, all of us concentrating our skills in a tour de force, supplying the old man with such an abundance of perverse felicities, that now he begs for more.

The homosexuals write as if they were women, satisfying their desire to be women. The timid ones write about orgies. The frigid ones about frenzied fulfillments. The most poetic ones indulge in pure bestiality and the purest ones in perversions. We have to cut out the poetry, and are haunted by the marvelous tales we cannot tell. We have sat around, imagined this old man, talked of how much we hate him, because he will not allow us to make a fusion of sexuality and feeling, sensuality and emotion, and lyrical flights which intensify eroticism.

Henry is reading the diary about Dr. Otto Rank and New York.

My first meeting with Kay Boyle took place in a Paris café. She was an intimate friend of Caresse's and I knew her only through Caresse. I knew about her books, her children, her life. We all admired *Monday Night*. Henry had written her a fan letter and she thought it came from a very young reader, who was praising her while imitating her style.

We met on a Monday evening, and I observed how fitting that was. I always have difficulty with people who are not openly warm, expressive. I need a certain sign, a certain invitation. Kay's face was inexpressive, a mask. She had a sharp profile, her talk was glossy and impersonal. We made no contact.

This time, in New York, I found her even more impersonal, like an Englishwoman. It was at a party for her book. Again the bird profile, words one cannot remember, no human expression of recognition. Thus, some people appear to us like paper cut-outs, one-dimensional, voiceless, merely because they have a blank way of looking at one, because their eyes convey nothing, not even the reflective quality of a mirror, and one *feels* anonymous. The slightest stranger I meet, I make an effort to single him out, to LOOK at him, to take notice, to identify him if I can, to separate him from the crowd. YOU. In the same way I seek to see deeply into whomever I meet, to pay attention, as I did the first time I met Kay Boyle, but her surface style was created to establish distance, to preserve a kind of human invisibility, and such distance cuts off communication.

[November, 1941]

Luise believes she can escape from her conflict by work, by not seeing me, but a résumé of our telephone conversations sounds like this: "No, do not mention me to so and so, he hates me. No, do not speak to me of so and so, he is angry with me. My agent wants me to act in a play I don't like." Producers, directors, fellow actors are frightened away. "I am withdrawing to regain control. You wanted to force me into analysis."

"I would not force you, Luise, I thought you were at a dangerous impasse. It is good I brought it up, for in recoiling from it you began to read all the scripts you had neglected, and now you have found Rachel, which you want to do."

If acting is the only avenue of escape for her, good, but when we last talked, that escape was blocked, too. She could not find a script she wanted.

Robert refers to our first meeting. "I feel I sneaked into your diary by the back door, I did not fascinate you the first time."

"That was because I had just been uprooted, Robert, I was still in mourning for what I had lost. I could not throw myself into new friendships so quickly."

What I do remember about our first meeting was that Robert, due to unsureness, talked obsessionally, overintently, overwillfully, as if he wanted to hypnotize me. His stare gave me a desire to escape, relax. Later, when we became friends, I remember how the fixity of his stare and uninterrupted flow of words still distressed me. It was as if he were impelled by a fear of getting lost, interrupted, confused, and must maintain a monologue, not a dialogue, as if a dialogue might endanger him in some way. Thus, our first meeting was like a failed hypnosis. I remember the room in the Cooneys' cottage. I remember the big fireplace, the wood fire burning. Jimmy had read me a poem of Robert's to prepare me for meeting him. The poem was beautiful. Then, when he came, I liked his appearance, the regular features, his stylized figure. He talked

159

fervently about the birth story. I asked myself often why his brilliance had not captured me at first. Then I realized it was because it was a solitary performance, he stood alone, and it was not intercourse, communion. I was a spectator.

I turned away, as one turns away from a locked-up garden to which one is not invited. I was fresh from the vital interchange, exchange, dialogue with Carteret, with Gonzalo, with Henry, with all my friends in Paris, except Moricand, who was also a monologuist.

Telephone call from Luise in her tenderest voice: "I love you, Anaïs. I have been reading about your father. I forgive you for wanting to take me to the analyst. I am not like June. I am like you. How alike we are! Why, you are writing *me*. And how like Odets Henry Miller is, and that part about your father wanting to lean on you when you were so desperately looking for a father to lean on."

"I'm so glad we are close again. No more misunderstandings. We need each other."

"You need me?"

"Of course I need you, because I love you, because I need people who feel. I am lonely with people who do not feel, and like Lawrence, I cannot love people who are all up in the head. I seem to meet too many of those."

Telephone. "The old man says none of the manuscripts you sent come up to the standard you set. They are more diluted."

The next day, another call from Luise: "I wanted to kill you when Henry says to June: 'Go away, I can't work when you are here,' because that is what Odets said to me. How terrible the confusions at the end, in June. When I get confused I run away. You live out the confusions until they become clear."

"Yes, they have to be lived out, only then do we know what we are, and only then attain clarity, and know whom we love. You can't run away from them. It's destructive."

Walk through Chinatown with Siegfried. He always brings gaiety and playfulness. The game he plays with me is that, being weary of playing the handsome man, he makes himself homely, makes himself into a Frankenstein monster (he is a good actor), and I pretend to be frightened. His laughter is feminine. I was telling him of my adventures with American publishers. One of them called me up after reading *Winter of Artifice* and said I was a skillful writer, a fine writer, but could I write for him a novel with a beginning, a middle, and an end? Could I write something like *The Good Earth*?

The idea of my writing something like *The Good Earth* made us both laugh so hard we could not stop. Every time he looked at me and said: "Anaïs Nin, *The Good Earth*," we laughed again.

Luise's agent said to me: "Put away your European work. It doesn't go here. Read *Collier's, Saturday Evening Post,* see how they do it, and go ahead."

Luise has not decided whether she is like June or like me. When she is June, she turns against me, when she is me, she fears my influence. "Write about a third woman, write about Luise."

I can never say: "I am writing about you, but in the diary." It makes everyone uneasy.

Henry is disturbed by the news that his daughter is ill. He said: "The past comes to haunt me like a jack-in-the-box. I thought I had pushed it all down, and it comes up now and then and strikes at me."

"The past cannot be pushed down. It has to be liquidated."

When the past haunts him he wants to run away. He is dreaming of living in California. He looks upon the illness of his daughter as a punishment, too.

When I say Henry is innocent, it is because he is not aware, except at moments like this. He ran away from his parents, he traveled, but each move he made, instead of freeing him, closed upon him like a net. The unpaid landlord keeps the trunks with books and clothes. Starvation creates illness. Papers not in order cause trouble.

I can see in Henry the inability to grasp the reality of money. I see in Henry's eyes first of all gaiety and clarity, then slowly a sadness as he becomes aware that he has earned in one year only a thousand dollars, that he is not free to come and go. A week of trouble.

While I am out Robert uses my phone to call his friend in Massachusetts. And I cannot pay my phone bill. Robert is another thoughtless child.

A would-be publisher promised to publish *Winter of Artifice*; he collects orders even though the book is not printed yet.

Gonzalo wants to work. We walk the streets discussing this. He hates the jobs he has looked into. He likes printing. Perhaps we could get a press and print books. I asked Dorothy if she could lend me two hundred dollars for a press. We would pay it back in work for her. Dorothy refused.

Eighty more pages for the collector.

I carry the money he gave me for the poets in desperate need. It gives me pleasure to be able to pay George Barker for his pages.

But I am tired of the great duels against destruction which I fought against June and against Helba. I cannot engage in the same duels with Luise and Robert. I have completed these experiences. I cannot live them over and over again. I have my work to do. I have an unfinished story on my desk. The Jean Carteret story. These stories, in which I seek the poem's perfection, the poem's abstraction, how difficult they are. I want the finite perfection of the poem, not a word too much. I want them to be magic stories.

When the so-called publisher had kept *Winter of Artifice* for months and did nothing with it, I took it back. Now Seon Gibben and Wayne Harris want to do it. Seon was working for the Gotham Book Mart. She met Harris there, a wealthy young man. They want to go into publishing together. They came to see me. She is masculine, exuberant, Harris is soft and feminine.

She was born in the Aran Islands. She can pilot a plane, do higher mathematics, studies Egyptian archeology. She is in love with man's achievements, but she doubts woman's access to truth. She came to challenge me. She looks at me as if I were a magician, and she must expose my trickeries. She is bellicose, "rational" she calls it. I can see that she is not.

I am revising *Winter of Artifice*.

Dr. Jacobson said: "You've lost five pounds in three months. There is nothing more I can do for you. You're spending yourself so fast no amount of injections can help you recuperate. Your heart is strained. You must rest. Eat at home, not in cafeterias. Get calm."

I am trembling from exhaustion. Taut. So I stay home two days, revise *Winter of Artifice*.

I stay away from Luise.

Robert, too. He has become aware of his frigidities. From the childlike ones, one expects warmth and tenderness in exchange for protection and nurturing. I discovered the coldness in Robert at the same time as I discovered it in Luise. I cast my own warmth around me and it is reflected in others. I believe in this warmth and humanity and suddenly find it is not there. Nothing repels me more than absence of feeling. In Robert's diary I found emotional chaos, impulses and hungers I mistook for feeling. There is a difference. They are hungry, amorous, they fall in love, but *they do not love*. They love the pleasures, the pains, the upheavals, the adventures. But they do not surrender. And I can no longer defend myself against the egotists.

I was looking for allies. I am not fitted for the role of cautious, wary friendships. I cannot love if I have to look out for myself, to parry certain blows, or sudden turned-off humanities. This is my first experience with withdrawal. Like Proust, I shall have to manufacture some handicap so as to be able to write instead of being consumed. What I cannot overcome is my own conviction that all one has must be shared, given, everything from physical to spiritual possessions, knowledge, discoveries, intellectual acquisitions, techniques, secrets . . .

Luise Rainer decided she was June, and not me. (They have the same birthday!) But she entered the personality of June in order to judge me. We began futile arguments in which Luise used the words "good" or "bad," which I do not believe in. It was not a question of being good or bad, but destructive or constructive, uncontrolled or controlled.

"I have my own demons, dear Luise. I am not a saint, I am neither good nor bad, neither are you good nor bad, neither was June good nor bad. We have demons, and we let them destroy us or we tame them." (In our talk I was referring to the one who cannot control his demons.) "If you cannot control your demons, whoever or whatever they are, you do harm to others. I found the way to cage mine, that was all. Anger, jealousy, envy, revengefulness, vanity. I locked them up in a diary.

"A veritable zoo I have locked up, of all my human frailties. June's demons were free. I depicted in June the instinctive forces which harmed her as well as those she loved. Uncontrollable, not deliberate, or consciously evil. Now I was wrong to think it was affinities which brought us together. I didn't believe you when you said you destroyed every relationship. I have had enough difficult relationships, and had dreamed of a peaceful, harmonious one. I thought you and I would never hurt each other, battle, or argue. Then suddenly I felt you were drawing me into your infernos rather than I drawing you into my world of work. The capacity to work, create, act, love, write. It is because you are in an internal conflict with yourself that you swing between wanting to be June and wanting to be me. Your pride was hurt when I tried to shed light on your confusions. But I showed you my own conflicts and confusions. So you retaliated by pointing up my errors, and of course my life is full of flaws. It is true that I tend to retreat from harshness into a world of children, like Robert, because I think that the young are at the beginning of creation, the beginning of the world, at the beginning of love, not yet corrupted, and there is a hope of entering a world without hostilities. But I was wrong. There is cruelty and hostility in children, too. There is danger in innocence, too."

Suddenly I understood the game Luise wanted to play. Instead of talking with a doctor, an analyst, whenever she was confused she resorted to dramatization.

"You, Anaïs, will play the part of the one I want to be, the lucid one, and I will play the part of June, which I recognize as part of me, and then by confronting each other, arguing, I will be able to find out who I am."

A spiritual punching bag. All this might perhaps be good for

Luise but where will I find the strength and the objectivity to play this game? I see my last image of Luise, standing at the top of her stairway, taut, stretching her little figure, made taller by anger, indicating that she is the biggest one of the three, shouting: "Now write a book in which I, Luise, am both you and June. A different book."

What was striking when Luise said this to me, as much as the words, was that she was standing at the top of the curving stairway to her bedroom, where we once sat together sharing a piece of music while she resisted answering Odets's telephone call, sharing our difficulties in relationships, our desire to cut off whatever had the power to hurt us, celebrating our sisterhood, our alliance.

But this time I stood downstairs in the living room, I was waiting for Luise, who was dressing, and as she came out at the top of the stairs and hurled those words at me, standing there, not calling out to me to come up or coming down towards me. There was no music, no sunlight on the window, but a delicately boned woman, drawn up to her full, willful height, commanding me to write about her as the most complete of three women, because she was a blend of June and myself.

I took Patchen's manuscript to Maxwell Perkins at Scribner's. I introduced him to John Slocum, the literary agent, who helped him to get his book published, and gave him fifty dollars, which I could not spare. But he talks badly about me. All of us have our demons. Mine is caged in the diary. That may be why I so often dream that the diary is burning. Every time I hear a fire engine I think the diary is burning. If the diary burns, this demon will be on the loose again, not chained. Not contained. In the diary I may record my coldness towards Patchen, but in life, the absurd code by which I live, I helped him.

Gonzalo's demon is jealousy and drink. When he drinks he is the opposite of what he is sober. What does that mean? Which is the real Gonzalo? This resembles my old question: Which was the real

Henry, the one I knew or the one in the world? Both. We all have a thousand faces then, and stand on turnstiles for each person.

In Henry the demon was the drive to write, to conquer the world, and to possess all women.

In Helba, unable to dance, disease became her theater, her Grand Guignol, and she gave terrifying performances by magnifying her illnesses, oppressing us with her imminent death. How many death scenes, how many paroxysms, how many near-deaths?

Paul arrives. He is faintly touched with sun always, golden, his eyes green, like new leaves, or moss. He has the profile of Louis Jouvet, only more refined. He always looks clear-eyed and innocent, even during the most perverse years of his life in France. He is graceful, charming, with a rich-toned voice and laughter. There is no sign of age. But at one moment of his unawareness, I caught suddenly on his face the lax expression of the child, the features suddenly deprived of the support of the will. I was surprised by the softness, the unformed quality of his face. I detected the bonelessness of the child within the body of the man, immaturity exposed within the structure of the full-grown man. Then it seemed as if he had been deteriorating as a perverse, prematurely aged child, and not as a man. I had caught the grimace of a baby's face when it is about to cry, the loss of control, the loose mouth, the disintegrated laughter, something vulnerable and easily crushed. Then just as quickly he tightened his entire body and became again the suave and controlled man, who had deceived so many women as to his preferences. He charmed Luise, who said he looked like the first man she had loved, the one who had died in a plane crash.

Caresse preferred him to George Barker and invited him to Ghost Town. Robert warmed to the glow he shed.

If on some days I can catch the mysteries of nature which does not mature us evenly, consistently, but in sections, portions, fragments, on some other days I see everyone in terms of gestures, theatrical gestures, or natural gestures. Gonzalo walks as he thinks and feels, in wide, uneven, asymmetrical zigzags, wavering, with a minimum of propulsion. Robert is stylized, erect, and only softens his gestures, walk and posture in the presence of men.

Henry is loose-limbed, agile, lax.
I am swift like an arrow, I move directly towards my aim.

Paul and Robert had a love affair, and I was caught in the middle as "confidante," charged with all their vibrations, currents, and drafts! Paul cannot understand how Robert can show so much frenzy during the night and then coldness during the day, even cruelty. I am not certain whether he, Robert, is warmed and ignited by Paul's passion, reflects, but does not share it deeply. This would exasperate his sensuality in an effort to arouse himself to the same pitch which Paul experiences from love. Or is it something I have sensed in our life here which I never felt in Paris, that sensuality is *vice* for Americans, and they are ashamed. It is always dirty and so they feel as men do after going to a whore: ashamed. And they visit their resentment on the one who lured, charmed or seduced them. There may be an added complication, if Robert does not accept his own homosexuality, or if they have one of the typical homosexual conflicts with establishing the passive or active role.

The cruelties of love take place when the love does not answer a need. Robert wanted a father, and Paul cannot play that role. Robert describes how once in the subway, when Paul laughed, he became aware of his immaturity exactly as I did once abruptly when I saw him in a lax pose. Robert became aware of the childishness of Paul and judged him for it. He likes violence and firmness. Another time Robert described Paul's passion for analysis, explanations, commentaries. Robert demands that one become lyrical with him, surrender to a mood, the atmosphere, the wild moment, ecstasy. "He is a scholar, not a poet."

I see my future work as a work of completion, for each day I *see more*. Even when I look back into the past, the figures do not grow less distinct but infinitely clearer, more meaningful.

For example, I never described my father's playfulness, which he acted out the way children make faces behind their elders' backs. He always performed his jokes, pantomimes, behind the back of Maruca, quickly, as if not wanting to be caught in the act, hypocritically, with a face ready to return to its impassible mask, gestures very swift, to be ready to return into solemnity if caught by the elder (like giggles in church, like children's love games, like schoolchildren's pranks), something of the child playing when he is not observed, and fearing to be caught.

Luise, in the same way, made a grimace to me in front of the door of Dr. Harding's office as if we were both in a plot to deceive her; if the door had opened unexpectedly, Luise's face would quickly have assumed a serious expression.

Reading Robert's diary was my only access to the inner Robert. Now that he can no longer work in my studio, and has taken his papers away, he wears a mask, he is detached. He felt I was throwing him out of the nest. The human contact, by way of the diaries, broke. One cannot reach him. Outside of the diary he is brittle, he is an actor.

While I read his diary we could communicate on a level where his cold rays could not reach, a level where play acting ceased.

In the diary he said he was devouring me like a food. It makes him write, to read my diary.

Man seems powerless to face the truth or the relative truth stripped of all adornment. Robert could not bear to look back, to examine, to interpret. His motives were oblique. He acted out illusions. He must have myths to love, but when they shatter, he stops loving. I argued this, that where the myth fails, human love begins. Then we love a human being, not our dream, but a human being with flaws. But Robert must peer forward into a new mirage. The moment we lost touch with the diaries, he lost his sincerity with me. Perhaps I lost mine, too. I would never have known Robert intimately if it had not been for his diary.

So now he exists outside, almost a stranger.

Robert thinks I am not writing a sketch book at all, that I am completing a work. "You are bringing in the characters fully, independently of you, and in person."

Scene with Robert. He came and asked for a loan for a trip. My eyes filled with tears.

"You weep only because you have no money?"

"I weep because I did not think you would ask me, knowing how indebted I am, how short I am. I thought you would spare me having to say no."

"Why do you weep? Just say *no* harshly, that's the end of it. I would have preferred that you get angry. Why don't you just get angry?" He made a grimace of disapproval. He said: "You are ineffectual in battle. You should *fight*."

The grin with which he invited me to battle was like a distortion, a Robert I did not know.

Because of my vision into the inner Robert I still refused to see how his behavior crystallized into coldness and selfishness. He always came in without a greeting. He went straight to the icebox. He was never concerned whether he finished the last carton of milk, or the last slice of bread, which meant I had to climb five flights of stairs to buy more of everything for dinner. He never helped to put away the dishes. He served himself, no one else. He monologued without regard for others' work or fatigue. I had to read all that he brought even if he found me writing. He invited his friends for lunch. At any time. When visitors came for me, he did not leave. Once, when he asked me for money, I showed him my empty pocketbook and he left without a word.

After breaking through the nonhuman Robert to reach the vulnerable Robert in his diary, again I had to learn I was casting my own reflections on him. I thought, With me he will be different. Knowing my struggles, he would not burden me. But he did. Furthermore, he demanded a harshness equal to his own. If I have to manufacture an equal hardness, then I do not want any friendship on such terms. I want to be able to trust, not live in perpetual self-defense.

When he rang the bell this morning I did not answer. I was in the kitchen when I heard him entering through the transom window.

I told him how I felt. He left angrily.

I made contact with the highest point of Robert's poetic intuitions, with the poet Robert, but all around this lay areas of confusion and coldness. This connection with the highest point of a human being can be dangerous to human life. You only love the potential and overlook the reality. Will I be able to love Robert as he is? Wasn't it I who told him, When you lose a myth about a person that is where human love begins?

Robert, *l'enfant terrible,* perverse and knowing. At times the softness of a boneless child makes him seem small, at others he stands up rigid and tall. His eyes are too widely opened, like a medium in a trance. His eyelids fall heavily, like a woman's, with a seductive sweep of the eyelashes, the feminine drawing of a veil; a man's eyelids never fall this way over the revealing landscape of the eyes. It is when a woman's eyes are about to reveal too much that the woman draws a veil, lowers the lid over the chamber of revelation. How often I have watched women cover the flame of mischief with a Venetian blind, especially the glint of jealousy, the flicker of envy, the gleam of anger.

Robert talked and wrote so much about his consuming hunger and his desire to be consumed in love, about his desire for renunciation and the protection of others. He talked about his quest for a father. With me he is not feminine.

My femininity annoys him. He loves me, but he would like me to be a boy. That must have been the meaning of the scene we had. He wanted a warrior, someone who would resist him. Not the softness of the woman.

Paul offered him a paradise somewhere, a beach where they could love each other freely, embrace day and night, a paradise of caresses. But this is not what Robert wanted. He was seeking the infernos of love, love mixed with suffering and obstacles. He wants to kill monsters (the parents), overcome obstacles (poverty), and know all the adventures of romantic, impossible loves.

At the same time, when he talked about Paul, there came to his face the same expression of obscene glee, of vain satisfaction, triumph, an inner uncontrollable celebration of his power to wound others, the female ruses and wiles and coquetries by which he had made Paul fall in love with him. The malicious feminine conspiracy to enchant, seduce and victimize.

He acted like a caricature of a woman. A bad imitation of woman. The woman without a womb in which such great mysteries take place. Only this travesty of the invitation, like the prostitute's, which will never lead to a magnificent fusion. Why do men love this travesty of woman and not the real woman?

No great love could take place in this wombless femininity. Only a travesty of love. Robert's fury. His angry words: "He overlooked the masculinity in me completely. He treated me like a woman. I want to be saved from becoming a woman. He handled and possessed me like a woman."

I added this page to the erotica:

Father, mother and three children lived in a two-story house. She was seven or eight years old then. Her father always took her to the attic to be whipped. He did not want her mother to hear her. The mother would interfere, get angry with him, and the struggle usually ended with a great battle between her father and mother.

So the punishment always took place in this low-ceilinged room with the slanting roof, cluttered with trunks, rags, broken furniture, old curtains, old books. She remembered how all of them hated this, and begged to be forgiven. The walk up the stairs was usually spent in trying to persuade their father that they were innocent and did not deserve a spanking. She wept bitterly and hated her father at such moments. But at the same time she felt that the hand which administered these violent blows awakened pleasure as well as pain, as if the vibrations of feelings had become crossed wires in her body, and messages intercepted or garbled. He awakened her dormant sensibilities. It was as if the spankings came too near to regions usually devoted to sensuous pleasure. Both pain and pleasure suddenly revealed to be in proximity to each other, physically and emotionally.

She never became aware of the short circuit, the link that had been established between them until twenty years later: She walked into a penny arcade near a theater section. She had already seen three or four short movie scenes, men and women rolling in the grass, women caught in their bath, whores undressing, and she was laughing until she witnessed the following scene: It took place in a schoolroom. Many little girls, between five and eight, sat on a bench, wearing the short, puffed little skirts she wore as a child. The teacher was growing angry at them. Finally, she beckoned one to come up to her desk and she scolded her. The little girl answered impudently. The teacher took hold of the little girl, placed her across her knees, lifted her skirt, pulled down her panties and began to spank her sharply. As she watched the scene she felt the most amazing wave of pleasure all through her body.

I never tire of hearing Gonzalo tell me about his birthplace: Puno, on Lake Titicaca. It is a port, populated almost entirely by sailors. There was a revolution while Gonzalo's mother was pregnant. His father was the mayor, and he was held as a hostage. Gonzalo's mother ran away, disguised as an Indian peasant woman, and Gonzalo's nurse hid her in the hut of her relatives. So Gonzalo was born in a humble Indian peasant's hut, while an order was issued condemning his mother to prison if she were found. It is a strange story, when one remembers that Gonzalo's whole life was one of revolt, revolt against Catholicism, school, his parents, his class; and even his marriage to Helba was an act of revolt, because she came from poor and ignorant origins.

At the age of two he was taken to their hacienda. At seven he was sent to the Jesuit school. He never went home again, except on vacations. Later, his family moved to Lima, where he worked as a journalist, reported on sports, took drugs, fought in boxing matches, and met Helba, the dancer. Gonzalo's description:

The mountains are made of metal, millions and millions of grey potassium cones in which the mica sparkles like glass. The soil has the color of chicken cooked with red peppers, the national dish. The desert ends in an arid mountain, denuded, crowned with the mouth of a crater of calcinated rocks, covered with ashes. This is the Misti, the sacred mountain of Arequipa.

The Cathedral of Arequipa is built of volcanic rocks, the color of honey and has remained looking young and fresh.

Arequipa is the great wool market, a market for mules, and revolutions. The houses are heavy-set at the base, they have stairs painted in laundry blue. The palaces are pink, the patios are laid with Spanish tiles from which sprout African date trees.

The llamas have wet, languishing eyes, small straight ears, mobile necks which pivot like that of birds, plump female behinds, and hide their bodies in thick wool. It was once a sacred animal. The Indians love it beyond permissible boundaries.

Where does the Indian come from? From Asia? From the Pacific? Did he come from the north by the Bering Strait, leaping over those stones we call the Aleutian Islands? Did they escape drowning in vanishing continents? Did they come in canoes from Polynesia? The Indian, by his gestures, reminds me of Asia. Puno sank its cathedral into the bullrushes of the muddy *laguna* through which Lake Titicaca is leaking out. Titicaca means "pewter stone," and it is truly the mat immobility of this liquid pewter which best describes this suspended Mediterranean. A desert of water in which is reflected the desert of sand between red shores. Titicaca, an aerial lake so deep that it is useless to throw an anchor, perched so high up, shaken by such violent storms, that one feels simultaneously sea sickness and mountain sickness. The Andes, covered by snow and ashes, the whitest clouds in all the world, a horizon like the edge of a saw. Man is said to have been born there.

Joy at the realization that I am completing a work, not just making notes, the joy of discovering that this is not a sketch book but a tapestry, a fresco being completed.

When Gonzalo mocks its being "hidden in a box," I answer that the very condition of the work required its being done in darkness, inside of a box, in secrecy. The very integrity of it depends on its secrecy. Like the stalactite caves, it would crumble at exposure, it would lose its sincerity, the very essence of its quality. It was born out of timidity. I lacked the audacity of the artist working in the open (I write my stories in the morning, my diary at night).

Secrecy is the very element which created this stalactite cave, this world of truth. As I grow further away from feminine reflection and nearer to art, to objectivity, I do not want to lose this drama of the process, from the first blurred reflections of emotional waters to the lucidities of the poet and analyst. I feel calm and lucid. At the beginning I was turgid, chaotic, occasionally clairvoyant, often blind, impatient, careless, living so fast, so much, writing in rhythm with it, negligent or excessive.

Now I write more slowly. Timidity marred my creative work outside of the diary. In the presence of others, I always wanted to wear my best dress. I assumed the ultimate defenses of perfectionism, I wanted to give only the perfect polished diamond. Inside of this shield my heart could speak simply. But I had to promise myself secrecy or I would not have been as spontaneous, or as sincere.

Every book I have written has brought me new friends, new realms of experience, new worlds. The imagination incarnates personages who lie in the obscurest region of one's being. In writing they come to the surface, take form, body, in the reality of the book. And then the answering character appears. I am sure that when D. H. Lawrence wrote *Lady Chatterley's Lover,* a real Lady Chatterley appeared.

When I wrote about D. H. Lawrence, Henry appeared. That is my essential reason for writing, not for fame, not to be celebrated after death, but to heighten and create life all around me. I cannot go into life without my books. They are my passports, my rudder, my map, my ticket. I also write because when I am writing I reach the high moment of fusion sought by the mystics, the poets, the lovers, a sense of communion with the universe.

There are passages in my books which are invitations, expectations, suspenses. Anyone reading them accurately would recognize a cue and feel, I can enter her life now. This is my clue. The atmosphere is propitious. Without the writing I am timid. Through lack of audacity I cannot enter without this bridge, a portable bridge I can lay down between human beings and myself.

It is quite possible that my father blew up this bridge and conferred this timidity upon me. With every friendship I face irreparable harm. Without my books I would often turn my back upon adventure and become a recluse. With my books I feel I have a task. I am an explorer. I must visit the lands I am to describe. When I write the book I use the book like dynamite, to blast myself out of isolation.

[December, 1941]

Everything is flowing, love, writing, talking. I talk with George Barker. He is so quick, so sharp, so focused, vital, electric. A taut mind and body, throwing off sparks. Turbulent. His wet Irish eyes, mocking, with that caressing slant towards the cheeks which indicates voluptuousness. At first I did not like his flippancy, his disguises. But when he said: "What can one do when one is removed not once, not twice, but a hundred times from one's real self?" at that moment I liked him, understood him.

We talked with suppleness, clarity, swiftness. Images appear spontaneously, a search for heightened living. His body is all keyed up for it. I am sure he makes love the same way, with nervous, feverish activity, as if a current of electricity were speeding through his body.

In America, poetry is being retranslated into prose. All effort to make the transmutation required of poetry, which is an alchemy of ordinary natural events into heightened myth, is taboo. Yet the very role of the poet is to exalt whatever he touches, it is to take ordinary reality and give it a fiery incandescence which reveals its meaning. Without this alchemy all writing remains dead.

I get the feeling that life and writing here are becoming as boxed-in, as monotonously symmetrical as the architecture. It is a dreary order, a mechanical structure, a functional practical servant.

Dr. Franz Horch, my literary agent, praises my work. But Wayne Harris and Seon Gibben are dreamers. Whatever money they had was sunk in a book of poems by Patchen which is not selling. One year lost. Caresse had also wanted to publish the book under the imprint of the Black Sun Press but failed to get backing. There is no protection for the writer. Anyone can come and say he will publish it, keep it in a drawer for a year, and then return it.

Meanwhile I am bound not to show it to anyone. The book is advertised as coming out, people send in checks, interest is aroused, then nothing happens. When it is mentioned again it seems like a hoax. And I am left to explain what has happened.

But I still have faith in *Winter of Artifice*. I have used decanting, thrown out all the unessentials to bring out the inner meaning. Attention is riveted on the inner drama. For that there had to be an elimination of upholstery, overstuffing. But people still want the old-fashioned stuffing, every door opened and closed, every window opened and closed, every bell rung, every telephone call registered, as in Dreiser, who mentioned the rent paid by each character. I used a roller to squeeze out all superfluous matter. It is compressed, condensed, a meal for modern tempo, even for parachute jumpers!

How to murder a writer.

He writes a spontaneous book. He is sent for. He is asked to write something to order, something like the last best seller, *The Good Earth*. After a few forced books, he becomes impotent. The falsity sterilizes him. I wonder how many good American writers were murdered in this way. Second method: Ply them with gold. The money throws them off course, off the atmosphere they know, and feel in tune with. They are thrown into false situations, become rootless. They dry up emotionally.

JAPAN OPENS WAR ON THE UNITED STATES. FIRST AIR RAID OVER NEW YORK. FALSE ALARM. SHOCK.

When these things explode, one gets the shock of people who were asleep, for none of us were informed enough to predict or prepare ourselves. We were all caught sleeping, dreaming, loving, working.

Gonzalo came to life. War makes him feel alive. He would love to be in the fight.

Henry's anarchism is excited.

In me there is always a slow awakening from my personal, my dreamed, my creative life. But what first awakens is my resistance to outer destruction. I do not sweep away all we are doing. I do not devaluate it. I am not instantly convinced that history is more valuable than human beings, because history is not humanism. It is the love of power. So I continue first of all to protect, preserve, bring to completion whatever sustains the human beings around me. Imperturbably I get my typewriter cleaned for more work because to me that means if the world loves war and destruction I won't go along with it. I will go on loving and writing until the bomb falls. I am not going to quit, abdicate, and play its game of death and power.

George Barker is terribly poor. When he comes, he is like a man sitting on a drill. He vibrates as if he would explode. His eyes are like blue porcelain, washed by the sea, his words staccato, like a typewriter. He wants to write more erotica. He wrote eighty-five pages. The collector thought they were too surrealistic. I loved them. His scenes of love-making were disheveled and fantastic. Love between trapezes.

He drank away the first money, and I could not lend him anything but more paper and carbons. George Barker, the excellent English poet, writing erotica to drink, just as Utrillo painted paintings in exchange for a bottle of wine. I began to think about the old man we all hated. I decided to write to him, address him directly, tell him about our feelings.

Dear Collector: We hate you. Sex loses all its power and magic when it becomes explicit, mechanical, overdone, when it becomes a mechanistic obsession. It becomes a bore. You have taught us more than anyone I know how wrong it is not to mix it with emotion, hunger, desire, lust, whims, caprices, personal ties, deeper relationships which change its color, flavor, rhythms, intensities.

You do not know what you are missing by your microscopic examination of sexual activity to the exclusion of others, which are the fuel that ignites it. Intellectual, imaginative, romantic, emotional. This is what gives sex its surprising textures, its subtle transformations, its aphrodisiac elements. You are shrinking your world of sensations. You are withering it, starving it, draining its blood.

If you nourished your sexual life with all the excitements and adventures which love injects into sensuality, you would be the most potent man in the world. The source of sexual power is curiosity, passion. You are watching its little flame die of asphyxiation. Sex does not thrive on monotony. Without feeling, inventions, moods, no surprises in bed. Sex must be mixed with tears, laughter, words, promises, scenes, jealousy, envy, all the spices of fear, foreign travel, new faces, novels, stories, dreams, fantasies, music, dancing, opium, wine.

How much do you lose by this periscope at the tip of your sex, when you could enjoy a harem of distinct and never-repeated wonders? Not two hairs alike, but you will not let us waste words on a description of hair; not two odors, but if we expand on this, you cry "Cut out the poetry." Not two skins with the same texture, and never the same light, temperature, shadows, never the same gesture; for a lover, when he is aroused by true love, can run the gamut of centuries of love lore. What a range, what changes of age, what variations of maturity and innocence, perversity and art, natural and graceful animals.

We have sat around for hours and wondered how you look. If you have closed your senses upon silk, light, color, odor, character, temperament, you must be by now completely shriveled up. There are so many minor senses, all running like tributaries into the mainstream of sex, nourishing it. Only the united beat of sex and heart together can create ecstasy.

Preparing for air raids. Buying flashlights. Tape for the windows so they won't break. Dark curtains. Again! In France, they said, it happened because we were too concerned with art, aesthetics, and not enough with politics. Here then? Where everyone thinks only of two things: politics and money.

Henry is working obsessively on the American book (to be called *The Air-Conditioned Nightmare*). The dream of Mobile is a beautiful section. I bring him a flashlight.

I write ten or fifteen pages of erotica a day.

Frances Steloff. Clear pale blue eyes. Clear skin. She is small and it is sometimes difficult to find her behind huge stacks of books, counters piled high, tables, desks with mountains of books. She wears an apron, she carries a paper with a list of books, or a bill, or a letter. She was one of many children, born in Saratoga Springs, New York. A Russian family.

There was too much work for her to do to be allowed to go to school. She had a great hunger for books. She promised herself someday she would live surrounded by books. Later she came to New York and her wish was fulfilled. She opened the Gotham Book Mart January 1, 1920, and was the first to keep it open in the evenings, in the theater section. I believe she educated herself this way, read and listened to the talk around her. Her main interest lies in theosophy. She has antennae, and a gift for friendship. She welcomes the unusual, the uncommercial, the avant-garde. As a result, everything converges to her store, small magazines, rare books, special, unique people, looking for special books. The place has an atmosphere, it is not slick, or organized, or impersonal. People like to come and browse. It is almost like being in a private library, with a familiar natural disorder. Because of her hospitality, there are many treasures in her cellar.

She took me to a light-organ concert. The concept was interesting. The colors impossibly weak and pretty.

Gonzalo and I searched for a job he could do and like. It was a dismal search, and Gonzalo grew more and more despairing. The only work he responded to was printing, because he had been associated with that on his brother's newspaper in Lima. He loved first editions, fine printing, and everything connected with it. But he could not get a job because he had no experience.

As we talked, I began to think again it might be good to have our own press. He could do my books or whatever else he wanted to do for his political beliefs, his Latin poet friends.

We saw secondhand presses for seventy-five and one hundred dollars. One of them operated like an old-fashioned sewing machine, by a foot pedal. The inking had to be done by hand. The man said we could turn out Christmas cards on it, but not fine books. Gonzalo was sure it would work. We would have to find one hundred dollars for type and trays.

I talked it over with Frances Steloff. She would lend me seventy-five if I could find the rest of the money.

Thurema Sokol lent me a hundred dollars.

I spent days looking for a loft. At the end of one afternoon of hunting, I tried a real estate agent on Washington Square. He took me to Macdougal Street, across the way from the Provincetown

Theater. It was an old house. We climbed the front stairs, then three flights to the top floor. As soon as he opened the door I knew it was the right place. It was a skylight studio, ideal for the work. An attic, with a ceiling slanting down to the windows on Macdougal Street. It was old, uneven, with a rough wood floor, painted black, walls painted yellow. There was a very small kitchenette. It was all a little askew, it had character, like the houseboat. It had a fireplace. Past tenants had left a big desk and a couch. Thirty-five dollars a month. I took it immediately. Gonzalo was ecstatic. It looks like the houseboat! We had seen so many places which we hated, dusty, plain, faceless, shabby, like prisons, with narrow windows, cold, damp.

The doors were uneven. The house was so old it had settled. The windows on the street opened outward, like French casement windows. The houses across the way were also small and intimate, a little like Montmartre. Everywhere there was a casual, artist life. One could see windows open on paintings, on pottery, on looms.

Gonzalo hung some of his own drawings on the walls.

The press will be delivered to 144 Macdougal Street. We went in quest of paper. We learned about end paper, small lots which are not usable by big publishers, but ideal for us. Good paper. We bought type. Gonzalo was glad to work with his hands. He loves machinery.

The press was delivered. We borrowed a book from the library on how to print. Gonzalo would run the press, I would set type. I started to learn typesetting. It took me an hour and a half to typeset half a page. We decided to start with *Winter of Artifice*.

I tried to interest Robert Duncan and George Barker in a communal press. We would all do the work together and bring out all the books we wrote.

I was cutting paper and typesetting when George Barker came to see me. I asked him if he wanted to help. I said if he helped me do *Winter of Artifice* we would do his poems next. He had come with a manuscript of his poems. He watched me work but volunteered no help and soon made his escape. Robert had worked with the Cooneys on their magazine, and did not seem interested in manual labor.

Had to console Henry for his first failure, the American book. It is an angry book. I do not know if it is a just anger. But no one likes it.

The reviews of *The Colossus of Maroussi* are not good. Yet I think this is a beautiful book, and I place it higher than the book on America.

The creation of an individual world, an act of independence, such as the work at the press, is a marvelous cure for anger and frustration. The insults of the publishers, the rejections, the ignorance, all are forgotten. I love the studio. I get up with eager curiosity. The press is a challenge. We make mistakes.

Once, following directions, I oiled the rollers themselves and for days we could not print at all. The inking has to be done by hand, so while Gonzalo pedals, I stand ready with the ink and the rag. We decided to use line engravings by Ian Hugo, using the William Blake method learned from William Hayter. That means setting the copper plate on an inch-thick backing, locking it in the tray, inking the platter carefully, making one print, cleaning the plate, and starting anew. Three hundred engravings. Typesetting slowly makes me analyze each phrase and tighten the style.

Robert came again, but we have a cool relationship. No more reading of diaries, no more intimacy. Such reconciliations are meaningless unless one can rebuild the broken trust. The vital bond is broken.

I go out to a party and meet the editors of *Partisan Review*. They sit there with unsmiling cold faces, uninviting, closed. Their talk is harsh, ideological, political, dry, neither warm nor human nor sensitive. They are tough intellectuals, without the slightest charm or wit or humor or tolerance. They are rigid. Clever in a cold way.

One of them asked me: "Are you related to Andrés Nin?"

"Not to my knowledge. Nin is a very common name in Spain. A branch of the Nins went to South America and have written books on Marxism. But I don't know about Andrés Nin. I left Spain when I was nine years of age, and have had no ties with it since. My father never mentioned Andrés Nin."

In the case of withdrawal from a friendship it is difficult to tell whether it is the withdrawal of feeling which kills the warmth, or whether the warmth was a reflection. As soon as I withdrew, Robert revealed his coldness, or was it always there? To what extent do people have an independent life or reflect each other's warmth? To what extent do we call into being what we believe, see, wish in others? Now I see only the unfeeling cold profile of Robert. Why? Because I rebelled against my mother role, because I rebelled against the troubles brought upon me by my exaggerated compassion and empathy. Robert wanted me harder. Sooner or later his hostile reaction to emotion would have revealed itself. I refuse to harden or toughen. But I will have to break with those who take advantage of it, for at first Robert did admit that it was this tenderness which revealed to him what a relationship might be, yet he did not know how to preserve this tenderness.

When I was writing the story of Artaud, putting together in an alchemized way all I knew about him, had observed, heard, I found it incomplete. I could not follow Artaud into his madness.

I happened to reread a section in the diary in which I recorded a visit I made with Jean Carteret to the place on the Île St. Louis, where they first brought the insane for questioning, classification and diagnosis.

I was struck by the resemblance in style, in repetition, in imagery and hallucinations, between a schizophrenic patient and the talk of Artaud. This could have been the language and even content of Artaud's madness.

The unfinished story (as taken from the diary pages on Artaud himself) and the reportage made of the schizophrenic patient matched like twin faces. I welded them.

Today I read in a magazine a letter written by Artaud from Ville Evrard insane asylum:

I must have heroin at any price and one must face death to bring it to me for the Initiates of Sickness have placed fabrics of terrible magic spells between that substance and myself and the police bar the roads in the occult no less than in the real. And I absolutely cannot live longer amidst this torment which pounds my nerves and bones day and night without hope of relief. Illness has done its worst and the Gestapo as well as the French police keep back the heroin to prevent me regaining my strength and to hold me here in despair and suffering. And I must open by magic the road to the Bohemians who are not of this world but who must introduce into it their powers armed with flesh and bone and the latter are numberless and you have among them your armies but I must be able to work to open to them the gates of this world.

You came to help me last Monday, Tuesday, and Wednesday, but through a magic displacement I lost you in front of the Matin at the angle of the Rue du Faubourg Montmartre for the illness prevented you from maintaining yourself there and you had to be in Morocco and take the boat, that is, follow what are called the normal ways. But the Bohemians who were at the Palais de Justice Tuesday evening and who burned it after having massacred the judge cannot follow the normal ways, they must penetrate our world from the same level and as one passes from ship to quai and their world which is the OTHER world will be installed in our own at the moment they come to meet me.

Compare this letter with my second half of the Artaud story, *"Je Suis le Plus Malade des Surréalistes."*

While writing the story of Artaud I remembered our last talk in Louveciennes. It took me years to understand what took place. I had just come back from the south of France, from a few days spent with my father to celebrate our reunion. I was talking with Artaud about it, telling him the story of the long estrangement, of our first meeting, our efforts to know each other. I was talking with elation about our discovery of each other.

Artaud at the time was preoccupied, obsessed with *Beatrice Cenci*, with his dramatization of it. It filled his imagination. The myth of the destructive father, the love between father and daughter.

In his exalted, mythical, dramaturgic mind the two situations, the two stories became one. He lost sight of the real Anaïs, the real father, and they merged into Beatrice Cenci and her father.

I did not realize what was happening in his mind. When he began in an accusing, theatrical tone to condemn, to judge this "impure" love, I thought he was distorting my life, my father, and me. I reacted to the distortion. When he said: "The most unnatural of loves," I retorted: "The most natural."

Artaud lived so completely within his own unconscious world, that for him theater, myth, and life were all one, conscious and unconscious. Personal divergences from the myth or the theater were unimportant. He could only see his play, *Beatrice Cenci,* and her father. And it was Artaud the judge, the moralist, the monk, the Savonarola of my vision of him (for I did see that aspect of his nature) which angered me as a grave act of injustice. If he had not judged Cenci-Anaïs, I might not have rebelled. We would not have quarreled. I would have accepted this superimposition of myth upon reality as I had accepted other interpretations, other hallucinations of his.

It is only in such human relationships that one insists on one's own identity and separation from myths. If in a story I saw Artaud as Savonarola, I never accused him in life of being Savonarola. But Artaud was denying me my own identity. He insisted I was Cenci and I was involved in a dark and terrible love.

The first proof print of *Winter of Artifice,* handset by me and printed by Gonzalo. His physical strength is needed for the foot pedal.

We learned the hard way, by experience, without a teacher. Testing, inventing, seeking, struggling. James Cooney came one afternoon and gave us a few tips. Robert, too. Robert brought his poems, but did not stay to file away the type.

We reset the whole page. It was too loose. Worked seven and eight hours a day. We dreamt, ate, talked, slept with the press. We ate sandwiches with the taste of ink, got ink in our hair and inside our nails.

William Hayter taught us the printing of engravings. A meticulous task. The engravings were not designed to fit any particular story, but Gonzalo chose those which harmonized with them.

Dudley, Seon, Robert, Harris, all between twenty and twenty-five, are child prodigies of intelligence, but absolutely devoid of feeling. All brain and without an ounce of humanity. I had to say to Seon: "Don't be so harsh." They treat each other with such brutality and venom.

I refuse friendships which are a constant form of dueling. Argumentative, aggressive, belligerent friendships. Pugilistic.

Seon said: "I understand much better Djuna Barnes closing her door to me than you opening your door to me."

As Robert detected, I am incapacitated for war. War is the great pleasure of people whose love is atrophied, who need war to feel alive, who find in violence and clash a semblance of relationship. Relationship by hatred.

I want to work. I have no time for battles. The relationship to handcraft is a beautiful one. You are related bodily to a solid block of metal letters, to the weight of the trays, to the adroitness of spacing, to the tempo and temper of the machine. You acquire some of the weight and solidity of the metal, the strength and power of the machine. Each triumph is a conquest by the body, fingers, muscles. You live with your hands, in acts of physical deftness.

You pit your faculties against concrete problems. The victories are concrete, definable, touchable. A page of perfect printing. You can touch the page you wrote. We exult in what we master and discover. Instead of using one's energy in a void, against frustrations, in anger against publishers, I use it on the press, type, paper, a source of energy. Solving problems, technical, mechanical problems. *Which can be solved.*

If I pay no attention, then I do not lock the tray properly, and when I start printing the whole tray of letters falls into the machine. The words which first appeared in my head, out of the air, take body. Each letter has a weight. I can weigh each word again, to see if it is the right one.

I use soap boxes as shelves, to hold tools, paper, inks. I arrive loaded with old rags for the press, old towels for the hands, coffee, sugar. Gonzalo's love for first editions prepared him for good taste in design, in choosing type, paper, in spacing. He loves the hard work of cleaning the press, taking out the discarded paper in barrels. He brings strength and *brio*. We study type faces while eating, and have read all the books on printing we could find in the library.

The press mobilized our energies, and is a delight. At the end of the day you can see your work, weigh it. It is done. It exists.

When Seon attacked my intuitive thinking, and I repudiated her love of battle, I told her that what made Djuna Barnes close her door is the fear of being wounded again. What made me open my door is that I never expect people to come as enemies. Until the person proves to be an enemy, I have no distrust.

But Seon, because of her weakness and uncertainty, is using me as a punching bag.

"You are hardening your fists against me, sharpening your teeth on me. Discovering others' weaknesses is not going to prove your strength. We all have weaknesses. The knowledge of human weakness is what gives a friendship its humanity. You must seek another protagonist. I do not thrive on war. War to me is the greatest weakness of all."

I seem to meet only people *sur un pied de guerre.*

Henry underlines a passage in Céline:

Did I love Rosalie? The question is meaningless. When a man is desperately at odds with himself, others do not exist. He is a battlefield of principalities and powers. His relationships with others are a caricature of this conflict. He is alone. And the more people he knows, and the more famous he is, the greater the solitude. In all relations to others I have been concerned only with myself.

I copied this out and sent it to Seon.

Robert is leaving for Berkeley. For once I did not elude battle. I told him what I thought of his behavior and what had alienated us. He could find nothing to attack except my ineffectualness in battle. "That is true," I said, "I'm not martial."

Robert said: "I must admit you gave me, while it lasted, the most wonderful relationship I have ever known, one in which *I was never hurt.* You showed me what a relationship could be."

Robert thinks that to bully or browbeat would prove my strength.

"I was not trained for prize fighting," I said, laughing.

"You did not fight Patchen."

"I had no wish to fight Patchen. When a friendship does not take place, I withdraw."

This combativeness is new to me.

In all of us there is a human weakness. The friend is the one who goes out to strengthen this weakness, but not to attack it. That was why June and Henry destroyed each other, because they attacked the vulnerabilities in each other. The desire to wound is destructive.

I was happy at the press. It made me forget the barbaric friendship with Robert. I was homesick for the care we all took in Paris not to hurt each other's feelings. A code.

A month of great labor, duels with the press, discoveries, failures, errors and triumphs. We gave ourselves to the press.

Helba increased her scenes. The more time Gonzalo spent at the press, the wilder her scenes. She once convinced him she was going blind. Gonzalo thought it was a syphilitic stroke, the beginning of paralysis.

I took her to Dr. Jacobson and he told me she was a hysteric, a malingerer, and he could prove it by taking a spinal fluid test. But Helba refused to take the test. Dr. Jacobson said: "She is resisting because she knows she will lose her last weapon."

The attack passed. Gonzalo went back to work.

Once there was something wrong with the press. It did not work. Gonzalo would not send for the workman, or the repairman. He literally battled with the press, as if it were a bronco, a bull, an animal to be tamed. His hair flew around his face, perspiration fell from his forehead, his centaur feet were kicking the pedals. The machine groaned.

It seemed almost like a physical battle which he intended to win by force. He towered over it. He seemed bigger than the machine. I never saw anything more primitive, more like a battle between an ancient race and a new type of monster. Both as stubborn, both strong, both violent. Gonzalo won. He was breathing heavily. The wheel suddenly began to spin again. He looked absolutely triumphant.

Again I appealed to Dorothy for a loan which we would repay in work. She refused. Her answer was: "I want to get a press for myself and do my poems on it."

People tell me Djuna Barnes is a broken woman. She sees very few people but will willingly talk to strangers at a bar. Should I see her? Should I reprint her *Nightwood*, which is out of print?

On my birthday: two pages done in three days.
February 23: Two pages in two days.
February 25: Two pages in one day.
March 4: Four pages a day. Jimmy Cooney helps us for an hour a day. His lessons saved us much time. We are now up to page 44.

Out in the world: fifty English soldiers bayoneted after surrendering. Women raped by the Japanese. Bali invaded. Java invaded.

Paris bombarded by the English. India rebelling against the English. Ships torpedoed. Pictures of Polish dead, camp victims, slow starvation, torture, murders. That is the world outside.

And what can one do but preserve some semblance of human life, to seek the not-savage, not-barbaric forms of life.

John Dudley had a breakdown. Flo tried to commit suicide with scissors.

[March, 1942]

At a party I met a young German doctor, about thirty years old. He looked worn and thin and strained. We began to talk, and I was struck by his anxiety and nervousness. He began to tell me the story Kafka wrote about the man who invented a machine for executing criminals. I knew the story, but I let the doctor tell it to me because what amazed me was the intensity, the hallucinated way in which he told it. "The inventor, when the machine was ready for an execution, began to feel such guilt he was unable to bear it. When it was set for the death of the first criminal he walked into it himself." At this point in his story the doctor's tension reached an unbearable pitch. He was perspiring.

I asked him: "Why does this story have such a power to disturb you?"

"Because I am the inventor of the fever box. You have heard about it? With it I have cured some tropical fevers as yet incurable by other means. But it is such a cruel form of cure, to subject the patient to an unbelievable fever heat, and I had to witness their suffering. This suffering preyed on me. It obsessed me, until I felt compelled to subject myself to it, too, to share their ordeal, even though I knew it might damage me forever as it only helps those suffering from high infectious fevers. I lost a hundred pounds and I am a nervous wreck."

Henry is up to the four-hundredth page of *The Rosy Crucifixion,* and writing like a fountain.

John Slocum gave up being a literary agent and became aide to New York Mayor Fiorello La Guardia and father of a boy.

Valeska Imbs is expecting another child.

Paul Rosenfeld is writing his biography. He asked me: "Where do I begin?"

I said: "Name, first of all, all the wishes you had, and then tell which ones came true and which ones did not."

Jimmy Cooney is writing erotica. George Barker is writing erotica.

Extraordinary talk with Henry on the everlastingly elusive truth of a life incident, a character. One would have to tell this incident, report on one's vision of a character every few years, to keep pace with one's change of view. I no longer see my father novel as the truth about my father. But even my father did not know the truth about himself, nor his wives, nor any of his friends.

Henry's objectivity is increasing. He is achieving a totality of vision. There are great changes in his character. Great changes in mine. We talk about Communism, memory, occult wisdom, of his desire to make money and find a paradise. I think Greece was the paradise he found and then lost because of the war. All the other paradises have become hells, Bali, Java, Hawaii, Greece.

We read Algernon Blackwood's *Bright Messenger*. There is a magic quality to his writing. He is one of the few transcendentalists. I thought transcendentalism had originated in America. But I see no sign of it in present writing. It is all one-dimensional. Blackwood seeks to express other dimensions. When he introduced the Bright Messenger and felt words could not convey the impression he made, he used music. Whenever he appeared, one heard music. His characters proceed by intuition, by faith in their sensations, in their dreams.

[April, 1942]

Take the letter O out of the box, place it next to the T, then a comma, then a space, and so on.

Count page 1, 2, 3, and so on. Select the good ones while Gonzalo runs the machine. Day after day. We are nearing the end. I have difficulties with the separation of words. And it is a problem in setting type.

(My separation of the word lo-ve became years later the favorite of the faultfinders!)

The writing is often improved by the fact that I live so many hours with a page that I am able to scrutinize it, to question the essential words. In writing, my only discipline has been to cut out the unessential. Typesetting is like film cutting. The discipline of typesetting and printing is good for the writer.

But no amount of work annihilates the undercurrent of monologues, dialogues, meditations, and flow of memories.

While I typeset, the radio plays one of my father's songs, and I am slowly, word by word, erecting the last monument to his failure as a father. To all the music from Russia, Germany, France, Spain, America, I weave the pattern of letters of metal proclaiming that the most important of all achievements is to be a human being. While I typeset one book, I am already writing another book. As fast as I typeset I also relive many periods of my life not included in this book.

I am often in Paris, seeking out the most forgotten incidents and places, reliving my experience with my father and seeing it differently.

If, for example, my father had not been my father but a friend, I would have appreciated his scholarship, his musical erudition, his gift for creating an atmosphere, his wit in the world, his talent for storytelling, his charm. But because he was my father, and a certain role was assigned to him, a certain expectation created in me, in childhood, and because in my eyes my mother's accusations seemed justified, all I could do was to draw a portrait of a relationship in which he failed to play the role he was assigned. It was by measuring his behavior according to the expectations of a daughter that I found him wanting.

Later I met other Don Juans and I passed no judgment on them! But they did not threaten the life of a family unit, they did not cause tragedy, loss, and uprootings. His travels, restlessness, escapes, would have seemed fascinating if they had not meant desertion, deprivation, and a constant anxiety inherited from my mother, concerning a wanderer who might never return home.

We are cruel when someone refuses to play the role in which we have cast him. We judge a person only according to his relationship towards us. The charm of my father was usually something he gave to others, not to his children.

I remember that at a time when I began to ask questions about the world, history, personalities, geography, astrology, astronomy, my father became bored with our curiosity and purchased *The Book of Knowledge* for us. (*Qui? Pourquoi? Comment?*) Some time later I found a lavish correspondence with a neighbor of fifteen, for whom he had taken the trouble of inventing an entire whimsical world of stories by which he seduced her into studying. When she moved away she gave me the letters because she felt I could learn from them.

The child expected protectiveness, loyalty, comfort, attention, help, teaching, guidance, companionship. His failure to be reassuring, present even, accessible, approving, companionable, dictated the judgment. If I had known him as a playmate, with whom roughhousing and games might be treacherous, dangerous even, and a matter of pitting one's energy and skills, or sharing adventures, he would have been my companion in dangerous experiences. Instead he became the awesome figure of the no-praise man, creating in me such a need of approval!

I relived my experience with Rank and understood it differently. He, too, was cast in a certain specific role. He was the doctor of the psyche. Although I encouraged his rebellion against the role of sacrificed doctor in order to rescue the artist in Rank, I could only have made this possible, I see now, by taking over the task of his analytical writing to free him for creative writing. That is what he asked of me.

This is what makes me rebel against the novel, which can only reveal a static fragment, freeze it, when the truth is not in that particular fragment but in continuous change. The novel arbitrarily chooses a moment in time, a segment. Frames it. Binds it.

A fragment does not give us that continuously changing truth. Perhaps we cannot bear a continuously changing truth. Perhaps we have to believe there is a TOTAL truth once reached and thereafter permanent, fixed. TOTAL. The capital T on the right-hand side of the box. The regular rhythm of the machine. It is heavy for the old floor, and I see the floor curving slightly under its weight, I hear the huge pulse, and hear the creaking.

I know that in *Winter of Artifice* I wanted to strip the psychological drama from too heavy an upholstery which obscured the psychic drama. I have gone into strange regions, woman's cyclical malady, insomnia, frigidity, neurosis, madness, anxiety, delusion, the failure of man's theories of behavior, the meaning of our father-quest as applied to the analyst. I have depicted the malady of to-day's soul. I have entered the dream with a powerful beam of light, to interpret, reveal its influence on our life, to focus on its influence, and the interdependence of fantasy and reality. I am writing with a sensitivity which our modern world is intent on destroying, not knowing that this is the only antenna we have to our psychic nature. Both our senses and our sensibilities are threatened with atrophy by the violence and brutality of modern life.

The young show signs of total emotional atrophy. I feel that I must remain an instrument of perception which must not allow itself to be destroyed by great violence, deafened by machine guns, calloused by harshness, though it is quite possible that I may not survive life in America.

I have not spared my hands. My nails are broken. I have not spared my book. I have slashed into its imperfections. It is shorter, better focused.

At night I lie in bed, write in the diary, write letters, copy lists for the announcements of the book's publication.

At parties I find only reflections of our life in Paris. The surrealists accept being feted, but for me it is all an echo of a dazzling, completed experience. Refugees repeat themselves. Some are ashamed of this survival and kill themselves, like Stefan Zweig. A singer who was adulated in Germany hanged herself with many colored scarves, on symbols of a colorful triumphant past.

While I finish printing *Winter of Artifice* the nightmare of the world grows immense, a chamber of horrors, a tortured world, bigger than I can bear to encompass. The madness of one man is terrible enough, the madness of millions, and a million Marquis de Sades is unbearable. Surely one has to create against this. One has to build private shelters against this not to be contaminated or maddened by it. The indifference and callousness that some resort to is not the way to defeat destruction and death.

Some are physically constituted for violence, and can deal with the wounds of the flesh. I can deal only with the wounds of the soul. Most of the people who can bear the great wounds of the flesh never dare to look where I look or touch what I touch, or deal with the insanities and horrors caused by the soul's fears and recoils. They will all deal with actual murder, actual torture, visible and touchable. I have given myself to the care of more mysterious anguish.

H out of the box of type, Henry has become an influence, a force, a magnet. G out of the box is for Gonzalo, a symbolic figure of our time. As in a play the same characters appear. There is again the father, the doctor, the astrologer, the novelist, the rebel, the conventional figures. You move to a new country, and you re-create the constellation. A for analysis, which to me has become a philosophy, the philosophy of understanding. Without it existence seems absurd and meaningless. With psychology I find the mechanism of motivation, and therefore meaning. M for meaning. Essential to faith. E out of the box, for elation, then period, then space, then a turn of the page, new letters.

The book was finished May fifth. Gonzalo and I printed the cover. The bookbinder was objecting to the nonstandard measurements. The machines were set for standard measurements. We finally found a bookbinder willing to bind three hundred books of an odd size. It was delivered all bound May fifteenth. The Gotham Book Mart gave a party for it. The book created a sensation by its beauty. The typography by Gonzalo, the engravings by Ian Hugo were unique. The bookshop was crowded. Otto Fuhrman, teacher of graphic arts at New York University, praised the book. Art galleries asked to carry it. I received orders from collectors, a letter from James Laughlin, offering me a review in *New Directions* by anyone I chose.

I chose William Carlos Williams, because of my respect for his work. An unwise choice, alas. His misunderstanding of the work began with his selection of a title: "Men Have No Tenderness."

He chose to emphasize a phrase uttered by a minor character in a minor situation and which never at any time played an important role in the theme of the book. He analyzed the book as biography, when it was a composite, and presented as a novel. He should have respected the fiction as fiction, particularly as he had no firsthand biographical information on which to base his erroneous assertions. When I wrote him gently about his misinterpretations, in time for changes, he was adamant.

Frances Steloff said: "I have never seen people react to the appearance of a book as they did to this one. They fall in love with it. Would you like to print Lawrence Durrell's *Black Book*?"

I was quite willing, but Miss Steloff did not follow up on this idea. She also wanted me to reprint my book on D. H. Lawrence, for which she has many requests, but none of us have sufficient capital.

As soon as she saw my book, Seon bought a press. Dudley, too. Dorothy said: "I want to do my poems." Édouard Roditi said: "I would like to review it for the *Psychoanalytical Review*."

Harvey Breit praised it for its sensibility. Alemany said it was "profound, audacious." The publishers had said "not universal." No one would be interested in a novel taking place in Europe. Yet one woman after another identifies with Djuna and Lilith. Without advertising or reviews, the entire edition sold.

Gonzalo will be able to earn his living, to be free. He is proud of himself. But he would not come to the Gotham Book Mart and receive the compliments due to him. He stayed outside, on the street, occasionally looking in through the window, like a wild animal refusing to be tamed.

Henry writes me from Hollywood. He is staying at the Gilbert Neimans' new home, and will see Budd Schulberg.

I had lunch with Paul Rosenfeld in an open-air garden restaurant in the Village. A summer day. Paul as ever pink-faced, warm, enthusiastic, with the good manners of other times, the capacity to admire so rare nowadays. He told me a wonderful story.

A Japanese Emperor was informed that his closest friend had conspired against him. He was obliged to condemn him to death. He was to be beheaded, but because of his high rank, and their long association, the beheading was to be a most ceremonious and distinguished affair. The entire court was invited to the spectacle. The beheading was to be preceded by the most aesthetic and artistic entertainment the Japanese court could provide. There were poetry tournaments, exquisite dancers, concerts, and plays. The condemned nobleman watched all the entertainment with interest for hours. But after a while he became restive. He addressed the Emperor: "I know you are offering me this last spectacle in honor of our past association, but may I say that if you once had regard for me and wished to treat my death with the greatest honors and kindness, I would beg you in memory of our past friendship, not to keep me in suspense any longer. Be compassionate and allow the beheading to take place at once."

Then the Emperor smiled and said: "But my dear friend, you have been beheaded."

No story has ever rendered in such a symbolic fashion the magic power of art.

A visit from George Barker. He is wildly propelled by tensions into sudden animation, restlessness, nervous buoyancy, spirited but shallow. His writing has the same sparkling but false tones. It is not emotion but a kind of brain fever. It is as if only the maximum state of tension keeps him alive. When the Westerner suffers from this electric short circuit he does not have the relief of the primitives, to dance all night, to drum until they fall to the ground. In George Barker it is agitation.

Because of the intimacy of *Winter of Artifice*, people feel they can confess to me, so that the tribute I pay to the value of intimate relationships is assured of continuity, of replenishing, of interlocking; it is so true that what you create becomes the living flow which attracts others of the same kind.

Robert admits his lack of feeling to Blanche Cooney: "I am a murderer."

Others are beginning to see the egoist in Kenneth Patchen. Paul Rosenfeld talked about his megalomania.

Horror in Europe spreads, grows vaster, unbearable, monstrous.

In July we worked on Hugh Chisholm's book of poems. In spite of heat waves, jungle humidity, swamp fumes, tar fumes of New York.

In August we went to Provincetown. The summer was peaceful. As in Saint-Tropez, we swam to the continuous sound of depth charges. We watched the pilots rehearsing for war. Underneath the aspect of joy, sun, swimming, runs the continuous tale of war and torment.

Helba choked on a fishbone and awakened the entire neighborhood.

I swam under water as if I really did not want to return to the surface, as if I wanted to stay below with the fish.

Then back to New York and to work.

Gonzalo entered a new phase. A magazine is being started to be called *Alianza Interamericana*. Rich people have given money. He will be the editor and the printer of the magazine.

At first he feared the responsibility and I thought he would elude it. Behind his fear lies his confession of inadequacy. He feels inadequate. And Helba's illness has always been his great alibi. But he is being pushed into this by a friend. I strengthened his self-confidence. At first he could not trust himself with money. He spent it all in one day. I had to dole it out or they would not eat. Slowly I began to test him. Finally I turned over to him all the gains of the press to make him feel independent. Soon he will be earning enough to live on.

Meanwhile Henry is going through great chaotic upheavals. He writes me contradictory letters. He says he is entering a phase of retreat, the retreat of the mystic. Life in New York has become intolerable to him.

Letter from Henry from Hollywood:

I just finished the Kerkhoven book by Jakob Wassermann a night or two ago. Effect tremendous, perhaps even more than the other book, because more intimately related to my problem. I was amazed and happy that he should have ended it on the mother note. I saw some correlations here with my own psychology. The innate fanaticism born out of lack of parental affection. When I gave myself to my father that helped me greatly.

I want to cite just a passage or two, to refresh your memory. Speaking of Marie's affection for Etzel, when at last they become involved as lovers he says: "As though in secret compensation, in inward justification, for having fettered all his youth to herself, she assumed deliberately, and in response to some mystic impulse, the role of mother with that of lover and thus entered into telepathic relationship with that distant, unknown woman who was his real mother and who, as such, was remote and strange to him also. She could not speak to him of this except with the utmost caution, for the slightest hint of the maternal element in her love filled him with nothing short of horror."

And Etzel's response to this? Here it is, next page. "All that Marie gave him, all that she was to him, was too little. The dream he lived, boundless as it was in its fulfillment, was a mere nothing to the dream whose fulfillment he desired. With unyielding demands he stood before her as before his fate, before his life, and stretched out open hands for more, for the immense, for the impossible."

That's a frightening and frightful statement! Altogether there is much in Etzel which reminds me of Julian Grant. The insatiable quality, the inexorableness, the search for sensation, the harsh pursuit of justice, etc. The narcissism. The implacable and ruthless . . .

Later Marie puts her finger on it—"You are all murderers!" And the author finally accuses him: "The man who murdered love." And now on this same page, comes an appraisal of Marie's attitude, which embraces her duality and duplicity, that made me open my eyes wide.

"She believed that hers was the higher courage, that it demanded of her more tact, more discretion, more consideration, more presence of mind and more self-sacrifice than were called for by instinctive frankness, which is the courage of the weak."

Could anyone have put it more succinctly? I sat bolt upright. I had to admit it was unanswerable. You always questioned the courage of my frankness. And now on the subject of my plans. Instinctively I have been trying to wean myself of irresponsibility for one thing. It was a sort of last desperate effort, coming out here and searching for work in the movies. I can no longer stand and watch you making sacrifices. I get along all right. I always have a roof over my head, cigarettes and food. With those fundamentals secured there is not much to worry about.

I don't like what I am doing—sponging on these poor people, but I repay in my own coin, and I know they do not suffer because of me. I eat out often with other friends, clean up my own mess, and in general make myself as inconspicuous as possible. If I only made twenty or twenty-five dollars a week I would be O.K. It is true I have seldom any money in my pocket, but then I don't need money, really. I have nothing to complain about. Only a slight feeling of guilt that in reality I have not solved the problem, only transferred my own problem to other hands. That can't go on indefinitely, I know. Send me only what you can spare. Anyway, not much has been accomplished so far. If I have to return to New York (because I may be a failure here) what then? Will I find something to do in New York or will I sink back into irresponsibility?

Second Letter:

If you, or anybody, make such sacrifices for another is it because the other has something more important to offer than the mere importance of his duty? The question in my own mind, as well as yours, seems to have shifted from the accomplishment (due to protection) to the means employed (dependence on others). Perhaps the whole trouble is that I am thinking as an absolutist.

All you're asking me is that I take a relative view of the problems and circumstances. Perhaps I have one great fear, unacknowledged, that if I compromise I will go under completely. I am possibly the only writer in our time who has had the chance to write only as he pleased. Perhaps this was bad. I wonder. One might say of me that I have always done only what I wanted to do, that I derived no pleasure from my so-called renunciations.

How can I answer that? Maybe it all boils down to this: If the present circumstances will not permit me to create then I should at least work, just as everybody else does. It's the old Chinese problem, of whether inaction (sometimes) is not better than action. Maybe there are two grand flaws in the above. First, that I might, if I have any genius, contrive to say what I please without contriving to bring about the suppression of my work. The only question is, am I up to it? Have I the ability? I have wrestled with that problem a great deal in my lonely moments, believe me.

All my life I have been tormented by the necessity of choosing between answering these demands and answering some other demand, some demand of my own which I make to myself—why, I can't explain. I think now that at the root of all my writing lies the fact that very early in life I lost the desire to participate with others on the basis laid down by society. All I have been doing, possibly, in my work, is to protest and explain wherein I'm different. And only recently the question has arisen before me: "Is that enough? Can you justify your behavior?" And then this question of causing others pain and suffering—because of my uniqueness. Am I to blame? Or is that something imbedded in the very heart of things, something inevitable?

For a long time now I have honestly never tried or wished to cause another pain. But to eliminate pain (to others) is almost an impossibility. Especially if it comes about only because I am being myself. Naturally, I will get what is coming to me, for being myself. That is right and just . . . that's one's destiny. I don't quarrel about that. All my troubles at the moment are caused by the mere fact that I am trying more and more to be myself. If this self is a monster, then the sooner it is recognized the better. By choosing to live above the ordinary level we create extraordinary problems for ourselves. The ultimate goal is to make this earth a paradise. But that's how I am trying to live all the time, as it were. I am the ideal citizen. I am ready but the conditions are absent. It's as though I had to live backwards, from some better condition of the world (which is natural to me and which I was born into) to some stupid and deplorable one. I have already lived the life people are dreaming of not only imaginatively but actually. So have you. The difference is that you adapt yourself better to the backward state. That's what you call being human, I rather think. You may be right.

Another difference is that with this criterion of *human* you emphasize the need for struggle. But to me the struggle is relatively unimportant. How can I struggle when I have already achieved? If you grow a flower isn't it silly to expect it to work—let us say to work towards making other flowers, better flowers, more beautiful flowers?

This struggle is on a level which I have outgrown. Both materialistic philosophy of the West and Oriental philosophy aim to lift man above this struggle. The kind of struggle I believe in is wrestling with myself. The irony of it is that it is these very utopists, the ones who claim that they are working to bring about this flowerlike condition of humanity, who mock the living flower. All this agitation in the breast of millions—I understand it—but they are agitated because they lack something. They are trying to help themselves by working together. They won't recognize individual work, individual germination. If thanks to you I have been lifted out of our time, even at the very worst if I am just dreaming (and how wonderful to dream! why is it such a sin?) nothing will put me back except chains.

Why is there always someone at hand to protect the artist, or are they helping to perpetuate something they vitally need? They are like the drones working for the queen bees. For me it is no problem to depend on others. I am always curious to see how far people will go, how big a test one can put them to.

Certainly there are humiliations involved, but aren't these humiliations due rather to our limitations? Isn't it merely our pride which suffers? It's only when we demand that we are hurt. I, who have been helped so much by others, I ought to know something of the duties of the receiver. It's so much easier to be on the giving side. To receive is much harder—one actually has to be more delicate, if I may say so. One has to help people to be more generous. By receiving from others, by letting them help you, you really aid them to become bigger, more generous, more magnanimous. You do them a service.

And then finally, no one likes to do either one or the other alone. We all try to give and take, to the best of our powers. It's only because giving is so much associated with material things that receiving looks bad. It would be a terrible calamity for the world if we eliminated the beggar. The beggar is just as important in the scheme of things as the giver. If begging were ever eliminated God help us if there should no longer be a need to appeal to some other human being, to make him give of his riches. Of what good abundance then? Must we not become strong in order to help, rich in order to give and so on? How will these fundamental aspects of life ever change?

The trouble now is that people are poor in spirit, low, mean, envious, jealous. The change they envisage is not towards the expression of greater magnanimity, but of protection against humiliation, protection of their petty egos, their petty pride, their petty prejudices. Anyway, you know that Capricorn is a steady climber, a steady plodder, a steady grazer. Now and then I rebel—I do lift my face heavenward. It seems at those moments that the world conspires to put my head down. Or, more truly, perhaps, I arrange it so that the world conspires against me. I haven't yet acquired a persecution mania, I hope you understand. I know my role and I know the world's role. And eventually we will get on together, the world and I. I am doing my best, always, even when I seem idle and perverse and stubborn.

Capricorn always tries, that's the hell of it. He never lets up. Don't you see how for me, with my nature, my destiny, my astral setup, that the greatest bliss is just to pause, to rest, to look upward, to be dazzled by the stars, to wonder, to dream, to meditate? What are we climbing heavenward for if not some day to reach the top and survey the world? That is where we fade out of the picture I suppose. I know I will never reach a tangible Shangri-La. I know already that it does not exist anywhere, except inside of one. I know what all my wanderings mean. But I can't learn faster than I do. I've got to work with these poor materials of which I am composed. As I can see, you are making the struggle to adapt to a bad situation. Whereas I make the struggle not to adapt myself.

I don't look back with any pleasure at the sacrifices I made. I consider it time wasted. Whereas I do not think it time wasted to be idle, to dream, to play. Very much the contrary, I think. It may be that the world is not yet arranged for people to live that way—but that does not prove that I am wrong.

Last night I read a little further into the Third Existence. Do you know what happened to the wonderful Dr. Kerkhoven at the height of his power? When he was just about my age? He went off on a wild-goose chase. He found he no longer believed in what he was doing. He left the wife whom he loved more than ever and went to Java—to study, to meditate, to experiment, to find himself. The world had accepted him as he was. He was at the top. But he was not satisfied with himself. He went out into the wilderness. And I'm in some kind of wilderness, too. And I'll find myself, no doubt about it. If I chose to make California the wilderness instead of New York, there is a reason in my madness. Time will tell. I am not anchoring here eternally. When I move I want it to make sense.

Henry has written ten books which everyone reads and yet they do not bring enough income for his simplest needs. His books are reprinted *sub rosa* and he gets nothing. People take advantage of him.

Meanwhile I struggle with the money problem, a hopeless tangle. After the Chisholm poems we have no other book to do. Caresse has plans but no money to carry them out. We printed the poems of Kay Boyle's daughter.

Paul Rosenfeld, with the best will in the world, writes a review of *Winter of Artifice* which is totally inaccurate because he treats it as exact biography and it is a composite. By dealing with it as biography he does not consider any of the lyrical, imaginative poetic flights (such as the long orchestra passage or the pages on dreams). He is so intent on showing his knowledge of the source of the portrait that he overlooks the alchemy produced by the poet. He creates a confusion between the diary and the novels. William Carlos Williams invents an antagonism between men and women which I never considered, which only exists in his own mind, revealed by his high-pitched, strained, a-sexual voice.

He is describing his own personal vision of woman, not mine. Those were the only reviews. Harvey Breit tried to write about the book but the new editor of the *New Republic* would not let him. Complete silence from the New York *Times,* the *Tribune.* My underground success continues from person to person, fervent, secretly and quietly.

I thought the press would solve our economic problems.

The five flights of stairs I have to climb every day when I get home seem to represent my difficulties. Somehow, on these stairs I climb after leaving the press, the fatigue and discouragement of the whole day attacks me. It catches me on the very first step of the worn brown rug. As I climb I think that Gonzalo needs new glasses, where will I get the money? Jacobson's bill for the care of Helba is overdue. Henry has to see the ear doctor. He also needs eighteen dollars for new glasses. On the first floor, I add the problems facing me. While climbing the second floor I add the possibilities of getting work for the press, how much we will make out of printing, how many days it will take. As I climb I feel heavily burdened and I see no balance possible. I am a worker, I am dexterous, but I am not talented for making money. On the third floor I sometimes sit on the stairs. There is a niche in the wall which once contained a statue. Probably a Catholic statue because the Village was primarily Italian. The empty niche becomes symbolical: I have no one to pray to, no one to turn to. I am a failure.

I am a failure in that realm in which Americans excel. They have a talent for turning everything into money. That may be why I am always absolving Henry and Gonzalo for that inadequacy in making money, in solving practical problems. I understood and forgave because I would have been in their place without the protection granted me.

But the protection granted me did not extend to my protégés. The qualities the three of us share, spontaneity, fantasy, love of creation, are incompatible with commercial life. For practical life one needs other qualities, prudence, foresight, discipline, control, etc.

When I arrive at the fifth floor I feel I have climbed a mountain of difficulties. And tomorrow I will have to climb the same mountain.

My lucidity gives me the deadliest weapons. I never use them. Dr. Jacobson tells me Helba is pathologic, a hysteric. That she cannot be saved because her "illness" is her strongest weapon against others. It is her one possession. He calls her *"l'emmerdeuse."* But Gonzalo could not bear the truth.

Frances Brown. The first thing I noticed about her were her eyes. She had two enormous, fairy-tale eyes, like two aquamarine lights illumining darkness, eyes of such depth that at first one felt one might fall into them as into a sea, a sea of feeling. And then they ceased to be the absorbing sea and they became beacons, shining with vision, awareness, perception. Wherever the blue, liquid balls alighted, every object and person acquired significance. At the same time their vulnerability and sentience made them tremble like candlelight or the eye of a camera lens which at too intense daylight will suddenly shut black. One caught the inner chamber like the photographer's darkroom, in which sensitivity to daylight, to crudity and grossness would cause instant annihilation of the image. They gave the impression of a larger vision of the world. If sensitivity made them retract, contract swiftly, it was not in any self-protective blindness but to turn again to that inner chamber where the metamorphosis took place in which pain became not personal but the pain of the whole world, in which ugliness became not a personal experience of ugliness but the world's experience with ugliness. By enlarging it and situating it in the totality of the dream, the unbearable event became a large, airy understanding of life which gave to her eyes an ultimately triumphant power which people mistook for strength but which was in reality courage. For the eye, wounded on the exterior, turned inward, but did not stay there, and returned with renewed vision. After each encounter with unbearable truths, unbearable pain, the eyes returned to the mirrors of the inner chambers, to the transformation by understanding and reflection, so that they could emerge and face the naked truth again.

And Frances has known plenty of ugly and painful experiences, as I find from our many talks.

She is lying down, her hip in a cast, and has been combating a serious case of sciatica which is improving after three months analysis with Martha Jaeger. I first heard about her from the Cooneys, when she was married to Lenny, and Lenny was corresponding with Henry. Now she is married to Tom, a pale, reserved young man.

She gave up dancing because of the onset of tuberculosis a few years before I met her. She did sculptures and drawings to take the place of dancing. She was doing sculpture when we first met.

We first talked about analysis and dreams. We have the most miraculous understanding of each other's lives although they are totally different. We met on the level of understanding. Our common language was that of symbolism.

She dreamt abundantly and richly. I dreamt less but I wrote what was the equivalent of dreams, *le rêve eveillé* of the surrealists.

Frances' skin is translucent and delicate. Her mother died at thirty of tuberculosis and I am concerned about Frances. I think of what the doctors say, that tuberculosis develops genius because the apprehension of death inspires a burning awareness of life's beauty, significance, transience. The bacillus breeds restlessness and hypersensitiveness.

How did she keep this gentleness and sensitiveness through a childhood full of poverty and brutalities?

She is just the opposite of Helba. There is a transmutation of physical troubles so one does not feel the presence of illness, only of a shining individuality. She has a fear of dying as her mother did, but I feel certain she won't because of her combat against illness on a physical and psychological level.

Frances' apartment has a window on Eighth Street. I see her bathed in light, like the clarity of her thought. Her voice is low and slightly husky. Every day she tells me a different story about her childhood.

Frances and I exchange lives. She talks to me, and I give her portions of the diaries to read as she is still lying in bed. As she talks, I look for reflections and echoes of this child she describes, and I can see the sense of humor and comedy, the playfulness, the lively intelligence. I cannot see the plain child her mother saw. I see the most expressive eyes, the translucent skin, sensitive hands, and hear her slightly husky but musical and modulated voice.

Her childhood seems almost unbelievable to me because it has not marked her speech, which is articulate and sensitive, nor deformed or embittered her. There is no anger, no resentment, no accusation of society as there is in Helba. Frances the dreamer, the artist, the one who passed unscathed through horrors, and preserved an inner world of unshatterable beauty.

As an artist, she could penetrate, understand, any world at all. This capacity to dream, to create beauty, had transported her safely through the darkest places, the same places which had made Edward Dahlberg snarl and hate in *Bottom Dogs*.

Tom, her husband, passes through while we talk. He is silent and expressionless. He does not seem to see or hear. He seems cold, and I cannot imagine what the relationship is between his coldness and her warmth.

The nightmare has not engulfed her. The only thing which remains is the desire to create another world. She reads to me from T. S. Eliot's *Four Quartets*, and we talk about music. There is utter confidence, and no fear of betrayal, because there is understanding. There is no passing of judgment. There is a similar, almost objective, passion for understanding. Sometimes I feel that because she has experienced the nightmare in reality she is better able to handle those created by our imagination or our anxiety.

Tom wants to be a writer. But perhaps because I am not used to that silent, monosyllabic, outward deadness, I cannot imagine a vital source and flow of writing there.

All the time Frances told me these stories I was impressed by the spirit which preserved this cell of the dream and creation of aesthetics, of intuitions. Where did she find time to build up her knowledge of music, poetry, where did she find time to grow those flowers of insight, these nuances of relationship as refined as Proust's?

Though she is younger than I, I can trust her clairvoyance and her judgment of people. We understand each other's anxieties. She is less prone to creating myth figures, and therefore less prone to disillusion. When we talk an alchemy takes place. We may talk about tragic incidents, but they become alchemized by understanding into adventure, into fascinating experience. The external events of our lives were totally different, the spirit and attitude similar. It was familiarity with psychological reality which made us so attuned to totally different experiences. The world of the artist was our common home. Symbolism was our common language. By our dreams we discovered the essence of our lives.

If anything, Frances is more classical in her taste than I am, because I, having been born in a classical atmosphere, am in rebellion against it.

I seek new forms, new structures, new sounds, freedom. I understand her when she says: "I could never marry anyone who did not love the quartets of Beethoven." *

The self-made woman I admire. Without the aid of a legendary background, of costume, aesthetics, external settings, Frances, the child of poverty, rises to clarity of vision. She combats her illness with intelligence. She treats it objectively. She never complains. Helba made her illness an instrument of terror and anxiety. Frances makes it an instrument of spiritual expansion. When her body is immobilized, her intelligence soars. Frances vanquishes the illness, creates out of it, finally exorcises it, so that in her presence one is never in the presence of illness, but of the vital challenge of it, and one believes she is resting while her luminous searchlight wanders over people and places.

A great deal of light falls from the large window on her bed. Her cheeks are faintly rosy, like the nightgown she wears. The black notebooks are scattered over her bed. Someone said it was cruel of me to share with Frances a life she would never know. The Village, limited means, an artist's life, was only one of my way stations, but

* This may have been a prophecy, because she later married the sensitive pianist Michael Field.—A.N.

Frances would never reach the places or the people I described. I disagreed.

Before I went anywhere, I possessed a rich world given to me by the writers; I was fed on books, and that is why I knew what to look for, what I wanted. I liked the flush on Frances' cheeks, her familiarity with heightened lives; she responded as if to a renewed supply of oxygen. She commented, tasted, understood. And because she knew my history, too, she protected me from that one fatality we might well escape, that of repetition. The pitfall of repetition. Her lucidity was never cruel: it was wisdom. Be careful, Anaïs. Just as I was seeking to protect her from her identification with her mother, with both her mother's creativity in life and with her premature death. I felt I was nourishing Frances with a desire to live, with a life she would want, aspire to, hunger for.

I wanted to know more about her childhood:

We were a poverty-stricken family. My young father was driving a cab at night to support my mother and five children. A penurious man, an indomitable struggler, he must have endured with rage and sorrow my mother's habits and interests. Theirs had been a love match, a passionate attraction which led to an elopement when they were virtually penniless adolescents, my mother a forewoman in a sweat shop, where my father worked at loading and unloading trucks.

Every fourteen months of their life together produced another baby. And this was her wish: "I want an even dozen." We, her children, were her playmates, the friends and the family she never had in her own childhood. The four-room, fifth-floor-walk-up tenement flat in which we lived was not a home, it was a children's playground which, while it had an ingenious teacher and guide in my mother, lacked a keeper. Dishes were forever piled high in the blackened sink; the table, its cracked oilcloth cover stained with congealed foods, was rarely cleared. A shoe, dirty clothing, books were merely pushed aside to make a place for my father's breakfast when he rose at three in the afternoon. He drank his coffee, snarling, from a cup without a handle; he cursed his grapefruit which was always cut the wrong way. A sled sat on the kitchen floor all winter long, skates, dolls, silverware were scattered there in the summer. The beds (we slept four in a bed along with my father in the winter and two in a bed in the summers) were never made, the linens were grey and torn. The contents of overstuffed drawers hung out and down to the floor.

There were no regular mealtimes, nor was there any expectation of supper, lunch or breakfast. We were fed whatever and whenever it struck the fancy of my starry-minded mother: cold canned spaghetti, cold canned spinach, expensive melons, dates, Post Toasties, candy bars, soda water, and condensed milk by the tablespoonful.

Perhaps the excuse she gave my ever angry father for her delinquency (and surely he must have complained—his own mother was a fastidious housekeeper and professional cook) was that she was helping to augment the family income. For she did do that by beading bags, huddled over her georgette-stretched beading frame, her fingers feeding beads and thread to her crochet needle like lightning. In reality, though, the money earned this way was not a help. It was spent, every cent of it, wildly.

I myself was once instructed by her to collect her earnings in Manhattan (a two-hour train ride each way) and buy whatever I needed for my twelfth birthday party. That was a saga in itself. I spent all of it but five dollars and lost that in the snow on the walk home from the station. As is common with the poor, the money was spent on absurdities; toys, picnics, movies, household fineries purchased on time, Rogers silverware, candies, fire-sale bargains that rose in a mountain of laces and silks on the floors of our sleeping quarters. It was madness.

Yet in her case, it was not just neglect, or ignorance. This setting was her cluttered and unintegrated unconscious turned inside out, as it were. It was the playground for her uninterrupted creativity and inventiveness with children, a battered setting for her endless crafts or projects. And nothing in the place was sacred when it came to materials for these projects: the portieres, the heavily beaded georgette, the yards of hand-sewn fringe, all were grist for her mill. The walls themselves served as background for rainy day murals, the peeling paint pulled off with purpose and decorated with decals, crayon scrawls, bits and pieces glued forever to the surface. Her way of finding a place to read her tomes, library books piled to the ceiling, was to inspire the children to their own inventiveness. What easier way to stimulate a child's pleasure than to peel off that first strip of loose, cracking paint to show her how to use crayon on a wall?

Frances possesses what I call "the magic sieve." In this sieve, the ugly experiences are sifted and thrown out, only the dreams remain. The child Frances inhabited a world I saw pictured only in the joyous paintings of Klee, of Chagall. People had wings, animals were peaceful and laughing, trees were heavy with fruit, the valleys were of festive colors, planets showered sparks, and all this could be seen as soon as one closed one's eyes and invented a world which in reality only existed in the Polynesian islands.

I never hear Frances accuse or blame anyone for a cruel childhood. She is too busy resconstructing herself anew each day, confronting the menace of an occasional nightmare, defeating it, dissolving her obsessions at the root. We do this together.

She is too busy painting her dreams, too busy planting new seeds of relationships, learning, expanding. Her love of life and human beings is stronger than her angers. She has no desire to quarrel or argue with destiny, which made her learn music from a wet charred book found in the ruins of a fire, while I fell asleep listening to Pablo Casals and my father playing.

She and I tracked the inception of sorrows where they are truly fashioned, not in events but in our reaction to them, and both of us spent all our energies creating a world according to our own desires and patterns, in disregard of the one the cynical deities had bestowed upon us.

"Perhaps what saved me," said Frances today, "was my capacity to turn events into a comedy, also my capacity for dreaming."

Frances' life makes me feel the inequality which I have spent my life trying to rectify, the contrast between the gifts granted to me at birth: a house filled with music, books, and interesting people, and Frances' cold-water flat. It is this inequality of privileges which has always bothered me, and made me favor the Henry Millers. It also dictated much of my obsession with sharing.

I am in a good mood. I have thrown away my much mended, much faded, dark-red kimono and bought in a secondhand shop a sumptuous black velvet evening coat, with a white satin lining, which I wear as a kimono. I have bought paints to repaint the now faded windows. I have bought a muff cushion and made myself a muff out of left-over pieces from my cut-down astrakhan coat, now cut to a small cape and hood. I have bought a cookbook and am cooking with care and delectation. I have washed my sea shells to their pristine whiteness.

Paul writes me from the army: "They gave us whiffs of the

deadly gases the enemy may fling at us. And do you know, there is one that smells like corn, another like heavy violets, and another like geraniums. What a shocking deception." At first he could not sleep because of the loud snoring around him, and he could not eat because he could not push his way to the food line.

Frances is writing a humorous book—about her childhood. Her dreams are real works of art, fantastic, ingenious, and full of surprises. Surrealistic. She carries on the most fecund underground life. We exchange dreams as we would the contents of a new film, a play, or a book. We admire them as paintings, as films, as plays.

Frances and I read the same books. We both feel the same mood when we hear the foghorns on the river. At times they sound like ominous signs of catastrophe. We think of dangers at sea, death, submarines, shocks, collisions, accidents. We feel the immensity of the city and its nightmares.

The same foghorns, on days of good moods, will seem like part of a concert of activity, creativity. The ships will sail gaily and escape catastrophe. The city is dressing for a feast. The night clubs will be crowded. We will listen to bebop, to Charlie Parker.

Frances and I talked about woman's hunger for an impossible bond with man. We wondered how D. H. Lawrence knew so much about how woman felt in sexual intercourse. How well he described two kinds of orgasms. One in which the woman lay passive, acquiescent, serene: the orgasm came out of the darkness, miraculously, dissolving and invading. In another kind, there was a driving force, an anxiety, a tension which made the woman grasp at it as if it would elude her, and the movements became confused and inharmonious, crosscurrents of forces, short circuits which brought an orgasm that did not bring calm, satisfaction, but depression. The first brought a flowerlike peace, the second, depression, as if the woman had not been possessed.

How did D. H. Lawrence find out about this?

Is it that in the sexual act of the infantile man, woman feels the lack of drive and it arouses her own strength? Or is it that in some women, as in some men, anxiety or panic causes a plunging forward, a desperate tautness which itself defeats the sense of union, and leaves a sense of failure?

Frances controls her irrational, as I do. Enclose the devil in his little box. Lock it away. I wish I could write END to the diary and begin the outside story.

I am interested in the theme of the development of woman. I would like to take the women I have known, their childhood, background, their underground life, their unfulfillments and fulfillments. I used myself only as a guinea pig.

The essential difficulty I see in the relationships around me is that the women, the wives, are willing and ready to help their husbands to fulfill their desires, their objectives, their development or careers. But in few of the husbands do I see the same helpfulness. There is a fear that the development of woman will make her less of a wife, a mate, that they might even lose her. Frances is attentive to Tom's writing, concerned over his struggles. Tom is not concerned with Frances' expansion or gifts. The same with the other women I know.

Frances tells me more about her past life:

There was one great summer, the marvelous summer we spent in a little wooden shack on a hill in Woodbourne. Woodbourne, which is now, I understand, a teeming section of the borscht belt, was then a quiet little town with many meadows, fields of daisies, black-eyed susans, apple, cherry, and peach trees, wild strawberries, perfumed forests where we picnicked in sun-lit groves. Paradise.

It began with my resourceful, poverty-stricken mother, who wanted only the best for us. And the best was the little shack on the hill for the whole summer. To amass the money to rent it she had the ingenious idea of having a book of raffle tickets printed (ten cents each, a book of twelve for a dollar), the prize to be a beaded bag she would make and raffle two months hence. It was still midwinter when she bundled my little sisters in the rusty-wheeled gocart, and together she and I pushed it for miles through the slushy streets of Brooklyn, stopping in shops and accosting strangers with her sales talk. This venture was repeated many times that spring. But by the end of it she had the money, and one cool morning in June we departed for the country.

There were five children, I ten years old and the eldest, the others ranging down to one. My mother was twenty-eight. My young father hauled the luggage out and strapped it to the top of his yellow taxi (borrowed from the boss for the trip) and seated us, while the sleepy neighbors watched in silent wonderment.

We waved good-bye and chugged off for the twelve-hour, exhausting ride which got us to our little house at sundown.

My father had to get back to his "hacking" and stayed only that night, leaving early the next morning. When he returned for visits he would come up on the milk train, arriving at dawn, decked out nicely in plaid knickers and knee-high socks, his cap at a jaunty angle and his mustache waxed (just like Adolphe Menjou, my mother used to say). It was always a joy to see him (although we never really talked together) and heart-breaking to see him go (although I never cried).

One morning, we spotted a fire a short distance away from the foot of the hill. That whole day we spent playing and picnicking as we watched what turned out to be the Bluebird Hotel burn right down to the ground.

Once again, an image comes up in light. It seems to have deeper meaning. It has to do with a holocaust, and out of the ruins some new and wildly wonderful unexpected flight. It must have been my mother's way that finally became my own when she was gone.

Your question about how and why I managed always to reap a reward from the ruins and thus move on to another level of experience may have its answer here. When the last stragglers departed from the terrible scene below, my mother led us down the hill to the scavenger's paradise. Once there it was a shock to see it: a small mountain of smoldering ruins; charred, soaking mattresses, twisted bedsteads, steaming, blackened linens, smoking bits of blankets, broken crockery and bent pots strewn around. The terror-stricken refugees had been housed in a nearby hotel, we discovered later from the owners. Hot and hellish as it was, it was all ours, and might have been the unhealthiest of summer playgrounds if not for my mother's find: a book. A large, nasty-looking, burned book with covers hanging by a thread and pages stuck together. Once she had it in her hands she was no longer interested in other possible treasures; she sat down happily on the wet grass, reading it as if she were in the Brooklyn Public Library. Calling me away from my fun with the ruins, she said, her finger tapping out a rhythm: "Here's something very nice." It was a book of folk songs and she hummed this one at sight. "It's a lovely melody, don't you think so?"

Like many Jewish mothers, and especially those who lived in poverty, she pinned great hopes on her children's talents. Mine, she thought, was a musical one, and since my sixth year had burdened me with painful practicing on the violin. "Such quaint words," she went on. "You take the alto, Frances, I'll carry the soprano." The others drew around (the show was on) and together my mother and I sang the first stanza of what later became a summer extravaganza.

> "I give to you a paper of pins
> To show you how my love begins
> If you will marry, marry me
> If you will marry me."

This short tryout satisfied her sufficiently to set forth confidently and immediately on her mission. Into the gocart with the sleepy children and off to the neighboring hotel we went. I was left at the foot of the porch steps to mind the children and my mother went right in, inquiring for the owners. In moments, the now familiar tune traveled out to us, embellished by faked chords and tinny arpeggios. A round of applause followed and she reappeared, surrounded by an admiring group, two of whom (the owners), to our delight, ushered us all into the dining room and seated us at their table. It might have been a Jewish wedding banquet. We started with soup and ended with nuts.

During the festivities I learned that we were to eat like this once a week for the rest of the summer, in return for a gala performance in midsummer. My mother had committed herself to writing, staging, directing, casting, costuming, and accompanying Roselle and myself in a playlet called *I Give to You a Paper of Pins,* and even more astounding, she had convinced them to let her write a version of *Cinderella,* and stage it with the hotel guests' children.

The proprietor, aflame with enthusiasm about her plans, offered to pay for the costumes. Still discussing plans, he hoisted us, carriage and all, up into his fringe-topped wagon, and drove us all the way home. Stuffed and sleepy, we were sent to bed while my mother in the soft yellow light of the oil lamp, wrote my father a long, detailed letter, listing all the paraphernalia he must bring with him on his trip up in the milk train. My sister and I sang *I Give to You a Paper of Pins.* Great success. My father had to drive up from New York for the performance. The next morning he appeared mildly hung-over and with half a mustache. The second booking was for the children's play, *Cinderella,* directed and costumed by my mother. At the dress rehearsal, Prince Charming fell into a herring barrel and Cinderella refused to dance the minuet with him.

Then came the grand opening. After this gala performance I was rewarded with my first kiss.

Racial memory. Is it a racial memory which stirs when I am shaken by certain scenes? I was deeply affected by the scenery of the Azores. I was disturbed in an obscure, mysterious way. Later I discovered it belonged to Atlantis; it is said to be one of its remaining fragments. It had for me the hauntingness of a dream, the ephemeral, fragile incompleteness of a dream, the black sand, the black rocks, the light, the multicolored houses.

In the same way, why was I so affected by Fez, in which I lost my individuality, where I fused with the city, the people, melted into the colors, textures, the eyes of the people?

Why was I so affected by the undersea explosions of Walt Disney's *Fantasia*, the section on the creation of the world, fire and water, the inner explosions? It is in this way that Atlantis disappeared. Why do these scenes have such strong vibrations in me whereas others leave me completely indifferent?

Atlantis has always bewitched me. It was said to be the place where people had a dimension unknown to us, a sixth sense, and a prodigious musical development. I made of this my true native land. Its legend suited my needs. It corresponds to my astrologic sign, Neptune. Clairvoyance, divination, intuition, and the ocean being the unconscious, which swallowed the earth.

Gonzalo fights the mystical concepts. He tells me: "Mysticism is like a powerful searchlight turned towards the sky. It becomes weaker and weaker as it points towards the infinite. Whereas look how strong it is when it is turned upon the earth."

As he says this, his own eyes are ardent, turned towards the earth always with an earthy fire and intensity. I tried in vain to explain to him that cosmic consciousness solves all dualities and divisions. People's ideas usually divide and separate. Gonzalo cannot grasp this, which is beyond and above ideological concepts.

Erotic moods are often colored by what happens in the world. The proximity of war, death, terror, and suffering intensifies life because it makes one aware of its fragility.

When Gonzalo was a very young man he was lured by a married woman to visit her in her hacienda, while the husband was visiting a property quite far away. But when Gonzalo was in bed with her the husband returned unexpectedly. The wife hid him under the bed. Gonzalo was young, had eaten and drunk heavily, had made love excessively, and so he fell asleep, having nothing else to do, there being no hope of escape while the husband slept. But Gonzalo was a powerful snorer—and he snored. The husband awakened. Gonzalo had to flee out of the window. The husband tried to shoot him. The bullet grazed his hip.

Colette is the modern image of my heroine, Ninon de Lenclos. I love Ninon de Lenclos because she lived for love to the very end of her life. She was generous with her house, her heart and her bed.

Colette lives in luxury. She is lively, sprightly, chic.

I envy them both the joyousness of their lives. Sometimes I think my anemia is like stigmata. Perhaps I do give others my very blood and substance. My desire to create in art as well as in life, to transform, transmit strength, has a miraculous power and has been a vital part of all my relationships. But perhaps there is a *leak* of energy, a loss of it.

When Gonzalo talked about the microscope, how gross our vision was, and what new worlds were revealed to the eye, I thought of psychoanalysis, and what gross vision people have who will not use it to interpret human behavior. How people resist understanding and prefer confusion and blindness which causes suffering.

Frances now lives on Charles Street, and the background is darker. Her paintings are on the wall. The windows of her bedroom give on anemic back yards. But the stories which I ask for continue to develop.

Back in the cold-water flat. The coal stove in the kitchen heated the whole place. No bath. I had an occasional bath in a tiny tub, or in the wash tub next to the sink. I had to go down to the cellar to get pails of coal in the winter and carry ashes down to the street on the way to school.

We would wait for summer, when the Fire Department opened the hydrants in the street so that the kids could prance in the water. I used to do this in a dress; I had no bathing suit.

We kids were put to work snapping snappers and sewing hooks and eyes on cards. At one point we must have been terribly poor. The children's work actually contributed to the daily expenses, I'm sure. Child labor! Yet, at a fire sale, my mother bought a crate of edging and applied herself to four days and nights of intense sewing: step-ins for everybody, blouses, camisoles, new trimmings on raggedy linens, dresses for imaginary dolls, drapes for nonexistent doll houses.

Enthusiasm always ran high. My mother replied to a Sally Joy Brown ad in the *News*. "A beautiful box piano given away." I can't tell you what that name Sally Joy Brown meant to me at the time. It was not only that she gave and exchanged objects which could never have been ours in any other way, it was the symbol she became, the magic fairy godmother, the miraculous giver, and her middle name JOY held all the magic such a word could hold for us children. Joy! So the box piano was sent for. We were to pay only for the carting.

I always remember the arrival of that huge upright piano, which seemed too big for our flat. After we received the piano, my mother lined us up and taught us how to play. She made us throw our hands at the keys while observing her hands and beating out the rhythm. Then she taught us how to read music. We all played in the same room where my father slept. In the beginning he groaned and cursed but eventually he got used to it, or learned to sleep through it. He himself was a great lover of opera, sang, whistled, and even played arias on his harmonica.

I'm sure he was secretly proud of my mother's and our supposed talents. It may have been the secret of their romance.

About this time I became aware of my appearance. My mother tried to persuade me that personality was more important than prettiness, and held up Queen Esther from the Bible as the model, the ideal, the woman who, although plain, had won the King despite the competition from great beauties in the land. Queen Esther used her talent for storytelling, her charm, feeling, wit. But I did not want to rely on these alone, so I saved pennies and bought a dimple-making apparatus advertised in the *Journal-American*.

I also slept on the handle of a knife to acquire a cleft chin. I sent away for a pamphlet on a steel mask which shaped beautiful noses. I took up stretching exercises to become taller.

When my mother discovered my hankering for external beauty, she made me a beautiful dress covered from top to bottom with bugle beads, with a heavy fringe of beads at the bottom. Then my mother had a hemorrhage. We were sent to different candy stores to beg for ice. An aunt was called to take care of us. When the doctor arrived, we were sent to a double feature. Just before I left, she gave me final directions on how to please my father: "Be sure and cut the grapefruit round-wise, and not up and down. Be sure the apples don't burst in the oven. Be sure the coffee doesn't spill over into the saucers. Be sure there are at least two and a half teaspoons of sugar in the sugar bowl." I tried to kiss my mother but she turned away. "Take good care of the children." I went to the movies crying all the way.

The picture was *The Kid* with Jackie Coogan. I felt suddenly that my brother was the Kid. My mother died and I took over the role of little mother. We were told we were to be placed in an orphan asylum. I never forgot our ride there in a taxi. But before that, there was the second-hand man appraising the furniture, my father's discovery of the long-paying installment plan for the now lost silver, and the lapsed insurance policies.

I was sent to the Metropolitan Hospital, on Welfare Island. I had to stay there for observation for six weeks. They had noted suspicious areas on my lungs.

When I was allowed to get out of bed, I did go on walks with a nurse who felt sorry to see a child among all these seriously ill and dying adults. On our walks we passed the narcotics ward, where the addicts clung to the iron bars, screaming obscenities. Then past terrible cottages which housed the poor who had incurable face cancers, noses rotting away, mouths missing, etc. The faces haunted my nightmares until I once made drawings of them, and then began to forget them.

After six weeks of this I was sent to the orphan asylum where I lived for three and a half years. I quickly became the intellectual (I read books), the comic entertainer (I sang, danced, and mimed). My sisters and I were given major parts in a Washington's Birthday performance for friends and relatives, and we were a success. I sang a solo rendition of "I'm Breezing Along with the Breeze."

My popularity with the staff brought me the privilege of a junior councilorship. A handsome senior councilor and I—at thirteen—fell madly in love. But the irate supervisor kept us apart.

One day the supervisor sent for me. I was then about fourteen, and well developed. He cornered me between his desk and the bookcase. I was straining away from him. He tried to win me by showing an interest in my reading. I told him I had just discovered the books of Mr. Freud. He seemed to derive pleasure merely from my proximity.

My father would come on Sundays and take us out. We loved the Orpheum, a big vaudeville theater, where I saw a pink-balloon dance done by a pretty, doll-like blonde in pink tights. I was deeply impressed by this dance. I suggested I could do the same for the orphanage program. The woman in charge expressed the most extreme shock, everything about her seemed to express shock, her tightly buttoned black dress, which covered all of her up to her chin, her black, kinky hair, her black-button eyes.

I did not interpret her shock as moral disapproval. I thought she felt it incongruous that I should appear as a pretty, feminine, fluffy balloon-dancer; I thought she felt I was not the type. It deflated my confidence, and so I ended by doing a parody of "Singing in the Rain," with big boys' shoes and a frayed umbrella.

Frances speaks of those who mistake tension for intensity. And I speak of those who mistake sensation for emotion.

Caricature of Anaïs: *Je prend tout par les sommets.*

Caricature of Anaïs: Dressed in black lace and taffeta, *froufroutante* and sparkling. Marcel Duchamp, Denis of the *New Republic,* James Sterne of *Time* magazine, and Marc Slonim, *à la Recherche des Jeux Perdus!*

At the Imbses I met Moira and her husband. She is Persian, voluptuous, dark-eyed and vivid. She wears a white satin dress, very dramatic in shape. It was a wedding dress she bought on Grand Street for a few dollars. "The only romantic style left to us is the wedding dress." It sets off her dark skin, brilliant eyes, her softly contoured neck, arms and feet. A round face with short curly black hair.

He a brooding Italian, remote, abstract. His painting fragile, artificial, surrealist. Paintings of fairs and bazaars, flying pennants, towers, castles, fiestas, but without the joy of Dufy, more like a preparation for the last day of pleasure, threatened by sorrow.

I was invited to her studio, where I saw his paintings and her jewelry designs.

A surface of charm, elegance, fashion, glamour. But my books always open the secret door to the underlying dramas. Immediately, I am not allowed to enjoy the decor, the elegance, the games with clothes and jewels and paints. I am taken behind the scenes, into the drama.

The drama suddenly erupts, dissolves all the aesthetic beauty, and reveals instinctive, primitive ferocities.

"Oh, the ugliness, the ugliness," cries Moira.

The mute, the dark, the jealous Italian aristocrat turns into a "tough," and hurls the basest insults. Bestial in hatred, animal pride, and savagery. Naked they stand now, revealing the demons. Revenge, self-love, envy, the wish to murder, destroy, all the crimes of the soul. Jealousy! The ugliest of all the demons. Jealousy, which makes a murderous savage of the most elegant and refined human being. Now we see Moira no longer made of white satin, feathers, velvet, coral, precious stones, and he no longer somber and mysterious, but both of them hurling foaming gutter words from the muddiest lower depths.

[Winter, 1942]

This is the thickest, heaviest notebook I have ever written in. Henry gave it to me. And such a light title I gave it: *À la Recherche des Jeux Perdus.*

In the darkest and heaviest days of history, because it is an unbearable moment in human history, I seek some world removed from pain and horror, not to be swept away into madness and war, to hold on to an island of humanity, no matter how small. The worse the state of the world grows, the more intensely I seek to create an inner and intimate world in which certain qualities may be preserved. Just as Dr. Jacobson fights the illnesses which are brought to him—he cannot do more, I cannot do more. I do not see any remedy. It is a contagion, an epidemic of hatred.

Wendell Willkie is preparing to talk about America's failure to help the Allies.

Henry is at the Gilbert Neimans, in Beverly Glen, in a place I cannot see or imagine. He has written a screen treatment based on *The Maurizius Case.*

Olga has a Rubens coloring, warm red hair, green eyes, milk-white skin. She is softly rounded, but not fat. She was born in Russia. She was one of the first poets to read to the workers. Her poetry must have sounded like a fiery political speech, contagious, I am sure, vehement, strong. She was very young then, fervent. She met her husband in Yugoslavia. He was a lawyer.

Whenever I come, she is dictating to a secretary, she is preparing an article. She writes in Russian and it has to be translated. But she is dressed in sophisticated Paris clothes, wears her red hair severely coiffed, wears bourgeois jewelry, pearl necklaces, pins, rings. There are Hermès cigarette boxes and clocks around. Chic travel bags. Expensive perfume. The leather, perfume, and silk smell of international elegance. The correct writing paper. Above and beyond all this—worldly manners, courtesies, amenities—there is exuberance, an exuberance which fills the room with oxygen, makes one dizzy and slightly intoxicated.

"In my family," she said, "we did everything with enthusiasm. We even *died* with enthusiam!" When she said this she propelled her body as if it were drawn into a mad waltz instead of carried away by death. She was carried away. A wonderful quality. The woman of the world could not tame this. Her husband was gently ironic about it. When he was filling out his papers to enter America and was asked: "Do you contemplate the overthrow of the United States Government?" he answered: "No, because my wife is not with me."

Olga gave her life to politics. She gave herself in a manner which gained the respect of the moralists, sociologists, missionaries, political party members. But my feeling was that she had run away from a confrontation with her self, from the task of training, nurturing, maturing it before giving it away. And now it was like an abcess which had been overlooked, ignored. It was festering. She felt useful, connected to the world, dedicated, but this tiny abcess in her soul was interfering with her proper functioning. And although I did not seem to fit into her disciplined, historical, legalistic, politically oriented world, she knew, and I knew, that I had the answer to one question at least, and perhaps the cure. Anyway, we were fascinated with each other's lives.

Her first creation was poetry, and even if this poetry was drafted, militarized, applied to the needs of the system, put in uniform, utilized, disciplined, she liked to bring it down to my studio. Her husband chided me about how little I knew about history, and I let him teach me. But I felt that they were escapists from another world, escaping from insights which blinded them in their very own political work, insight into human beings.

While they had a definite role to play, there would be no drama. But I always saw in her face the plea of a prisoner, a prisoner of duty, signaling distress . . . ashamed of having a personal distress at all when there was so much to do!

Moira on the brink of disaster. The Persian woman of the legends, once veiled, refined, and subtly shaded by her life in France, still aureoled and robed in fashionable clinging textures, with the perfume of Byzance exhaling from her hair, still *malgré* her contemporary chic, lifts up the fantail of a silver peacock to pass the black kohl dust along her eyelids. Petite, luxuriant, seemingly all emotion and chaos, but behind the grilled Oriental windows of her dark eyes watches a modern woman, capable of insight and detachment.

By way of Jung's interpretations, by way of Martha Jaeger, a Jungian analyst, she regained power over the chaos created by her husband's attitude.

As a child in Persia she lived in a big house, with a vast garden, a little city in itself, with many relatives, many servants. From the roof of her white house she could see the people passing by, vendors, beggars, costumed Persians, going to the mosque.

Moira's skin was golden, just slightly tanned. In school, she had a friend whose great sorrow was her dark skin. Moira offered a remedy. Every day she used a pumice stone on her, until the girl could no longer bear the pain.

At seventeen Moira left the Orient, veils, secret femininity, to study painting in Paris. She still retained an air of being veiled. She still conveyed the impression of restraint, and of being covered, sheathed. This feeling of secrecy was due in great part to her inarticulateness.

In Paris she suffered from an unshatterable timidity. It had the effect of concentrating all light, all messages, all signals, all communication within the eyes. So that Moira, while dressed like a European woman, all chic, flurry, feathers and flounces, still talked only with her eyes, with the stabbing brilliancy of those eyes in the Orient which had to pierce through layers of white cotton to reach a man. The desire to speak was there, after centuries of confinement and repression.

She laid out cards and told fortunes like the women of the harem. She began her conversations with: "I had a dream last night," because at breakfast time in the Orient, over the first cup of coffee, everyone told their dreams. Her desire to be noticed was still manifested as in the Orient, by a bit of plumage, a startling jewel, a spangle pasted on her forehead between the eyes. Her husband had not understood the signals: "Look at Moira, the woman of the Orient, who wants to be a woman of tomorrow." At first, she painted meticulously on small canvases. Colors of the Orient. Small flowers, serpentines, confetti, metallic-lace paper, roses and butterflies. In the same art class with her was a dark, silent, timid Italian. Those who approached him felt such a shriveling timidity in him, such a withdrawal, that they remained at a distance. The two timid ones observed each other. Both had Oriental interiors, without windows on the external world.

A Gallic playfulness pervaded the painting class. The atmosphere was warm, gay, physical. But Moira and her husband remained in their inner patio, listening to birds singing and fountains playing. They painted the same inner landscape, the same moods, the same gaiety always threatened by a sorrow.

They were revealing their dreams to each other, by way of their paintings. And thus they entered each other's world.

At first they married to hide together. In his hands she is being remolded, refashioned, stylized. He initiates her to severe aesthetic values. He cannot remold her body. He is critical of her overabundant breasts. This makes her shrink within herself and plants a seed of doubt of her feminine power. He bound her femininity as the Chinese bound their women's feet. He polished her language, her manners, her impulses.

Her marriage was a second veiling. It was the aesthetic veil of art and social graces. He designed her dresses. She became the women in his paintings. His women were transparent, they lay in hammocks between heaven and earth. Slowly she became more absorbed in his paintings than in her own. The flowers and gardens disappeared. He painted a world of stage settings, static ships, frozen trees, crystal fairs, lace palaces.

Moira protected and sold his paintings for him, nourished and sustained his faith and work until her health failed.

The dream of every maternal love is: "I have filled him with strength. Now he will be strong, and I shall rest upon his strength."

But her loss of strength unbalanced the marriage.

When the marriage exploded, Moira bought large canvases and

painted. She was free. Free to unbind her breasts, to speak, to laugh, to keep open house.

In Paris I had helped my father's old secretary Lantelme until I could no longer do so, and I was bothered by regrets. Joaquin, observing this, decided to tell me the truth. Lantelme was not, as I had thought then, a victim of my father's selfishness. He had been a partner in a musician's agency for concert tours. My father had met him in this capacity. The agency collapsed. It was discovered that Lantelme was responsible for this, had been misusing funds. It was at this moment of his disgrace and poverty that my father took him in, charitably, as secretary. When Lantelme was seventy, my father wearied of his burden. Lantelme became spoiled, did not help very much, and my father asked him to retire. He had children who were comfortably off, who could take care of him.

Lantelme then came to me. I believed his story that when he had ceased to be of use to my father, my father had thoughtlessly discarded him. I took on the burden. I never thought to inquire about the story. Did I choose Lantelme as a living proof of my father's selfishness because this was the image my mother had created in me? Did my unconscious make the choice that would confirm this belief? Could I have found, equally, proofs of my father's unselfishness? We choose the verdict and then proceed to substantiate the fact. Thus, we add to the portrait only proofs of our assertions, of what we *seek* to prove, to believe.

If one can get lost in the labyrinth of emotions, one can also get lost in the labyrinth of analysis. I found this out with Rank. One can believe one is objective and defeat one's self in life by using analysis. An hallucination can be confused with a vision. Fear can create an image as clear and distinct as clairvoyance or prophecy. Interpretation and analysis are still dependent on the interpreter's fallability. A greater structural harmony, semblance of logic, is possible to analysis because it moves in the realm of objectivity—but this objectivity is treacherous and full of traps. Objectivity is just as fallible as the instincts, just as self-deceptive.

Gonzalo's intuitions and instincts are often just as accurate as my attempts at objective interpretation. Because the objective interpretation precludes a perfect self-knowledge. Without self-knowledge you are not capable of objectivity. Only of rationalization. When you have self-knowledge you know what areas of your judgment are not to be trusted. The only difference is that the higher mathematics of analysis can construct a semblance of balance, continuity and consistency, whereas the exertion of the emotions often presents an image of chaos, contradiction and waste.

We select our proofs. Because a businessman's sympathies were with capitalism, he managed to see and hear only what made capitalism seem justified. He accumulated facts in its favor with apparent objectivity, but all the while it was his unconscious desire that capitalism should be right that dictated his sources of information and his selection of facts. The day he experienced emotionally a revolt against the system, due to an act of flagrant injustice, he was able to consider other sources of information and gather together all the other facts with equal ease. Once he was converted emotionally, all the "proofs" came his way. He admits this, though he is a man of justice, control, and seemingly guided by an objective intelligence. But all the while it was his emotional self which was guiding him to protect, sustain, and maintain his a priori theories.

In the same way it is people's inner demons which create wars, and which they will not recognize. It is the inner demon of a man which makes history. But America is still looking for the devil outside (the inner life, implies Houghton Mifflin, in rejecting my book, at this moment, is so trivial!).

The actual world would be vital if people knew what is essential, but they confuse the actual with contingencies and petty immediacies, fads, fashions, modes, mores, all of them evanescent, puerile, futile.

Auguste Bailly on Joyce:

The life of the mind is a symphony. It is a mistake, or, at best, an arbitrary method, to dissect the chords and set out their components on a single line, on one plane only. Such a method gives an entirely false idea of the complexity of our mental make-up, for it is the way the light falls upon each element, with a greater or a lesser clarity, that indicates the relative importance for ourselves, our lives and acts, of each of the several thought-streams. But in the silent monologue, as transposed into words by Joyce, each element seems of equal importance, the subsidiary and the essential themes are treated as equivalents and an equal illumination falls upon these parts which were, in reality, brightly lit up, and those which remained in the dark background of thought.

I prefer the analytic method, which doubtless eliminates something of reality, but eliminates only the superfluous and neglects only the negligible. Joyce has perceived—a fact that is psychologically correct but no novelty—that our mental life is composed of a continuous monologue within, which though it adjusts itself to the object of our activity or immediate preoccupation, is apt to desert this and wander far afield, to yield to other influences, to distractions, internal or external, and sometimes to be influenced by almost mechanical associations. In fact, we may listen to this inner voice yet be quite unable to control it.

It follows that if the writer wishes to give a complete and accurate study of the mood of one of his characters, we must no longer employ the classical method of analyzing and segregating thoughts, or seek to emphasize the nuances by deliberately ignoring the chaotic turmoil in which they are involved; his object is, rather, to give expression to this turmoil, its fermentations, its stormy nebula of gestation, with all its extensions, contractions and vortices, and even, so to say, its shortcomings. . . .

The necessity of recording the flow of consciousness by means of words and phrases compels the writer to depict it as a continuous horizontal line, like a line of melody. But even a casual examination of our inner consciousness shows us that this presentation is essentially false. We do not think on one plane, but on many planes at once. It is wrong to suppose that we follow only one train of thought at a time, there are several trains of thought, one above the other. We are generally aware, more completely conscious, of thoughts which take form on the higher plane. But we are also aware, more or less obscurely, of a stream of thoughts on the lower levels. . . .

Finished the story of Conrad Moricand. Called it "The Mohican."
Rereading a note I copied from a book on Dostoevsky:

The question of jealousy preoccupied Dostoevsky unceasingly. In his characters, jealousy brings a suffering which is not complicated by any feeling of hatred for the rival. Dostoevsky seems to establish in the human soul a kind of stratification. First, the intellectual, remote from the soul and whence proceed the worst temptations. Therein dwells the treacherous demonic element. The second region, of passion, ravaged and desolated by storms. There is a region deeper still, where passion does not exist. . . .

Nearly all Dostoevsky characters are polygamists: I mean that by way of satisfying, doubtless, the complexity of their natures, they are almost all capable of several attachments simultaneously, without jealousy. Here is the mysterious essence of Dostoevsky's philosophy and of Christian ethics too. The individual triumphs by renunciation of his individuality. In all Dostoevsky we have not a single great man (intellect or will)— no hero.

I cannot abandon my love of the hero. I see this quality in Frances, and admire it, and I do not admire Helba, who lacks it altogether.

It seems to me that all my creation is an effort to weave a web of connection with the world; I am always weaving it because it was once broken. But as I want these webs to be always truthful, I do not know how to break the false ones, such as the artificial one with Dorothy Norman.

She seeks me out, and if I try to explain how I feel, she will not understand. I feel as Dostoevsky that the intellect by itself is the seat of trouble. Falsities. I prefer the seat of the passions, even with the storms. There are times when one sees a friendship as hopeless, basically so, and it is useless to argue about the little errors, the small falsities, the small misunderstandings. It is a fundamental incompatibility and one hates to express this.

Letter from Henry from Hollywood:

Just got your letter telling me that you might resume your role of analyst. Yes, I do think you could do that well. Glad you mentioned Kerkhoven, in this respect. One feels, in reading Wassermann, that he realized that what the analyst needed was the poetic touch, the ability to leave things open, in fact to increase the mystery surrounding everything. Kerkhoven was a mighty figure, one that Wassermann himself fell far short of, I imagine, in actual life.

As to the fundamental weakness of the Kerkhoven type, I leave that for you to discover for yourself. You know, when it comes down to bedrock, I don't think it's so much a question of caring for the sick, as you put it, as it is one of getting results. You can see the results of creation, dealing with your neurotics, and that's pleasurable. It also puts you out of the competitive world, which is so abhorrent. You may remember— I said it to you more than once—that if you feel you must minister to the weak and ailing, then you should do it with all your heart and soul. You can't play at analysis any more than you can at art. Remember this, that you will profit more from it, in the end, than your patients. Because there is something defective in the analyst which drives him to this work—it is like the relation between master and slave—so I firmly believe. Don't fool yourself by thinking you are doing good, that you are alleviating misery, and so on. No, you will be treating yourself, that's what I think.

In this way, and maybe only in this way, can you complete your own analysis—and then see beyond it. This is not to deter you—on the contrary. I think it will be excellent. And don't tie it up, your work, with the idea that it is a solution to our economic ills. Do it for its own sake, purely. Enjoy it! I want you to put an end to your anguish about my physical comfort. I want you to get like a rock and not worry whether I sink or swim. There's undoubtedly something wrong with me, or I would have solved this primitive question long ago. Better let me face it. But I don't want you to think that I ever get the idea that you failed me. No matter what you did you couldn't fail me. I hold myself responsible for whatever happens to me. You, having greater wisdom, probably have more fear of what may happen than I in my blindness.

The last three days have been marvelous. Such perfect weather! Almost as good as Greece. Would be, too, if there were the Mediterranean, the ruins, the people, the tradition, and so on and so on. I always think of Rank here. You said he liked it so much. Now I see why. I get more and more crazy about it.

You mention Frances, the wise one. It seems such a great pity that she has to lie on her back in a place like New York. This place here is paradise, comparatively. She could be up and about here, I'm sure of it. The very light in the sky would do something to her. I feel enriched. One doesn't need people, theaters, bars. Just to step outdoors, see the light on the hills, the stars at night—that's enough. People in the East think it is a bizarre place, because it's Hollywood. I have almost nothing to do with Hollywood. I might be a thousand miles away, for all it matters. It drives me nuts sometimes, to think that one can't live where one wants, especially when this place is not the moon, not the Antarctic.

Places are important, just as important as food or other things. I'm going to return, but I tell you this, as long as the war is on, about this thing, living in the right place, the right climate, nothing can convince me that I'm wrong. I look to New York with loathing. Two days, such as these two, wipe out years of living in New York.

Anyway, what I'm trying to tell you is this, the West is utterly different from the East. It's enough for me to exchange a few words with the grocer, or with Honest John, the Greek who runs a hash joint up the canyon. People stop and talk to me—they always do, you know. But I don't care whether they do or not. I get to the point of complete enjoyment of life, and then bango! the old question—how do you make a living? I'm not a bit sorry that I didn't land a job in the studios, callous though that sounds. I've had a rich, wonderful time of it, these four months. Margaret and Gilbert were wonderful to me. And, if I did drain them a bit, I repaid them in other ways.

I'm going to talk to Tom Brown and Frances when I get back. I don't see why they should drag out a miserable existence back there in New York. You know, I meet more people who know Frieda Lawrence than you can shake a stick at. They all tell me what a wonderful life she leads up there in San Cristóbal, New Mexico. Somehow Frieda has solved her problems in a very humble way. She must be a grand person, quite different than we think from reading Lawrence. I begin to suspect that she was the bigger of the two, when it comes to life. And that's what I'm getting at all the time, to arrange things so that one can live simply and easily, very humbly perhaps. I don't need cities any more. You can always have music and books, even in the most remote places. And sometimes it's good not to have even these, but to be thrown completely on your own.

So many personal dramas: Moira and her husband. Caresse's low peak, low financially, and low in publishing ventures. Her life becalmed. The surrealists becoming *objets deluxe* for the galleries and merchants. The oppression of the Negroes which I witness every day through talking with Millicent when we eat together, when I hear the stories about her friends, and her relatives. The political nightmare, Communism against democracy, but a democracy partly corrupt, hypocritical.

The drama of Moira is very significant, it is the Orient against the West. She could have stayed in Persia and found happiness.

But there she could not have developed her strong artist personality. She was brought up like a little primitive in a big property, allowed to run wild. She dreamt of France. And she married an over-refined, perverse, feminine Italian. He is complicated, deceptive, elusive, inhibited, ingrown, obscure. Her suffering began. Once she ran away from him, back to Persia. He came to get her and took her back to France. Back of all her actions there is a creative intent, a need of beauty, a need of the myth. She felt her husband was a *twin*. The twin to her bound self, perhaps, for he was equally bound, but not the twin to her expanding, developing self. He not only did not free her, but he imprisoned her. He was, in fact, no different from the Persian men she wanted to escape, the ones who cloistered woman.

The drama of woman's development is very painful, for in each case the man seems to punish all growth. So the woman intent on growth chooses a yielding, passive man who will not interfere with this growth, with her evolution. But in the end, his weakness destroys her.

To be the mother of children demands immolation and abdication. Moira evaded this, but preferred to become the mother of the artist, who needs protection and support. She recognized that the artist needs protection because he has a work to do, and the world usually does not protect him. He is helpless in the world. Her fulfillment lies in a symbolic giving birth, giving birth to an artist. But the real child, the child of nature, grows up as the mother grows older. He becomes strong in turn, he may even turn around and become her protector. However, the artist-child never grows up, never grows stronger. And the woman finally collapses under the burden. If she wearies, gets ill, fails in her role, she finds herself alone, deserted. When Moira fell, became ill, her husband turned to a tall, giant masculine woman for more protection.

This is a phase in the evolution of woman. She wants to divert her strength from biological motherhood into other forms of creation.

But she needs man's blessing and man's help.

In Moira and her husband, in their war, there was another aspect of Orient against the West. Moira has a natural wisdom, and he none. She longs for harmony, subtle concordances, suavities, and he shouts, insults, attacks, makes violent scenes. She clings to the myth, and he destroys it. He vulgarizes her. He vilifies, he distorts the issues, reduces them to quarrels about possessions, money, studios. She seeks to embellish even the break, so that it will not leave any poison.

She moved out of the studio on Forty-second Street and took one on Washington Square. Moira can make any place look beautiful with garden furniture, flowers in hanging pots, birds, bright felt curtains and pillows. I found friends who would work for her, gluing sea shells, painting earrings. I worked with her now and then so that we could talk, interpret what had happened so it would hurt less.

Her decor changed. She returned to her Oriental atmosphere. There were pillows on the floor. She sat on the floor. Her cooking smelled of spices. The colors around her were Oriental, emerald green, shocking pink, purple and turquoise. Once more she believed in astrology, in card readings, palm readings, which her husband had mocked. Once more she believed in magic. Once when she was cooking, meat was frying in a Pyrex frying pan. Moira was making susurrating sounds with her voice to silence the jumping grease. She said: "My mother had a magic power. When she did this the grease never leaped on her." As she said this the glass frying pan shattered.

Moira's explanation of this failed ritual was illuminating. "I have lived too long with people who did not believe in magic," she said, "and so I have lost my power."

Moira, by being herself a dream personage, reinstated the dream faculty in me and turned all my imagination to Morocco, and by writing the "Labyrinth" story I escaped from the nightmare of life in New York, the press, money problems. The high cost of living gives us not a moment of pleasure or relaxation. Window opens on Morocco. Chimerical worlds, but no mere escape into fantasy. Fantasy leads to storytelling. As you begin to tell yourself tales they begin to take shape. Moira re-creates Persia in her studio, and tells me all about her life. It is a magic ritual. The demons are defeated.

One's courage is renewed. Who spoke of ivory towers? Laboratories of the soul. Where essences are manufactured which defeat ugliness, poverty, debts, humiliations, defeats. Moira spreads the vast cardboard trays with rosy sea shells, pearls, beads, pins, small mirrors, and with glue we turn them into fantasy earrings and pins. On a large table she also designs textiles. Her black hair curls around her forehead, around her ears in small ringlets, she looks like a harem woman, her eyes dark and glistening, but she is another one of tomorrow's women.

Letter from Henry:

Last night I finished the Céline book [*Death on the Installment Plan*] —at long last! It was tremendous. I was howling with laughter here all by myself. . . . Such verve, such gusto, such a racy style. Even in translation the language is new, like ultraviolet rays. And what a piece of grim surrealism, in the last analysis. What surrealist has written like that, aside from Lautréamont?

This morning I was rereading the last pages of my *Rosy Crucifixion*, and do you know, I found it almost as good. I was delighted with it. Wondered if it was really me who did it. That's the truth . . . and this leads me to say, that I am sure I can both work for a living and do my writing too. So many men and women have done it. And done it well. And I'm sure everyone will be much happier when I've solved this little problem. I've lost that fear now. I don't much care where I go or what I do. I feel happy and will make what I can of what's around me. I repeat we're fortunate not to be involved in the war business. You must read Frederic Prokosch's book *The Seven Who Fled*. He's achieved a splendid style for that kind of writing—pure, imaginary description, which is so much better than reality, it seems. It's morbid and somber in tone, but excellent, excellent writing. It had me in a trance. Well, Lafe has arrived. I'm going to meet him now at the Satyr Book Shop. Give my regards to Frances and to Tom Brown.

To help the press along we are doing a book for Caresse. It is a reprint of a book she had done for her Black Sun Press: Drawings by Max Ernst, text by Éluard. She wants to recapture her prestige as a publisher. But she does not allow Gonzalo the freedom to design the book. So we are copying the typography and have lost all interest in the work.

Max Ernst comes now and then to see how his drawings reproduce. He is short, very slender, very stiff, with the profile of a bird. The blue eyes are set close together, the aquiline nose dominates the face, the mouth is small, the cheeks lean. He has a small, stingy smile, innocent eyes, but the whole of the face gives a cutting, shrewd impression.

I remembered the story I was told about the time he was married to Eleanora Carrington. She was a beautiful English girl. The surrealists, as a group, encouraged her neurosis to the point of madness. She was a painter. She would paint a canvas and lay it against a wall. A few days later she would look for it and would not find it. The story was that Max Ernst needed canvases and had painted over it. But he would say to the girl: "Are you sure you painted anything? I never saw such a painting."

Now Max Ernst is married to Peggy Guggenheim. She saved him from a concentration camp. Her collection of Max Ernst paintings was impressive; with this marriage it was complete.

Max Ernst gave me a feeling of stratification. I could see him born of the swamps, the nightmare, the lunar foliage he loved to paint, the overgrown, mossy, secret caves. I could see him part of the bird world, predatory worlds. Once he looked like Merlin the Magician; now he is subjected to the taxidermy of wealth. He has no antennae, he seems made of sawdust. They all enter, talk, sit, eat, but like performers, brilliant, glowing, nonhuman. Politically, they tear each other apart.

I believe that what estranged me from the surrealist group was that they were content to find the sources of images and free associations, the surrealist element in life and art, but I wanted to go one step farther, I wanted to unravel the meaning of the unconscious and bring it into consciousness so that our very life could be lived in harmony with its fertile, unending richness.

When I meet Eleanora Carrington in Dr. Jacobson's office, she amazes me by saying that her greatest concern is that the source of her images in painting or source of material in writing might run dry. This has always been the last of my concerns.

It seemed to me that by unearthing the unconscious one found an infinite source of creativity, and the problem lay simply in how well, how eloquently to express the rich diggings. Eleanora had gone far, too far almost to return from those regions. How could she speak of the fear of running dry?

I feel that so many of the surrealists simulated their dreaming. They simulated the unconscious, the mad, the fantastic. Simulation always betrays itself by leading to barrenness. Much as I was seduced by the theories, I always felt in their presence, as a group, that the unconscious was summoned by the intellect and made to perform. None of them walk, weep, laugh, feel. When the unconscious manifests itself genuinely, you are like the primitive possessed. No, the surrealists are in full possession, it is a game, a game of wit and brilliance. Those who were truly possessed lost their minds.

Letter from Henry:

You know, if I just wanted to float around forever, I could. I get all sorts of invitations from all over the country, to put up with people. In Chicago I have the pick of four houses to stay at. Another in St. Louis, another in Minneapolis, and in Kenosha, of course. In New Orleans three places. It's strange that in New York the only offer of this sort came from a pest.

You never did read that last part of *Rosy Crucifixion*, where I turned into a dog, did you? That was marvelous. A savage bit of symbolism. Sprang from a remark of June's I overheard when descending the staircase—about being just a child. That will bowl you over when you read it. It ends with Woof! Woof!

I was thinking yesterday, in a fine mood, that the only way I can get on with the book is to remember certain people who enjoy reading me, write with them in mind. Put blinders over my eyes, sink into it.

God, it's so hard for me always—to really become totally absorbed in what I'm writing. When I read a big bloc I get this feeling, get the hang of it again, and realize all that I want to do yet—the immensities of the vistas stagger me. And at the same time I realize that one must not and cannot wait for the perfect situation—to write thus. One must write, and live too, as if today were the last day, the last chance.

Had a letter from Houghton, enclose his carbon, which he always sends. He's finished another book! Great Scott! And he works at a job. And Céline worked in a clinic. And Élie Faure scribbled his notes on his cuff, while visiting his patients. Makes me ashamed of myself. As I said to someone, your guru friend Frances can do more lying on her back than healthy people standing on their hind legs. I must do as everybody else does and then see if I can boast of being wise, serene, gay, etc. I have been living a lie, and writing it, I guess. Yes, I have run away from so many things—and finally I've had to face them all. So much has to do with the fact that I find the work of the world ugly and stupid. Perhaps this bugaboo will disappear too, now that I am face to face with it. And yet I feel that on my dying bed I will raise up on one elbow and have a last say at the world—"Don't work so hard, you poor fools! Give over . . . do as little as possible!!"

You see, it isn't the easygoing, happy-go-lucky people who cause sorrow and misery in the world. It's the go-getters, the reformers, the conquerors, the fanatics, the hard-working ones. They think that paradise is created by sweat and labor, by making everyone think alike. *That,* that sure knowledge that at the bottom of all this toil and effort is simply a miserable, gloating sadism, that's what kills me. Well, as the monk said in Shangri-La, I'll be moderately industrious.

I don't know what day I felt: *No puedo más* (I can't bear any more). But it came with such violence that I broke down. First came an extreme weakness, so extreme I could not climb the stairs to my home. I had to take them like mountain climbing, resting between each step. Then came the weeping. Uncontrollable weeping. It seemed to me that I was broken for good, physically and spiritually.

Fears, doubts, confusion. The work at the press too heavy. Strain. Unbearable tension. Such painful tension. I had driven myself too far.

I telephoned Martha Jaeger, Frances' analyst.

A beautiful, compassionate face. I yielded to her like a child, weeping, confessing. Immediately she released the tensions by her words: "You encompassed too much. You had no sense of reality about the body—the limitations of the body."

As I talked to her, abandoned myself to her care, I felt less hurt and less confused.

It was as if I had been given absolution and the permission to rest, relax, and give up my burdens. She was amazed at all I had taken on.

The second time when I left her, I fell asleep in the subway, and at home I slept, slept, as if for the first time. I thought of nothing. I gave up all my cares and responsibilities. I became like a child, and admitted my weakness, absolute loss of strength. The tension broke. I could rest. She said I had a right to rest. I had done all and more than I could.

The third time, she explained the urge that had driven me into this superhuman effort. "Woman communicates with the cosmos, the cosmic, through the earth, through her maternal self. So you became the all-mother, giving out endlessly. You attempted to take care of everyone. You attempted the infinite with a finite human body."

Each time she mentions this I see the enormous loves growing immense and finally crushing me. And all this immense effort is reduced, simplified, and I stand naked and free of the giant task, a child again, relaxed and insouciant.

That was the first liberation from the wild, straining heroics. I felt like a convalescent. Weak but peaceful. The nightmare was over.

This is a new drama. The father is absent from this drama. This one is the drama of the mother, of woman. I have been drawing closer to all women, lately, aware of their particular tragedy. I had been reading about the three stages of consciousness. Woman is only now becoming aware of her individuality. But also, as Jaeger said, of her different way of relating to the cosmos. It is a difficult, a deep problem for woman to commune with the cosmic. She can only achieve it by a universal motherhood or else the priestess-prostitute way.

I crumbled because of the immensity of the burden. And the emotional substance I used for it, the psychic and emotional expenditure. For it is not only protection which obsessed me, but the giving of strength, spiritual and psychic nourishment. Jaeger made all this clear.

It is strange how I turned to the woman and the mother for understanding. I have had all my relationships with men, of all kinds. Now my drama is that of the woman in relation to herself— her conflict between selfishness and individuality, and how to manifest the cosmic consciousness she feels.

There are depths I have not yet entered, which I struggled to express when I argued against Henry and Durrell and wrote about woman in creation. I reread this tonight and only begin to understand it now because of what Jaeger said about the cosmic life of woman running underneath. It is strange, like a recurrent dream, to find her living by the river. The flow again. Where she lives, the Hudson is wide and beautiful. But hers is a peaceful barque. Her home is situated on *Haven* Avenue, and before we talk about the cosmic mother she has been washing her husband's shirt. And this touches me, the world of woman.

To console Moira I began to talk to her about this larger woman she had been trying to enact also.

It is strange that I have described these feelings and made the somewhat similar statements Jaeger makes, but emotionally and unconsciously, and I'm fully aware of their meaning now in her presence, as she talks. The diary must be unconscious and emotional and so even with it and within it I can get lost and can only regain my vision through the objective eye of another.

The first morning I went to her it was like a nightmare. I got lost in the subway, came out too early, and then was met by a violent wind. I could hardly walk against it. I thought I would never reach her. I remembered then my first visit to Rank, the sense of confusion and being lost.

After three days I stopped weeping.

How necessary is this periodic removal of guilt. It plays the role of the old confession and absolution. What a change of mood after one is operated on, and the well of guilt cleansed.

Psychoanalysis is our only way of gaining wisdom because we no longer have religion.

There was in me a confusion between love and devotion. I

thought all my acts were acts of love, yielding up of the self, the personal. But I did feel hurt that they were all willing to immolate me, and felt unloved according to my own definition of love: sacrifice.

I felt that in love the self must be shattered, love was abnegation, effacement of the self. My revolt goes back to all the concessions and sacrifices I made out of love, friendship, devotion. Jaeger was shocked by the story of the burning of my books by Gonzalo so I would stop dreaming and become a Marxist. I revolted against the *misuse* of my gifts. The waste. My first gift of a typewriter to Henry hocked and money spent on drinking.

I thought I had always been identified with my father, but as a woman I acted more like my mother, who was a sacrificed mother. My father was the ego, my mother the sacrifice.

I was deeply hurt, maimed, suppressed. Must I fall mortally ill to prove to my children that they have overburdened me?

Letter from Henry:

Two nights ago I met a friend Lafe is staying with, a young man of twenty-six, Pierce Harwell, a composer, who works in a drugstore as a soda-fountain jerker, to support his mother. One of the most stimulating, fecundating meetings I have had in ages. He is a homosexual, a student of astrology since the last few years. He has a positive genius for it. Lafe gave him my date and he told me the most astounding things about myself. I haven't heard the all of it yet. We talked for six hours, and had only made a dent in it. He reads me like a book.

It was most encouraging too, all he said. I won't bore you with the details, but he did say I had found myself. He added that I would never go to the bottom, that no real mishap could ever befall me, that I would be protected always, no matter what I did, and that I would probably live to ninety or more, and enjoy good health. . . .

Analysis is the real thread of Ariadne.

The only repetitious theme is that of doubt of the love, the first trauma.

Peggy Guggenheim looks like W. C. Fields. Guests at her house are often invited to exchange husbands and wives. One artist told me the following story: "Someone designed for her a bedstead of aluminum. It looks somewhat like an abstract tree. It has branches which overhang the bed, flowers, and leaves which flutter like mobiles at the slightest breeze. It is quite an elaborate contraption. It has one inconvenience: at strategic moments, it shakes, tinkles, to the accompaniment of wind chimes and electronic sounds. I can assure you that it does not act as an aphrodisiac."

Letter from Henry:

A few words about the *Seven Gothic Tales*. They are Gothic, all right. There is an irritating, bewildering quality about them, I find. I've read the first one now, about the flood, and reread "The Dreamers." I can't read more than one at a sitting. What's irritating for me is the mystification, and not the mystery. As though the author herself were confused in her own mind. Maybe you can read them with keener insight. I'm curious to know. Maybe I shouldn't examine them too closely. There is a certain enchantment in the style, but every now and then the skin breaks and a broom handle shoves through. But with all that, she is a sort of Northern Arabian stroyteller—the weirdest mixture I have ever seen.

I like the names and places very much—all so outlandish. But have you noticed, all the characters speak alike? It's always the same mellifluous rhythm, tinctured with, it seems to me, a rather antiquated French jargon, no?

When I first read "The Dreamers" I thought immediately of you. But there is such a mixture of symbolism that I am more confused than at first reading. You ought to be able to tell me a lot about it—because much of the famous Pellegrina Leoni is you. (Does Pellegrina mean anything in Italian?) Every descriptive piece she gives is like you to a T. Starry being, winged lioness, saint of the first magnitude, a soul two-parted, the enormous eyes, heaping benefactions out of a horn of plenty, the sensation of flying, the milliner-revolutionist, the absence of shadow (no fear, no regrets, etc.), no black around her or in her, the boundless life in her, her agelessness, etc.

A wonderful line where she describes her as a swan in the lake of life everlasting. Marvelous that, and it fits you perfectly. Also true of you: "She made you feel as safe, above the abyss, as in your own chair."

And this: "To be the manifestation of all that was lovely, great, elegant, and brilliant—in this lay her happiness."

And finally: "In spite of her good sense she was ever a Donna Quixota de la Mancha." There is one thing she says which contains a lot of meaning: "Never again will I have my heart and my whole life bound up with one woman, to suffer so much. From now on I will be many persons." When she recovers from the accident (the fire wherein she lost her voice) she admits she had been very selfish—always Pellegrina, Pellegrina. To have such awful things happen to her as happened to Pellegrina— that would be too much to bear. And then a strange thought comes to her—that never more would there be a Madonna in the skies to smile on her poor audience. A tremendous self-idolatry or self-consciousness, no? A strange assumption that the ability to spread beauty and happiness was supremely hers. And so, to enjoy life a little more, she decides on many roles instead of one blazing one. And with that comes such a complete loss of memory that she does not recall who any of her lovers were.

Of course, the loss of memory and the loss of shadow go hand in hand. And then, in death, she becomes one again—the great Pellegrina. You can fool the world but you can't fool the Creator. Is this the story of what happens when one loses one's true role in life? Does it mean that one should not attach too much importance to a role, or on the contrary? I can't make it out. Or does it simply mean that if one is born to be a radiant star nothing else will ever satisfy one?

I can understand that to a starry creature the world must always seem drab and incommensurable to one's powers. And yet that is an illusion. Because if one is truly a star then all one demands is merely to shine. And a star would not be dependent on such a trivial thing as a "voice." A star would have a thousand ways of manifesting its radiance. And perhaps in losing the voice Pellegrina lost her connection with the world . . . her medium of transmission—the star—became dead, as they say about the radio waves. I don't know. I'm mystified. And I get more and more mystified.

I know that a similar thing happens to you when you are prevented from radiating peace, joy, and munificence. When you can't function as a resplendent, bounteous Venus you go dead. And if someone says to you, What is the matter? you fly away, just as Pellegrina did. I've noticed what importance you attach to that word "climate," your special climate. But do you realize what that means? Not the warm, tropical places you imagine, but this atmosphere which you ever strive to create about you—of bliss, understanding, beauty, opulence, etc.

Pellegrina was not vain because she demanded magnificent trappings in her stage roles: it was an expression, on a mundane plane, of her opulent and exalted nature. If I knew more about astrology I would be able to say more about the role of Venus in such lives. I would hazard this, of course, it's almost banal to say it, that where Venus is afflicted (or exalted) everything pertaining to love must be acted out on the highest plane. The sacrificial element then is seen to be the true exaltation of Venus, which in lowly parlance, becomes interpreted as a poor "afflicted" Venus. This Venus is not meant for the earth, but for the heavens. Her role is to ennoble and exalt. When she tries to do this through illusion she fails.

Pellegrina identifies herself with Pellegrina the actress. She wanted to bedazzle instead of to illuminate.

You didn't make that mistake. Perhaps your only mistake has been to attempt to transfer your powers. And that because you are mistaken as to the source of the power. I say "perhaps." I am not absolutely sure. But I think sometimes that people endowed with great gifts, especially magnetic, prophetic powers, are apt to forget that they are simply a medium of transmission, that these powers are loaned them, and that they can never be lost so long as they do not try to possess them for their own or bequeath them to others.

If I mention this it is because I have often been struck by the fact that the great illuminati seem never to be in danger of exhausting their powers. They blaze forth until they die. Even in the act of dying, if you will notice, they are capable of raising the dead.

In Pellegrina's case, the reverse happened. She had a tomb erected over an empty space, over her supposed dead body. With the loss of her name she seemed to have lost her substance. She was neither alive nor dead. She hovered between two worlds. The image which the author perhaps unconsciously chose was very telling—that of a star that had fallen from the heavens.

Yes, the rest of her life was like the passage of a fallen star across the firmament. Having left the center she fell out of her orbit. It's true that she left a blazing trail behind her, but the light was finally extinguished. She did die in the fire. And could we say of that disaster that she was consumed by the artificial blaze which she sought so desperately to create? Is that far-fetched? I may be a million miles off the track.

I read it almost too intensely, first knowing that it meant something to you, and second, being puzzled as to exactly what it did mean to you. Maybe it's so simple that I missed it altogether. Certainly in the highest correlations, Pellegrina Leoni and you have a tremendous affinity.

I can imagine your surprise. But you've said all these things infinitely better. That silly schoolgirl preface by Dorothy Canfield shows you the only way the public gets these things is through the pretty artifice of a pseudo-Arabian night tale. I think it was curious that the author should be Danish, don't you? I'm wondering if all the stories have to do with roles? The first one about the actor was remarkable, though a bit forced, it seemed to me. She seems to be vastly interested in the astrologic features of her personages. They are not real people, but the shadows of their matrices, or the adumbrations, rather.

I imagine Moricand would have liked these tales immensely. I see types parading before me, and as with Houghton, the incidents and settings are nonetheless true for being unreal. I'm not ravished by her style, though. She is definitely baroque. And sometimes a bit rococo. . . .

Letter to Henry:

Every word you said about "The Dreamers" (Isak Dinesen) corresponds to my feelings. I was puzzled by the same thing and I see the difference clearly. She had wealth, and her voice. She possessed the horn of plenty. I had the desire to be Venusian, and I had the desire to give but I was not wealthy. And so to live this out and bring magic and creation around me I was not content to sing (write) but I had to give real food, real nourishment. And as I didn't have plenty I had to deny myself. And ended by collapsing physically. I felt responsible for everyone. I was not content with singing, or to give as you do of your talk, reading, writing. You gave what was easy, natural, abundant. I gave up all I needed, vacations, good food, rest. The strength of the body is not infinite. That was my error.

The most intricate and fascinating detective story in the world is the tracking down of incidents and misinterpretations which create a distortion of reality. Neurosis plants only the seeds of death in every relationship. Re-evaluation. Reinterpretation, objectivity. Could I make a work of art of this? Reveal the magical effect of transmutations, transformations, the magical effect of analysis?

The magic consists in the fact that the changes you affect within yourself in turn affect others. Anxiety breeds anxiety, doubt breeds doubt, fear breeds fear. As you get free of yours, there is a chain reaction on all those around and close to you. Tranquillity is contagious, peace is contagious. One only thinks of the contagiousness of illness, but there is the contagion of serenity and joy. Neurosis is the real demon, the only real possession, the real evil force in the world. *And it is curable.*

Letter to Henry:

In Spanish they say: All saviors get crucified. Well, it's a question now whether I'll resuscitate in due form! It's true I don't feel like writing. I feel like Pellegrina after the fire—the mother was properly consumed, buried, and what survives I don't quite know.

Dreams: Jean appears, luminous and joyous. I am happy but concerned about having to take care of him. I seek *La Belle Aurore,* the houseboat, again, I find it, I rent it, plan to move in.

Winter of Artifice is the pure essence of the personality, stripped of racial characteristics, time, place, the better to penetrate the innermost being, the deepest self. Description of states: insomnia, obsession, coldness, split. Because I myself was free and beyond nationalism, uprooted, and possessed of an X-ray of the inner life of others, as well as my own. Describe people as composed of climate, elements, race elements, foods they eat, animals they resemble, books they read. As layers, living in past, present or future, in ideas, dreams or daydreaming, absent, or preconscious, conscious, seeing themselves or blind, atrophied or superaware, and then all this must be stripped away in order to reach the subconscious essence which is a superimposition of all these elements, in a web, a cellular interdependence.

There are day people or nocturnal people, constant and variables, deflected, focused, or reflective.

Virginia and her friends dress like schoolchildren. Baby shoes, little bows in their hair, little-girl dresses, little-boy clothes, orphan hats, schoolgirl short socks, they eat candy, sugar, ice cream. And some of the books they read are like schoolchildren's books: how to win friends, how to make love, how to do this or that.

They prefer the radio, the movies, recordings, to hearing tales firsthand, to hearing experiences directly. They are not curious about people, only their voices over a machine and their faces on the screen.

Helba's confusions, madness, are like some infectious, engulfing darkness in which Gonzalo is hopelessly tangled. He aspires to order, discipline, creation, but she pulls him back into chaos. He never comes to the press before three or four o'clock.

I have to cut the paper, which is heavy, I have to take out the discards, which are heavy. I have to clean the press in order to start. He says it is Helba who gives him errands to do. Undertows. I cannot work in the evenings. Gonzalo said he would, but he never does. Because of the press, he says they have to eat in the restaurant. He has no time to shop. So he needs more money. His mother sent a cable that she was ill, wanted to see him, wanted to help him obtain his inheritance.

Gonzalo dreads facing his bourgeois family; he is a failure in their eyes. He fears being kept there while they pretend to disentangle his inheritance, taken over by his brothers. He fears a trap on the part of his family.

He prefers this life, with all its ordeals.

Martha Jaeger's face is all compassion. Her eyes are clear. She knits while I talk. She receives me at the door with playfulness, as if we were going to begin a game instead of a serious talk. She shows hesitations. She does not pretend to know all. The talk seems wandering, desultory, meandering, yet each time I take a step forward. Each time I face a new truth.

I fell into a trap because of my compassion. At what point does self-injury begin? I injured myself. But Jaeger tells me there is a way to give without injuring one's self, of being compassionate without masochism. Masochism. The word is out. My concept of love as sacrifice. All that I needed I gave away. For years I did not even have a fountain pen, but Henry had one and Gonzalo. I had no records, but they did. When I was alone, I ate badly, to save money. I didn't have money to take all my diaries out of France. This winter, I had no gloves in freezing weather. Gonzalo buys books, and I take mine out of the public library and they are filled with bedbugs.

Henry gave my birthday date to Pierce Harwell, the young astrologer from Hollywood.

Good lord, I haven't come down from the stratosphere yet! Her chart is an experience. While every chart is something of a spiritual event in the astrologer's life, Anaïs's chart is one of those symphonic things which fill the brain and the soul with the music of the spheres. Libra rising. But Mars rising therein and retrograde symbolizes a passion for life, but passion which is trying to justify and purify itself. Passion which is ever trying to balance soul intensity and body intensity. It is also a symbol of tremendous energy. The spiritual energies become physical power, and the physical energies become spiritual power. Her effect upon other people is that of spontaneous combustion. She herself glows, but when they touch her they break into flames. Another effect indicated by Mars rising is hopeful for her present affliction. Mars rising indicates a remarkable power of resistance and regeneration. She can pull herself back from death's door.

Her chart contains the most beautiful pattern of aspects I have ever seen or imagined. I get almost lyrically ecstatic when I think of it. There are two aspects—patterns which form the folded wings of an angel or dove. Like this:

The eastern half of this pattern is burnished and gleaming like gold. The western half is all silver and opalescent. It is like an unspeakable dream in the limitless mind of William Blake. Language is too puny to express it. Only music could approach the telling. Her chart contains a wonderful and tragic example of something we were speaking about last Sunday.

Venus is the most malefic influence in the whole horoscope. Love is a kind of sickness in her. Love is her bondage, it exacts day labor from her. She is a drudge and a chambermaid to her own tenderness and frantic sympathies. It demands that she sacrifice herself to the passional service, not merely of just men, but of Man the father-son-God-brother-Christ-lover-king-beast-man! So free yet so enslaved. Her Venus is the old pagan Venus rising from the sea.

Pater's words are a perfect expression: "Men go forth to their labors until the evening; but she is awake before them, and you might think that the sorrow in her face was at the thought of the whole long day of love yet to come." The eclipse degrees have been falling on Anaïs for several years. It is the cause of her present physical collapse. It is indeed a wonder she has not collapsed before this!

Henry came nearer to a true surrealism because he was spontaneous and sincere. It was not conscious simulation of surrealism. I came nearer because I live by a natural fusion of fantasy and realism, symbolic surrealistic living. Unilateral writing, literalness, shrinks dimensions.

I feel that by my very nature I can fuse physical and spiritual, conscious and unconscious, and I should be able to reach that in writing. Surrealism reached an impasse by separating dream from human life, but the dream feeds the action and action feeds the dream, they are not separate. The only difficulty is superimposing them for people who are intent on separating them and keeping each level from connecting with the other.

When Millicent saves pennies on the shopping, she opens the little box on my bed after breakfast and says: "Now go and spend it on yourself." So I buy a pair of stockings.

In the bus an old lady clinging to her handbag, her umbrella, her gloves, clutching her glasses as if they were going to be taken away from her, as if she knew she would soon have to separate from them because we do not believe in burying the dead with their possessions.

It is always the same story one is telling. But from a different angle. At times it is an image made small by layers and layers of glass, which is time, the past, and the figure receded, to the point of diffusion.

For a human being, war between the parents, or war between couples, or between friends is just as devastating as the large world wars. The human being is equally torn asunder, equally shell-shocked. The parents feuding and dividing, nations warring. The sorrow may be enlarged, transferred, but it is the same sorrow: it is the discovery of hatred, violence, hostility. It is the dark face of the world. Childhood is never prepared for strife. It seems to enter the world with expectations of paradise and of playgrounds. To force the tragedy of hatred and destruction upon a child is to force too great a burden on its receptivity. It cracks.

Through the microscope of analysis I see the dispersed and sundered being, every little piece leading a separate life. Occasionally, like mercury, they fuse, but remain elusive, unstable, and not welded.

How to live as divided cells—*voilà!*

Something always eludes the scientists, the poets, the stargazers, the biologists, the anthropologists. Something eludes the informers, detectives, police, lawyers. It is the dream. And what lies in the deformed mirrors of the dream and haunts our sleep is the secret of everything.

Perhaps I felt in both Joyce and the surrealists an *imitation* of the unconscious, one intellectual and scholarly, the other by willful derangement of the senses. Perhaps I felt they had not entered the unconscious, but made a literary equivalent of it.

Henry came nearer to true surrealism in his flights. Surrealism reached an impasse by listing unfinished, incomplete dreams considered by themselves. But the dream passes again into reality, affects reality, and from the acts stems the dream, and it continues to make an interlocking chain which contains the mysterious pattern we must unravel. We cannot merely contemplate or register it. It is an interdependence which produces the highest form of life, an expanded consciousness.

I have always been able to make this passage. You can only take a farther step when you know the meaning of the last one. It is the discovery not of the image but of its meaning which leads to the next chamber. It is a technically difficult thing to register. When to fly, when to decipher, when to analyze. I am approximating a discovery.

I know that in the Jean Carteret story lie further and further layers, which at one point will weld and become a symphony. I know that the diary should be written in two columns. I know that the dreams should be completed. It is not enough to penetrate into the subterranean chambers. It is not enough to illumine separate cells with a partial light. Some total process must take place, some miraculous synthesis. I want to find the true dialectical writing.

My problem is that in action people repudiate the invisible world which has formed their acts, dictated these acts, as they repudiate the influence of the dream, not the direct influence of the dream as such but of the *unraveled* dream.

I am filled with elusive perceptions. I am approaching something new.

Letter from Henry:

Pierce said he got your *Winter of Artifice* and wrote you a big letter. He found all sorts of marvelous things in your book, as he does in everything. Indeed, he seems only to look for the marvelous. He's a wizard in the body of an adolescent. More like Rimbaud than anyone I can think of—and with all of Rimbaud's faults too. To have him around is like having a comet in the house. But I never met anyone who can offer—and at lightning speed—more amazing interpretations. Finally, though, you have to throw him out, like a dirty sock. He knows no laws, no limits. Burns like a geyser. Knows no fatigue. Has no hang-overs. He's free if ever a person was, but it's not an enviable freedom. All of which in no wise lessens the power of his words.

I was giving a party. All the lights were on, plus candles. There was music from the phonograph. The windows were open, the three windows which open onto the fire escape. We were laughing, talking, and dancing. The record came to an end. And just at that moment, in the strong light which fell on the fire escape, there appeared a neighbor from the floor below. Half of his body showed in the light as if startled by the scene he had not expected; he had stopped climbing. There was a moment of silence, because we were equally startled by his sudden appearance. He was a man who walked with difficulty because of polio. He had red hair and watery blue eyes. He was ashen pale. He had walked up the fire escape and stood transfixed.

I was about to ask him if he wanted to come in when he spoke like a zombie, mechanically, lifeless. He said: "My wife died. She was a saint. Why should a saint die of cancer?" And without turning around, walking stiffly down the steps so that he looked as if he were falling down a trap of some kind, he disappeared. He looked as if he had sunk from our sight, like a ghost we were not sure of having seen or heard.

[January, 1943]

How many evenings spent lying down, writing in the diary, reading, listening to music. Do I lie content, savoring Giraudoux, or ruminating the story I want to write, or improvising in the diary? Evenings at Louveciennes, with the countryside asleep around the house like a giant foster mother, evenings when most people feel at peace, lulled, drugged with memories. But Anaïs cannot rest. Warmth, perfume, rugs, soft lights, books. They do not appease me. I am aware of time passing, of all the world contains that I have not seen, of all the interesting people I have not met.

My imagination pulls me out into the night always. I want to be everywhere. Lying down, I am missing the heart of passion, drama and adventures.

I dream of fiestas, Indian tribes, Mayan architecture and I am in the salon of Olga, meeting heroes of the Spanish war. I dream of Tahiti, of Japan, of South America, of Peru, of Lake Titicaca, and I am in the salon of the Imbses, and Bravig Imbs is playing the virginal, a lady is singing old English songs.

The scene is frozen like a daguerreotype.

The evenings pass. I get panicky. Time is passing. Time. Time. I am stirred, awake, stirring. Restless. I cannot rest. I dream of voyages.

I am like a winged creature who is too rarely allowed to use its wings. Ecstasies do not occur often enough. Giraudoux, whom I had once misjudged, has created an intoxication by his great subtlety and playfulness. The delectable nuances of experience, the elusiveness, and the mysteries which lie imbedded in his fantasies. In Paris I did not understand him, I did not hear his subtle musical microscope. I thought he indulged in the cascades and waterfalls of language, but it is not so. True, it sounded like a virginal, a spinet, but it was a subtle Oriental tale, quarter-tone writing.

At the window of a secondhand shop on Greenwich Avenue I look hungrily at a small organ. Every now and then I have this great return to music, music from which I want to extract the secret for writing. I must wring its secret for volatile dematerialization, its flow, its fluid penetrations.

What I have to say is as fragile as snow, but as strong as the deluge. Shall I have the voice of tomorrow? Shall it be the power of my feelings which will inundate and water the cement and concrete cities of tomorrow with the necessary fecundating water, amniotic fluid, the fluid of tears, the fluid notes of feeling?

How can I believe this when some of the young I know are as feelingless as robots? Music may disappear from the world of tomorrow, painting, writing, dancing. What will water the roots and cause the ultimate flowering, fecundate the million cells revealed by the microscope? I now see the smallest grain as well as the largest. This circulation of ideas quickening like that of blood, what will come of the smoke and nebulae? Fermentation, leaven to uplift an entire universe. I am a small package of yeast. I have operated in secret through mysterious channels. People cannot even see what I have accomplished. They do not recognize me. In the face of my incantations they are silent. I am as always invisible, because I am the voice of the unconscious. I am aiming at the center of being.

I feel them seeking to speak through me, these women who have taken longer to speak than man because what stirred in them were states which are not articulate in the language of man, but perhaps in the language of music if this music could be frozen in the air to catch the words it forms.

Sibyl, sibylline. I'll be found one day at a fiesta, dancing, but what I will write will be full of gravity. Only when I die will I become visible, and then some publisher will be seen bending over my manuscripts and perhaps bidding for them, but while I lived he took no step to prolong my life, or reveal my work.

Meanwhile it is to Josephine Baker that the world gives a palace in Marrakech!

Yet I have served so many uses, and I have dispensed the drug of clairvoyance.

Work at the press.
Dinner for Joaquin.

The well of guilt emptying. Jaeger with a giant sponge is erasing the guilts.

My concept of love clashed with my desire to create. Everyone's life and work were more important than my own. Creation I considered a danger to my loves, my human relationships. In creation I would reveal what I was, in opposition to the roles I played to be whatever anyone needed.

But the silence of the world around *Winter of Artifice* distresses me. No reviews. Silence from James Agee, Robert Fitzgerald, Charles Henri Ford, Joe Sadow, Veronica Jennings, Kay Boyle, Harry Bull of *Harper's*, Harry Hansen, Peyton Boswell, Allene Talmey, Marc Slonim, New York *Times*, etc.

I am practicing scales.

I study the prodigious virtuosity of Giraudoux. I study my three gods of the deep: Dostoevsky (instinct–unconscious), Lawrence (instinct–unconscious), Proust (unconscious–analysis).

I seek in science new and concrete imagery for tomorrow's writing, new symbols. Metabolic altitudes. There are people who are weightless and better able to travel deeply or far psychically, fluid, invisible, mobile, able to melt into other forms, into propitious disguises to be able to divine, to love, to penetrate, to fuse. Flexible, to be able to follow all the curves, ellipses, detours, byways, cycles of love. The heavy ones, overloaded with earth, travel at snail pace and with snail vision. American literature at present is in this state. It needs expansion of consciousness.

Very often I would say I rebelled against this and that. Much later it occurred to me to question this statement. Instead of rebellion could it be that I was merely asserting my own belief?

Jaeger, by being a woman, by her particular intuition as a woman, has caught a truth not known to any male analyst: the guilt for creating which is strong in woman. Creation linked with femininity and a threat to it. A threat to relation with man.

In a woman who loves man as much as I do, it becomes paralyzing. The feminine and the maternal having developed protection and nourishment, not war, destruction, or revolution for the sake of new worlds. I had guilt for writing about those I loved, exposing the character of the father. Henry never weighed the consequences of his portraits. I feel them as a danger to love. Secrets. Need to disguise. The novel was born of this. If I used myself as a character it was because it was an experiment with the suitable object, as in chemistry. It is easy to work in one's own mine, to dig for oil or gold on one's own property. I never met any character but Henry capable of living out so much. The desire to know intimately drives one back into the only honest "I" who tested and lived out what it describes.

Otto Rank, in *Volonté du Bonheur.*

According to Freud, the individual is, in the deepest part of himself, acquiescent to the great laws of nature (submits to the inevitable repetitions), whereas his personal self is composed of a multitude of identifications for which the parental images serve as a base. It may be true for the majority of people, but not of the creative type whom I already described in *Art and Artist* as the failed specimen.

In this brief reference I would like to define the creative type; it is a being gifted with an aptitude to use instinctive factors, elementary ones, for an ultimately willed creation, a being apt to push the development of his power beyond identifications, beyond the mores of the superego of the parental pattern.

He is one who wishes to guide and consciously dominate this creative will into the making of a personality. The main thing is that he draws out of himself a personal ideal, selected by him, and which he seeks consciously to fulfill.

The myth of the hero proves above all that man wills. The religious myth that man must. In heroic myths, on the contrary, man himself appears as a creator, that is to say, it is his personal will which causes his responsibilities and his suffering.

Psychological reality is feeling and not thought, and it is not necessarily action, except when this action flows from emotion and is in harmony with it.

If normal, healthy, happy man is capable of accepting as truth the appearance of reality, the suffering of the neurotic does not stem from whatever may be painful in reality, but from the fact that he has arrived for a long time at the point where psychoanalysis wishes to take him, he has penetrated the illusion of the sensorial world, the falsity of so-called reality.

The enormous difference between the relationships you need, and the one you deeply want. The need is created out of an accumulation of negativities, planted by traumatic experiences: fear, doubts, anxiety, dependence, weakness in certain realms, inadequacy, incompleteness. A certain relationship can remove the fear, calm anxiety, supply a certain completion, replace a loss, fulfill an organic insufficiency, lull an insecurity, supply a substitute love.

But it may not be the love one would want if free of all these negativities. A negative element dictates the choice, much as a climbing plant seeks a wall to rest on, and prevents a positive choice.

Gonzalo remains bound to the woman who will fulfill his greater impulse towards self-destruction. There is a rebellion against the relationship you need, the one you cannot have, because of the bondage to the need. It is not, for example, being attached to the mother but to the groove, the habit of such a relationship, making its very repetition the source of familiarity. It is not that you may love your sister or a sister surrogate indefinitely, it is that whatever relationship you had with her is the one which created a groove, a habit, a familiarity which is comforting.

His autocratic ego needs her devotion, her enslavement, her faithfulness. He would prefer it if she looked like a movie star and were eighteen, but she alone plays the role his fatality requires, a love which is not discouraged by his avarice, his selfishness, his unfaithfulness. She never bores him. They play a game. She gives the correct answers. She rescues him. He does not believe in the other women, he distrusts them, distrusts young girls.

I considered Henry's work far more important than my own.

I tried to efface my creation with a sponge, to drown my creation because my concept of devotion and the roles I had to play clashed with my creative self.

I opposed creation, its sincerity and revelation, to the disguised self. Creation and revelation threaten my loves; threatened the roles my love forced me to play. In love I played a role to give each man whatever he needed or wanted at the cost of my life.

In creation I would reveal what I am, or all the truth.

I have a fear of public recognition.

Those who live for the world, as Henry does, always lose their personal, intimate life.

I told Jaeger the lamentable story of my publications.

D. H. Lawrence, published by Edward Titus a few months before his divorce, which caused him to go bankrupt. The book was but partially distributed, half lost, not sent to reviewers, and no royalties, and not even copies for myself.

Michael Fraenkel loaned me the money to print *House of Incest,* but lost interest in it when it was out and did not distribute it as he had promised. No reviews.

Lawrence Durrell backed the publication of *Winter of Artifice.* Obelisk issued it a week before the war. No distribution. No reviews.

Can Jaeger say to all this that the veil which concealed me was of my own making? Had guilt suffocated my work—does it envelop me in a fog, guide my destiny? What is fatality? *Fatalité intérieur?* Other women who produced far lesser works have gained reputations.

I thought my obscure destiny was that of greater mysteries and subtler influences.

But Jaeger smiles. Guilt. Guilt everywhere.

I did not want to rival man. Man was my brothers, younger than I, Joaquin and Thorvald. I must protect them, not outshine them. I did not want to be a man. Djuna Barnes was masculine. George Sand.

I did not want to steal man's creation, his thunder.

Creation and femininity seemed incompatible. The *aggressive* act of creation.

"Not aggressive," said Jaeger, *"active."*

I have a horror of the masculine "career" woman.

To create seemed to me such an assertion of the strongest part of me that I would no longer be able to give all those I love the feeling of their being stronger, and they would love me less.

An act of independence would be punished by desertion. I would be abandoned by all those I loved.

Men fear woman's strength. I have been deeply aware of men's weakness, the need to guard them from my strength.

I have made myself less powerful, have concealed my powers.

At the press, I make Gonzalo believe he has discovered this, he has suggested that improvement, that he is cleverer, stronger. I have concealed my abilities like an evil force that would overwhelm, hurt, or weaken others.

I have crippled myself.

Dreams of Chinese woman with bound feet.

I have bound myself spiritually.

I have associated creation with ruthlessness, absence of scruples, indifference to consequences as I see it in Henry. (His story about his father and mother, a cruel caricature.)

I see strongly creative women crush their men. I fear this. I have feared all aggressiveness, all attacks, all destruction. Above all, self-assertion.

Jaeger said: "All you are trying to do is to throw off this mother role imposed on you. You want a give-and-take relationship."

Jaeger, by being true to the woman, creating the woman in me, by her particular intuition as a woman, has penetrated truths not observed by either Allendy or Rank. The creator's guilt in me has to do with my femininity, my subjection to man.

Also with my maternal self in conflict with my creative self. A negative form of creation.

Also the content of my work is related to the demon in me, the adventure-loving, and I do feel this adventurousness a danger to my loves.

Guilt about exposing the father.

Secrets.

Need of disguises.

Fear of consequences.

Great conflict here. Division.

If only I could invent, invent other characters. Objective work which would not involve guilt. Rank said woman could not invent.

Will begin to describe others minutely. I was more at ease with myself as a character because it is easier to excavate on one's own property. I could be used for all experiences, was protean, unlimited.

When I started out with an invented character, based always on someone I knew, and then sought to expand, I found myself inside restricted forms, limited outlines, characters who could not go far enough into experience. I felt in a tight mold, and returned to my experience which I tried to transpose into other women.

But this was a misconception. You do not get rid of the self by giving it away, by annihilation. When a child is uprooted it seeks to make a center from which it cannot be uprooted. That was a safety island, but now I must relinquish this too.

Letter from Pierce Harwell:

I believe, Anaïs, that you are approaching a new discovery, not only new in the sense of your own work, but also new in the art of language itself. All utterance is magical: somewhere every hour the word is spoken that could change the earth. The failure is in our trivial intent. Our words are like the moon, only half-illuminated. The other side might mirror the galaxy. Language has become so closely identified with the intangible habits of thought, that our words and phrases have lost all their tangibility, all body, all vital flesh form, as you say.

Remy de Gourmont gave much attention to this empty condition of language, but his suggestions on the dissociation of ideas have proved themselves, I think, only artificial and very brief stimuli. The question does not concern ideas, for ideas continue to be expressed satisfactorily by the old habitual association of meaning. As a matter of fact, the field of ideas is so limited that the thirty or forty possible basic ideas had all been completely expressed before the dissolution of the Roman culture.

But, though the gamut of ideas is limited to the mind, the infinite scale of sensation is not limited to the body. There is a spiritus in us that vibrates to bodily sensation: the nerves of God begin where ours end. If language can attain to a new substance, a new rhythm, a more fleshly impact upon the very skin of the mind, if it can by-pass the empty center of thought and permeate like tone the integument and firm tissues of consciousness, then what an instrument it would become! What an orchestral experience for the soul, perhaps even surpassing music, for it would remain in the consciousness while music is volatile and its substance is gone almost in the instant of its appearance. Music is such a high experience because the vibrations of sound envelop us all at once. The consciousness of sensation is not auditory alone, but the surge of the sound waves breaks like a tingling surf against the responsive of our hair, our hands, our throats, our lips, our eyes. We should listen naked to music, with our pores, the littlest lanugo, the soles of our feet. Language, by its very nature, cannot do this unless it is recited, but then the vibrations of the human voice change it into a kind of music.

Written language, to obtain that effect, should enter the brain and explode like a rocket sending showers of palpable, scintillating meanings down through every fiber and to the terminal delta of every nerve. It should envelop us from the inside out, as music envelops us from the outside in.

I am tremendously interested in this new path you are following, for if there is anyone who is perfectly fitted for this artistic pioneering, it is you. Your chart is like a wellspring of clarity. You can go as far afield as you wish without risking complete loss of meaning. This crystalline guarantee will redeem your values when others have fallen into turgid bankruptcy.

The role of woman will be extremely crucial. Tomorrow's woman bears the burden of redeeming mankind's emotions. Out of herself she must create the new harmonies of joy, the new faculty of emotional counterpoint.

As human beings we are rapidly losing our capacity for real feeling. We are growing cold and insensate even as we draw closer together. It requires a more intense shock to move us than it ever required before.

The young see everything as it is, and therefore they see nothing. They feel everything exactly in its proper relation to practicality, and therefore they feel nothing. The Arian age, its end, was not marked by the loss of feeling as ours is, but by the loss of direction and social purpose. The responsibility of tomorrow's woman is to re-educate the human heart. We await the coming of Superman as the pre-Christian cultures awaited the Messiah. But, if women do not take upon themselves the birthing of a new spirit of poetry and gentleness and joyousness of life, Superman, when he comes, will be little more than a Marxian gorilla, a powerful robot with a battery for a heart and a radio tube for a brain. Your own birth chart is a prophecy of what woman can become in the salvation of the Piscean age. If your spirit of life could somehow be transfused into women all over the world, the gloomy patterns of history would break and the satanic circle of necessity would change into an ascending spiral.

You ask about myself. About three years ago my real life ended, and with it I destroyed everything I had written, all the music I had composed, even every letter I ever received. It took two days to burn everything in the trash incinerator. Until recently I had not so much as written a postcard.

But since Henry sent me your birthday I seem to have broken out in a red rash of writing. I even surprised myself with a sonnet the other day when I finished reading *Black Spring*. That seems like the last straw. If I'm not careful I'm liable to come back to life again, which would only be to return to the realm of pain and restlessness and frustration. I suffer from supersensitivity. I am almost like a seismograph. One slight tremor a thousand miles away tears me up like an egg beater.

Almost the only music I can bear to hear is pre-eighteenth-century music because the intervals of the fourth and fifth sound to me like tremendous discords. And the diminished or the dominant seventh nearly knocks my teeth out. Other people seem to be calloused against these sensations. The mere touch of a finger tip sends me into a whirl. I can tell you it is just as bad to be too sensitive as it is to be too insensitive. If only I could distribute some of my feelings to a few of the hard-boiled eggs in the world. It might do wonders for both myself and them. My prison is my sensitivity.

Friday morning I went to Jaeger with all my notes on creation. My material is novel, and in a sense adds to an unsolved problem. Jaeger is concerned with this. It was more than analysis, I feel we are beginning to create together. She is my guide, but I can see that I am a good subject. I feel elated and strong because something is being created, and I feel something is being discovered which baffled men analysts. Rank always admitted that man-made psychology might not apply to woman. He honestly threw up his hands at Jaeger's problems.

What I consider my weaknesses are feminine traits: incapacity to destroy, ineffectualness in battle.

"I am the same," said Jaeger.

It is strange and wonderful that the analysis was conducted this time by way of the emotions. It was her feminine compassion, her feminine intuition which discovered the maternal complex, and the conflict before creation.

I represent, for other women too, the one who wanted to create with, by, and through her femininity.

I am a good subject because I have lived out everything, and because contrary to most creative women of our time I have not imitated man, or become man.

It is the creative self which will rescue me. Constitutionally I am more or less doomed to suffer, and I have had little relief from anxiety and doubts, but the displacement is taking place harmoniously and I am entering a larger realm.

Jaeger quoted the legend of the woman who was ordered to cross the river and would not, because she did not want to leave love behind. But when she finally crossed she found love on the other side. I brought up the fear of disconnection and solitude.

The evolution of woman. I am living it and suffering it for all women. I have loved as woman loves.

The process which takes place with Jaeger is one of flights into great depths and discoveries. She is helped by my articulateness, I am guided by her objectivity. She is inspired by the richness of my material, I am calmed and strengthened by her clairvoyance.

I have truly been inundated three times by my unconscious. Three times Atlantis sank, but each time psychoanalysis saved me from catastrophe.

Pierce Harwell writes me:

Your words are little clay pellets with hieroglyphs on all sides, on top and bottom. Their meanings are not philologistic, but telepathic and cumulative.

Analysis has to do with flow. I am flowing again.

Giraudoux (like me) cannot finish his stories with categorical resolutions. Being suspended in infinity, there is no end to them. They vanish in smoke, because they never end. So should Moricand remain suspended, and Jean.

Letter to Henry:

Today I received your gift. I didn't want you to send so much—you
may need it. I did two things with it, I took my radio out of the repair
shop, and I bought paper to print my short stories on. When I finish
the book for Caresse, I will print the stories. When you wrote me what
Dudley said, I felt sad and ironic. Yes, I was wonderful, he said, wonderful enough to use, to take from, to feed on. His rich nature demanded
freedom to be an artist, but at the cost of mine. He helped to cause the
collapse.

Pierre de Lanux, who talks like Giraudoux, like Cocteau, Saint-
John Perse and Louise de Vilmorin, says to me: "Wake up, and start
writing in French. The French language has many levels of meaning which can never be rendered in English. English is one-dimensional."

"I don't feel that. I feel it was used in that flat, one-dimensional
way, but it can say everything."

Martha Jaeger admits that it is sometimes difficult to tell the difference between masochism and the natural suffering that life demanded from whoever wanted to give birth to children or a work
of art.

But I am learning the difference between guilt suffering and real
suffering due to normal, inevitable causes (illness, war, separation).
I have learned the difference between human tragedies and those
caused by a guilt-ridden soul seeking atonement.

Blanche is a beautiful Negro girl who wants to be as white as her
name. She is a hostess in Harlem, is taken up by society, corrupted
by them. So now she knows nothing about jazz, she thinks *Native
Son* too depressing, she sprinkles her talk with names, social events,
charity affairs. She has disguised her soul in white robes. Poor lost
Blanche. She prefers to wear a hat to conceal her own lovely black
hair. Every word she utters is a repudiation of the blackness, a
denial of the dark Blanche. Blanche *à la chaux*, renegade of her
lovely blackness, the enemy of her black self, of her night self. Paro-
dying the snobs, the socialites. Insipid and diluted by her aspiration

to erase her heritage. Betrayer, intent on her artificial, acquired manners. Snobbish. Oh, Blanche, of the lovely, sensitive hands wrapped in white gloves, of the powdered face, of the restrained laughter, demanding that a doorman with an umbrella run across a half block in gentle rain, to bring her a taxi.

Anaïs, rise to the surface. Dress up. Go and take a look at the surface world. Meet the world which glitters. Go to a cocktail party at Colette's.

There is Genevieve Tabouis, who looks like a gentle, white-haired grandmother you would confide affairs of state to, any secrets at all. Felix Rosen the banker, Mary Frost the art critic, Louis Jacques Daunou, of *La Victoire*. Later, Colonel Isham, the very symbol of the man of the world, suave, subtle, formal, distinguished, enchanting, with a fund of marvelous stories told expertly. There is Elsa Schiaparelli.

All of it shines, the dresses, the furniture, the glasses, the silver, the ice, the satins, damasks, but you must not look within. Pandora's box. Attention. To distill pleasure you must accept the *feux d'artifice*.

Aptly enough we talked about GOLD. Caresse's gold mines, Caresse's gold sun-worshiping ring from the tomb of Tutankhamen, the gold treasures in southern Ireland, hidden from the invaders and now being rediscovered. The Irish who first discovered it threw it away, saying, "It is the gold wheel from the chariot of the devil." It was later rescued by a museum treasure-seeker.

I talked about the gold stories of Lake Titicaca, the chain which surrounded the lake sunk before the Spanish invaders and never found. Caresse had gold suns inserted in the cover of her Black Sun book of Harry Crosby. The gold woven into Indian saris, the gold of Bangkok temples, the gold of minarets. Each one of us had a gold story.

I wanted Caresse and Colonel Isham to meet. I thought they would fall in love. He was a man who would have had as adventurous and interesting a life as her own. Colonel Isham was certainly suitable. They could sit by the fireside and exchange stories endlessly, and never bore each other. He had been the friend of

T. E. Lawrence, and T. E. Lawrence had read Caresse's poems in his tent and had once written her a letter. They had known the same friends, the same places, the same hotels, tents, boats, castles, towers, windmills, and read the same books, heard the same music. He was a collector of Boswell's papers, an Intelligence Service man, a war hero. His stories, touched with fantasy, appealed to her airiness.

Caresse was delighted with the colonel. But the colonel was silent. The two tired adventurers did not decide to rest together by the fireside. Colonel Isham thought her charming, but she reminded him of his first wife, who made him suffer a great deal and who was unfaithful to him. Caresse was delighted to think that Colonel Isham would run away from her power, be afraid of her, she was delighted and flattered. She ended by saying laughingly, "And do you know, I think he is right. I am sure I would have been unfaithful to him." So there was Colonel Isham, already won, married, betrayed, a sufficient victory to satisfy any woman.

Evelyn and Milton Gendel are youthful and breezy. They have a big, high-ceilinged apartment on Washington Square, top floor. It is almost empty except for paintings. They keep open house for all the artists, tirelessly hospitable.

Almost every week we meet there: Lipchitz and his wife, Paul Goodman, Matta, Pajarita, Noguchi, Kay and Yves Tanguy, Moira, André Breton. It is informal and casual. They call up. We come. But I will never know them any better, nor why they want us there. It is our favorite salon because it is roomy, vast, casual, nonchalant. No one fusses over you. You can come and go.

There is Kiesler, kissing hands, Kay Boyle, reserved, George Barker, explosive, Zadkine, joyous. One night, I met Laurence Vail, who had an exhibition of his decorated bottles, made of collages, wax, etc. Moira, who only heard that he collected bottles, asked him: "Oh, you collect bottles. What do you do with them?"

"Oh," said Vail, "I make myself very small, I enter the bottles, and then *je fais des collages.*"

"I will show you my Arab bottles," said Moira. "They have very long, tall, narrow necks."

"From these bottles," I said, "you'll never escape."

"Enough! Enough!" said Vail. "This is a bottleneck!"

One night, after hearing a John Cage concert, we all gave an imitation of it, with pots, pans, water-filled glasses, paper and tin.

Milton Gendel and Evelyn asked us if we would all come with crayons and paint their large table as Robert painted my benches. So each one of us painted a fragment. Catherine and John, Moira, Milton himself, and I.

I met Peter Blume, a vulgar, red-haired lion, who painted that surrealist painting of a huge Mussolini head, and a city wallowing in war and torture, with earthquake fissures cracking open, disaster, hangings, fires.

[March, 1943]

At Canada Lee's. A big apartment on the river. When I first hear his warm voice say "Come in! Come in! Hang your coat," I feel emotionally moved. I seem to hear for the first time, since I have come from Europe, a warm voice which means what it says wholeheartedly. Wholeheartedly. "Come in!" The place is crowded. Half white, half black. People from the theater. Left intellectuals. Artists, doctors, sculptors, architects. Warm, cordial, natural, spontaneous. Here I feel at home. There is talk, laughter, and a physical tenderness. People embrace, they touch each other. It is a climate of warmth and humanity. No deadpan faces, no silence, no closed faces. Handshakes are meaningful, sincere, faces open, there is much laughter, vibrations, flow, humor.

In a corner sat a Negro who seemed carved of wood. So definite his features, his stiff, straight grey hair cut like a brush, his lean, rigid figure. A voodoo figure, imposing. I talked with him. He began to tell me a story:

When I was a young man in Haiti, I participated in a revolution, was caught, condemned and sent to Guiana. I was tied by a chain to another prisoner. The heat and dampness were unendurable. The guards were sadistic. It was the same place, the same conditions as in the days of Dreyfus. I was seventeen and condemned for life. We worked at our escape for two years. We planned it well. We found ourselves in deep jungle, miles from the sea, where friends awaited us with a boat. We fed on fruit, and slept in caves, and inside of dead trees. We were bitten by insects. The chain binding our two arms made walking difficult. We had no way to cut this chain. It was too heavy to wear down by scraping against a stone. We tried that every night. On the third day, my companion drank polluted water, on the fourth day he died. And I was chained to a dead man! I freed myself by cutting his arm off at the shoulder with a small knife. But I had to carry with me his dead arm, covered with ants, all the way to the boat.

I finally made it to France. I learned how to cut fur in France, worked for the *couturiers*. Came to America. Have you met my daughters?

He introduced me first to Josephine Premice, who is about sixteen, lively, humorous, impudent, with a turned-up saucy nose and contagious laughter. Her sister Adele quieter, gentle, self-effacing. Canada was a generous, warmhearted host. He seemed to be whipping up excitement and expansiveness, creating a sumptuous creamy evening. His warm voice immersed you, his warm hand led you here and there, linking people, fusing them.

We found a café, the Bistro, on Eighth Street, below street level. We decided to meet there evenings. The Italian patron served an inexpensive white wine. There was sawdust on the floor, plain tables, baroque Italian woodwork, artificial flowers, faded and dusty, a fat bar man.

Great animation. Stuart Davis, Sam Cootes, Marie de Rothschild, the Rattners, Peter Blume, Frances Brown, Louise Varèse. The evening began wonderfully. We had found our café life. We felt intimate and expansive. All went well until one of the painters turned on the radio to hear the baseball game. Fini café life, fini.

George Davis invited Richard Wright to stay in his house in Brooklyn. An amazing house, like some of the houses in Belgium, the north of France, or Austria. He filled it with old American furniture, oil lamps, brass beds, little coffee tables, old drapes, copper lamps, old cupboards, heavy dining tables of oak, lace doilies, grandfather clocks. It is like a museum of Americana, which I had never seen anywhere.

Many people stay there, live there. W. H. Auden. Carson McCullers. George Davis is like an overgrown child, soft, round face, smile, occasionally cynical. He was born in February. So was Auden, so was Carson, and so I call it the "February house."

When I came to visit we sat in the back yard. Carson came in. George had told me she wanted to meet me. I saw a girl so tall and so lanky I first thought it was a boy. Her hair was short, she wore a cyclist's cap, tennis shoes, pants. She came in and pushed through the group like a bull with its head down, looking at no one, not saying a word. I was so put off by her muteness, and by her not even looking at me, that I did not even try to talk with her. I did feel that *Reflections in a Golden Eye* owed a great deal to D. H. Lawrence, and was overpraised, but considering her age it was a feat.

But I am fully aware now that people do not judge literature objectively, as a work of art. A book is judged almost entirely by a person's need, and what people respond to is either a reflection of themselves, a multiple mirror, or an elucidation of their time, a concern with their problems, fears, or a familiar atmosphere which is reassuring by its familiarity.

The kind of reading I did, to transcend my own life, to reach new lands, new boundaries, new relationships, to live other lives and other selves, I do not see around me. Or the other kind of reading I do, which is like listening to music for its quality of expression, beauty, perfection, virtuosity, I do not see around me either. An apt, accurate, perfectly carved phrase can give me the pleasure of a perfect harmony. There is more narcissism here in America than in Europe, here where the SELF is banished from conscious talk and admission, perhaps just because of that. We led individual lives and were concerned with individual growth, admittedly so. Part of this growth was expansion of the self and relation to the unfamiliar.

In the different quality of the pity I feel, in the different way events affect me now, in the new freedom from suffering, I felt that something had changed deeply. It was as if some core of the self where pain is lodged had dissolved. Some core has dissolved which made the love and pity greater but less personal. I asked myself: "I do not feel in the same way as before. Yet I can't say I am not feeling, or dead, or indifferent. It is myself I no longer feel."

Suddenly I realized the meaning of my "wheel dream." I had seen a very large wheel turning and I was afraid it would crush me. But as it turned I found that I was one of the spokes, turning with it. The ego has died, and with that suffering. It is the ego that suffers, that is vulnerable.

Intense work on Caresse's book. Two days before the end. Finished printing *Misfortunes of the Immortals*.

I would like to be writing. I have stories to tell. Story of Moira's inflation following analysis. Plans for her birthday party.

I gave a party for the Premices, Albert Mangones, Olga, Moira, George Davis, Evelyn and Milton, Lionel Durant, Charles Duits, Gerald Sykes, Ellen and Richard Wright.

The party was a dream, a dream of Haiti. Premice and his voodoo face, long and very dark, austere even, with his hair standing straight up as if he were carved of wood, a mask. His two daughters, Adele and Josephine. Josephine is an inspired dancer, abandoned, savage and violent in her gestures. Adele is sedate and learned. Immediately they show affection.

I respond with all my warmth. Albert Mangones is almost white (his mother was Spanish), an ivory white, with softly waved hair, soft burning eyes, a soft voice. He has just won the gold medal for architecture at Cornell. He plays the drums and sings. He is well educated and refined. He sang while he drummed, and Josephine danced. Olga was effervescent, finally boiled over, and read a Russian poem with all the color and drama of an actress. Then she recited a scene from a Russian play, showing extremes of comedy and tragedy, making us laugh and weep without our understanding the words. All fire and effulgence.

Canada Lee was enamored of all the women at once. Evelyn's sea-shell skin looked translucent, Moira looked medieval in a *robe de style* of black velvet and a bit of crystal pasted between her eyes like a maharani. Catherine was the English beauty, with her long gold hair, worn loose and flying as she danced, and John sad, dreamy, and caressing.

All this was infused with the colors of the windows, my modern cathedral windows, by the colors of the candles, of the painted wooden boxes and benches, the sea shells and my collection of shoes from all over the world, by the two lanterns on the feast table from Spain, a glittering glowing evening born of the incubation of many dreams, the wine of many desires.

We sat in circles on the floor. Albert told the story of the moving trees. The trees take advantage of the night, to change places. Children often stay awake all night to see if they can catch them moving. Plants, flowers, bushes, trees, animals, fish, insects, all have personalities and individual characteristics, and are inhabited by different spirits. There are always the evil ones and the good ones. There are the plants which kill and those which save life. There is always the idea of sacrifice, of offerings to the spirits. They believe in zombies. These are the dead which are ordered back to life to serve as slaves. They obey mutely and blindly.

I wanted to know how this came about. Was the zombie a relative, an enemy, or someone who deserved such punishment? Was he black or white? A zombie, I found, could not be described. He was simply a man whose soul had left him. There was only the body left. This body obeyed his master.

"Would he kill?" I asked. "Is it hypnosis? Is it a drug?"

When you question a mystery, then all the Haitians, even Albert, with four years of college, fall silent.

A hot night. We took off our shoes, we danced.

The porch was dark and cool. The lights low. Gerald Sykes' companion kept her hat on, and it was humorously incongruous, this hat in the middle of shoeless, relaxed Haitians, with their white shirts open at the neck, no ties, no coats.

I grew lighter and gayer.

"There is an innocence in them," said Frances.

Catherine, shaking her mane of gold hair, prancing and rearing rather than dancing, masculine, muscular and spontaneous, with a strong voice and an anxious soul. She was analyzed by Jung, by many others, unsuccessfully. She went of her own will into an asylum in Paris. She broke away from a wealthy middle-class family, and delights in saying *"merde!"* at parties. She suffers from sexual hysteria. After years of puritanism, she never has enough men. She is one of the only genuine cases of nymphomania I have ever known. She begged the doctors to operate on her, to deprive her of her feminine attributes.

John's sadness is now explained. He is faithful, loyal, he is there to console, to shelter, to help her. He never judges her. He is quiet, retiring. He has a dolorous face, his manners are gentle. He has intensely blue eyes, a lunar skin, beautiful teeth, a sensual-emotional expression. He is her feminine soul. She is the male. They live in the Village in great poverty. Her pottery is beautiful. It has an incandescence which I have seen only in Egyptian pottery at the museum.

I see the mutual seduction between them, I see the currents that pass between his body and hers, between his black hair and her light hair, between his big fingers and her slender ones, between his small child mouth and her full one, between his laxness and her tenseness, between his laziness and her activity, between his deep emotional awareness and hers. They are both throbbing before they even touch each other, they seek a proof of it, they ascertain it, his hand seeks the fountain of pulsations, and they are inundated in pleasure.

Why does a gesture, a walk stir your blood? What a mystery this is, desire. The love sickness, the sensitivity, the obsession, the flutter of the heart, the ebb and flow of the blood. There is no drug and no alcohol to equal it.

[May, 1943]

A vernissage for the Max Ernst book.

The book we had printed was admired. André Breton, Peggy Guggenheim, Sydney Janis, James Johnson Sweeney, Pegine Vail, José Maria Sert and his wife, Olga and her husband, Frances Brown, Fritz Bultman, the Gendels, Carol Janeway, Zadkine, Albert Mangones.

Mangones invited us to his studio for dinner. He invited my Haitian friends, too. Mangones is twenty-six. He could easily pass for a Spaniard, or a Cuban, but he does not deny his African father. His skin is the color of coffee with much milk and a touch of gold. His mouth is full, soft and sensuous. His hair dark and softly waved. He is gay, sincere, natural. He looks made for pleasure, but he is planning to return to Haiti to build low-income housing.

We danced, ate our Italian dinner. Albert and Josephine sang, played the drums.

The next day Albert came to visit the press. Then we walked around the corner to visit Catherine's pottery studio, and with her we went to Albert's studio, where he showed us his sculptures. He wanted an opinion of his work and we took one of the realistic statuettes to Lipchitz.

To hear them talk together was fascinating. Lipchitz all intellect, abstractions, theories. Albert receptive, understanding, responding to the vision of Lipchitz, but not with an obsessionally overdeveloped mind, fusing mind and flesh, instinct and thought into an integrated balance. Lipchitz seemed like a monstrous excrescence of premeditation, calculation, theory. Albert poised, never leaping into a void of geometric abstractions, pulling back towards nature.

No one has described fully the horror of this illness called anxiety. Worse than any physical illness, this illness of the soul, for it is insidious, elusive, and arouses no pity. You have just been caressed. You are walking into a summer day. No great catastrophe threatens you.

You are not tragically struck down by a fatal disease, the death of a loved one at war. There is no visible enemy, no real tragedy, no hospital, no cemetery, no mortuary, no criminal court, no crime, no horror. There is nothing.

You are crossing a street. The automobile does not strike you down. It is not you who are inside the ambulance being taken to St. Vincent's Hospital. It is not you whose mother died. Not you whose brother went to war and was killed. In all the registers of catastrophe your name does not appear. You were not attacked, raped, mutilated. You were not kidnaped. You were not on the clipper which sank into the sea with twenty passengers. You were not in a concentration camp, not on the refugee ship which was not permitted to land anywhere. You were not jailed in Spain, your family was not tortured by Franco. None of that.

But as you cross the street the wind lifts the dirt and before it touches your face you feel as if all these horrors had happened to you, you feel the nameless anxiety, the shrinking of the heart, the asphyxiation, the suffocation of pain, the horror of the soul being stabbed. Invisible drama. Every other illness is understood, shared with other human beings. Not this one. It is mysterious and solitary, it is as ineffectual and unmoving to others as the attempted crying out of a mute person.

Everybody understands hunger, physical pain, illness, poverty, slavery. But no one understands that this moment at which I crossed the street is more annihilating than a concrete catastrophe. Anxiety is a woman screaming without a voice, out of a nightmare.

Could it come from a participation, an empathy with what is happening to others? Is it the only link we have with the fate of other human beings? If it is unrelated to your life, must it come as vibrations from the lives of others? If it gives you happiness only to corrode it with a poison which denies this happiness, then must it be born of the ordeals of others? Must it be part of one's brotherhood with others?

Dream of paradise: I landed like a bird on an island, the sea was golden, and warm, the sand silky, the light dazzling. The tropical sunlight whose sparks enter the head through the eyes, like fireworks.

Ladies and Gentlemen: Just because I started in the opposite direction from the general run of adventurers, that is, I started with tragedies, not comedies, with the difficult and not the facile, it does not mean that having lived deeply and tragically I will not be able to entertain you further with more and more enticing stories of seductions, abductions and deductions. I have many surprises for you, many enchanting adventures yet to come.

I am still in quest of the lost games of Paris, of pleasure. I went to the Haitian Fiesta.

A large hall, two bands of Haitian musicians. I met the Haitian poet Jean Brièrre, who looks like a Hindu prince, straight fine nose, classical features, sleek, and slim and stylized, standing firm and proud. I danced with Albert, and other Haitians. Josephine performed her voodoo dances. Canada Lee arrived at midnight. A climate of utter gaiety and warmth. Warmth and tenderness. Premice made a speech. "I am not an intellectual."

Fanatic eyes. A noble race. They do not have the wide African nostrils, they look like Hindus. They dance like the waves of the sea, boneless, but never vulgar. They have Spanish, Indian, Oriental blood. The older people sit on chairs on the side. They are dressed very formally, with long dresses and evening suits. They wear gloves. They danced a minuet with dignity. There is a humorous decorum. The young wear hats, carry umbrellas and gloves. They make flowery speeches, straight from sixteenth-century France.

Canada Lee asked me when I would come to see him. He is still acting in *Native Son*, and is only free Monday evenings. I promised to come.

When I arrived, five or six persons were cooking spaghetti. A drunken visitor was making a political tirade. A young red-haired actress was studying her part. Canada and a Jewish boy started a political argument.

I tried to make friends with the actress but she was hostile. I suddenly realized she was jealous. I tried to reassure her. Every time Canada put his arm around me, she watched him.

The telephone rang. Canada and I went into the bedroom to answer it. It was for the actress. I had just been saying to Canada: "I think I should leave and come another time."

When she came into the bedroom to answer the telephone, she was in a turmoil.

"I'm leaving," I said, putting on my coat.

"No," said she, "I'm leaving." She went off tempestuously.

Canada and I sat talking together while the others continued a heated political argument. I heard a noise outside the window. Canada had his arm around me. Someone was walking on the terrace. He laughed. I saw he had no fear.

"What is it?" I asked.

"It's the actress," he said, "she just went out and stepped onto the terrace." This time I buttoned my coat and left.

All through my life I have been unable to cause other women the slightest pain or pang of jealousy. It is as if I were always reliving the pain of my mother suffering from my father's infidelities.

[June, 1943]

Albert, his girl, Olga and her husband, the Premices, all of us went to George Davis's house to serenade Richard Wright. We went like troubadours, carrying drums. We gave him an evening of singing, dancing, drumming, with a flavor of Russia, Haiti, Yugoslavia, Spain, France.

Richard Wright is handsome, quiet, simple, direct. His speech is beautiful, modulated and smooth. His ideas clear.

Albert is the image of joy, beauty, and nature. He is the sea, the island, the tropical dream, languor, softness, siestas, hammocks, the sun, dance, song, drum.

George Davis, whether because of his own reserve, or his destiny, seemed always to remain eclipsed, the host, the protector, the recluse, although he had written an interesting book, had been an editor, and everyone knew him. When *Time* magazine wrote up his house in Brooklyn, so often filled with famous personages, they left out his name. He was one of the invisible ones. I have known many. Is it that they chose invisibility? Or that their wavelengths were too subtle, too indirect, acting upon others but never identified, never even thanked. It has nothing to do with talent or gifts.

Albert, Josephine, and I went to the Blue Angel to introduce Josephine at an audition. Albert drummed for Josephine. While she was dressing, Albert and I sat at the bar.

With all the island gentleness, the indolent movements of his body, he still has the erect proud carriage of the Haitians. They live, even in New York, a kind of tribal life. When I invite Josephine and Adele for dinner, six or seven come with them. They move in groups, stay in groups. Close to the families, and close to each other. You never see one alone. They are always on their way to an evening together, always with the drums, the songs, the storytelling. The mind is quiet. It is the island life, the life of the senses. Dances, parties, trips.

Jean Brièrre is not like that. He is tense and nervous. His black, fiery glance is more like a stab than a glance. The women so beautiful and desirable, bodies joyous and flowering. A refined sensuality. Emotion. Subtlety.

Both Albert and Jean must return to Haiti or be drafted.

At the Premices' house in Brooklyn, generous hospitality. Joyousness and naïveté. The mother works in a factory that makes stuffed animals. She brings some of the failed ones home. She comes home and starts cooking, quietly and without nervousness. And music, always music.

Jean Brièrre came to visit the press. In a black suit, with a hat, an umbrella, and gloves.

He presented me with a poem, and then sat on the edge of a chair.

He spent fifteen months in jail for revolutionary activities. He looks somber, smiles rarely. He has a finely chiseled face, the close short Negro hair, a fine straight nose, a full but not exaggerated mouth.

Albert is his opposite. He is tender like his island, tranquil like his island, vibrant like his plants.

Jean talks in a literary way. À la Baudelaire, à la Verlaine. He recites. But in their presence one feels like a woman, a desirable woman. There is a constant magnetism and seduction, a mutual responsiveness. The atmosphere is charged with responsiveness. How far I am from the dead evenings of other groups.

Olga objected to so much music and gaiety. She said that the Haitian music prevented talk, and that we must not yield to the primitive forms of expression like music and dancing but must bring our own expression, talk, to them so as to get to know and understand each other.

"My dear Olga," I said, "there are many ways to understand and to know others, and it is not only by music, dancing or talking but more importantly, by loving. Music and dancing create more intimacy than talk."

She insisted on seeing Richard Wright without the troubadours. I was not certain how Richard Wright felt about our last evening, so I yielded to her. But when Richard Wright found out the Haitians were not coming, he was disappointed. His disappointment made me aware of mine, of my own detachment from talk and cerebral activity.

Richard Wright is dignified and sensitive. We sat on the porch. Olga talked overwhelmingly, incessantly, and I remembered Albert saying: *"Elle me fatigue."* Wright's wife, Ellen, is a handsome, quiet, warm Jewish girl. The evening was lovely.

Wright admired the idea of the press, thought it was courageous. He is unhappy in America and dreams of Europe. Spoke of the void in which the American writer is born, with nothing to support or nourish him. And how this void later becomes a real danger, an aggressive threat. How the response to his *Native Son* was mostly a cheer, such as is given to a baseball player. He objected to a phrase by a critic: "Richard Wright hit the jack pot!"

"What kind of response is that," he said bitterly.

He also talked against the New York hostesses who were so willing to invite him when he became successful, a best seller, but who objected to the friends he brought, who hesitated when he appeared at the door with an unknown, unsuccessful friend.

He has finely shaped hands.

When he and Ellen left, George Davis talked about their problem. When he invited them to live in his house, there were difficulties with the neighbors. His superintendent, a faithful Negro who had tended the furnace, resigned because he would not tend a furnace for another Negro. The Negro's condemnation of Richard's marriage to a white woman.

Rent at the press four months overdue.

The vision of Haitian way of life has made my life drab by contrast. The highly artificial evenings at the Bernard Reises, for all the famous artists. The drabness of my artist friends' lives in cold-water flats. The absence of beauty, music and nature. Too much talk, dear Olga, too much talk, hollow words, words, words.

I took the Haitians into my devastated life and into my diary as one places fragrant flowers in a book, my life blossoming anew because of them. Singing, drumming, without savagery or harshness they came, soft like their songs, tender like their climate, tranquil like their islands, vibrant like their plants, rich like their earth, to keep their innocence and luminousness.

I gave them only the perfume of my suffering, for there is a suffering that can bear a perfume, a fragrance of the soul, there is a suffering that is without bitterness, which can give birth to a deeper knowledge of joy, to a deeper reception of joy, to a deeper love for all.

In each moment of joy there was a magnetic miracle of love that knows the beauty of what it loves, knows it deeply for all its deprivations, for all its denials, for all its openness to pain. There are so many to love. A full rich world. New worlds, new lands, new souls.

The Haitians, Albert the image of joy. Hair which has not been dampened by nightmares and insomnia, which curls dry as leaves, eyes which have not wept, a mouth which has not known bitterness, teeth which have not gnashed in anxiety.

Flesh never poisoned by sorrow, sex pure and strong. Nerves that never knotted and tangled, rhythms that were never broken, a voice that was never wounded, flesh that was never stabbed, lungs that were never suffocated. Because they take their nourishment from the sun and plants, their pleasures from the body, from music and dancing. No darkness, no moonless nights, and their gift to me was an assurance that such joys exist, can be attained.

Gonzalo is designing a beautiful book for *Under a Glass Bell.*

Frances has the clearest insight of all. Like a diamond. She has an acute clairvoyance, arrowlike, penetrating, uncanny. The day she first came with the Cooneys I loved her, felt the beauty of her intelligence and comprehension. I poured my passionate life upon her, gave her the diaries to read. We exchanged lives. But hers had been less tumultuous, less varied.

To her I must have seemed a kind of June, living by impulses and chaos. She could see beyond appearances of people and experiences and clarify them. She could guide me. And on the other hand, I am sure, when she was up again and began to live, I inspired her. She dressed for me. I found her beautiful. I carried her along into my life, swept her into my activities. We could rush into activity and then sit quietly unraveling it. What gifts we made to each other. A climate of intuition. Dreams, analysis. In her own dreams, I played the rescuer. But I trusted her mind, her objectivity.

Siegfried arrives, sunburnt, with his brilliant smile and his chanting voice. He is now working in a defense plant, his operatic career postponed. He showed me an apartment he wanted to rent, in a dead-end street. I took him to the press and showed him the book being printed.

We sat on a park bench in Washington Square, watching the old Italians playing chess. As usual, he was both clownish and playful, serious and dreamy.

What I liked about the apartment he was going to take was the tree, a tree which almost grew into the room. It filled the window space, and made the apartment seem to be a tree house.

A summer night. The shivering of the leaves is paradisiacal. The flight of the clouds innocent. We meet Albert and his girl walking.

I feel a real love for the Negro world. I see them in the Premices' neighborhood. I feel close to them, to their emotional sensitiveness, their sensory awareness, their beauty, the soft velvet of their eyes, the warmth of their smile, the purity of their violence. They are human.

That hatred should fall upon them is inconceivable, except when one sees that the origin of this hatred is fear and envy. What the Negro has, the white man has lost, he is diluted, without vitality and without power of sensual enjoyment.

It is the whites who are decadent, and therefore jealous, envious, dangerous to the Negro.

Witness the neurosis all around me. So much impotence. Impotence to love, to create, to enjoy, to live.

Summer nights in connivance with lovers, interchange of sun, air, wind, caresses, voices, laughter in the streets, sharing in everyone's embraces, and I moving slowly towards a dream of happiness learned from the Haitians. The fluid of happiness, from uncorrupted, flowerlike nature.

When you are sorrowful, the shivering of the leaves is a sad event, like watching a child suffering from cold. The displacement of a cloud is a tear of separation, farewell. When you are happy the shivering of leaves comes from pleasure; they, too, have been caressed.

Paul and Pierce Harwell had been corresponding about astrology. They fell in love with each other's letters. All of us loved Pierce's letters. But none of us knew what he looked like.

Then I had a dream in which I saw Pierce Harwell. He was tall, rather lean, thin, blond-reddish hair, thin features, pale-blue eyes and freckles. And it was all true.

When he rang the bell, there he was, just as I had seen him. Something of a young Dr. Caligari, the young-old, the divinator, the mediumistic, the magician, the astrologer. Huckleberry Finn and Rimbaud.

Just before coming, he had written to me:

"More light" is what Goethe meant to say. The atoms themselves are composed of light. How then, could there be more LIGHT? Yet you accomplished this miracle of which Goethe, dying, dreamed. You create more light by seeing more light.

The Bright Messenger. He brings music and air. I took him to Frances. She was charmed with his intuitions. She offered him the little guest room next to her apartment. He played a composition of his own. In Hollywood he shared the life of Henry and of John Dudley. He observed a Henry immune to suffering because, very long ago, "he got into a boat and threw anchor, mast, oars out." He felt that Henry did not understand me. He did not like Henry's essay *"Une Étre Étoilique."* "It is not Anaïs." He did not like the *Scenario.* "It is not *House of Incest.*"

Pierce sings his chaste songs of fleshless caves, illumined planets, stars as cells of the bodies, and dreams. Every time he enters a room it is to reveal mysteries and make predictions. He is illumination. Frances' richest life takes place in her dreams, long, rich, abundant, violent, vivid dreams.

He analyzes her dreams, reads her horoscope. He said of her: "She swallowed a mirror."

He has a body which does not inspire love, all bones, freckles. He has a wide cat smile which remains fixed on his face long after his eyes are not smiling. His eyes are faded, pale blue and watery. He is a reflection of spirit, a mirror, a fortuneteller.

When I took him to Frances he said: "You are a pregnant woman. You are about to give birth." Frances answered: "Perhaps I'll adopt you."

Mystically he began wooing and courting everyone. Charms, enchantments, hypnotic all-night talks.

Pierce and I walk beside the East River, through the ghetto.

Pierce experiences anxiety, too. He says that this is the shadow self, the psychic self to which catastrophes do happen, great shocks, but not apparent to the conscious self. They manifest themselves only in anxiety.

Dream of Haiti over. A farewell party for Albert. Albert singing the same songs, dancing lasciviously.

Pierce tried to nestle into our lives, to be loved by all, to enter into every home, every ménage. And failed. He wanted to talk all night, had no respect for time, or for work, or for fatigue. He drinks, he creeps into a place and stays. He began to use astrology to strike terror in all of us.

He told Frances she would die at thirty, which is the age at which her mother died and which she has always considered with fear. He made dark prophecies to me, to everyone I introduced him to, to the Imbses, to Leo Lerman, to George Davis.

Everywhere he went he found a husband, a lover, a friend who played a major role. He was always the child, the guest, not vitally needed or loved. He could not inspire desire. He wanted to be part of the family, inside the marriages, he tried to separate all of them. He tried to wreck all the bonds.

When he began to make deadly predictions to others, I told him it was a criminal thing to do, to bring out all the terrors and fears, unless he could at the same time exorcise them.

"Yes, I know," he said, "but I am unconscious at the time I do it, I am merely a medium. Afterwards, when I become conscious of the destructiveness, I feel bad and I want to be punished for it. I know people always end by hating me, by closing their doors."

"You *wish* these things to happen, Pierce. You have found no love and so you are envious of all of us."

Frances had told him: "All this comes out of *your* own unconscious."

At the same time he imagined all the women desired him. He would appear wearing only a bath towel around his waist, hoping to seduce us.

Lucas Premice is about fifty. His nose wrinkles up when he laughs. Big mouth and big teeth. Worked on ships so that he could travel. Wanderlust. He was exiled from Haiti for political activities. At thirty he landed in America, was gravely ill in a hospital, met his loyal and devoted wife, married her, fathered two daughters.

He is a tyrant. Josephine often rebels against him. He works as a fur cutter. Organized the workmen and lost his job. Talks bad French and bad English, almost unintelligible. Wanders when he talks. Has no sense of time. He is homesick for Haiti. Practices a noble and generous hospitality.

Adele is about twenty. Wears glasses and is a little heavy. She has no confidence in herself and is afraid of her father. She is self-effacing, kind, has a beautiful voice and plays the piano, but is totally eclipsed by Josephine, whose zest and aliveness are dazzling. Josephine is bright, flaming, has a beautiful body, breasts carried high, long legs, the backside almost as buoyant as the breasts. Her singing is husky, her dancing almost epileptic. She is full of humor and improvisations, mimicries. She is magnetic and flirtatious.

Invited by Olga and her husband. I arrive in Stony Brook, New York, with my hair floating loose, and Olga makes me pin it up. Her husband teases me gently about how little I know about politics. I say it is difficult for me to take an interest when I don't feel I can be of any help (the old argument). He was disillusioned.

Olga tells me about her friendship with Valentina Orlikova, the first woman captain. A beautiful girl. She became our heroine. We all wanted to look like her. We all rushed and begged for masculine evening suits to be converted into military-style suits. Identification. Love. The heroine. Olga is writing about her life. Born February twenty-second. Valentina faces death every day, separation from her husband and child.

We washed dishes, swam, sunbathed, sewed, made beds, talked of clothes. I listen to her husband. I see traces of past luxuries. Aristocracy.

Olga seeks to control her Russian, ebullient nature by her role of the chic *soignée* woman. Every little red hair in place with brilliantine. A tiny, well-ordered bay to swim in. Conventional clothes. My Bohemian life amuses her, but she lectures me. She knew Pierre Quint, who wrote an excellent book on Proust. She knew Guglielmo Ferrero. Lived a political and worldly life. She tried to dress me like a lady, to formalize my hair. I let her, as if I were a doll, knowing I would soon return to my Bohemian freedom. Olga in her tailored suits, categorical. But vulnerable, too, and responsive. She said: "You have gone deeply into all things. I deal with them more objectively."

"I love your life in action, your dramatic life. What happens to me is less extroverted, less visible, more underground."

"But my life reads like a cheap novel. Yours is deeper."

I do love her ACTION, the outward life. We are always beginning to talk. Because she proceeds cautiously into the inner life, it is not as with Frances, an immediate entrance into the underground world.

We sat under a tree, knitting, her bare arm was soft, the skin so fine. She talks about the real captain of a real ship, and I think about my symbolic guidances, guiding Henry's barque, Gonzalo's barque, so they will not sink or hurt themselves. The invisible captain, captain of Rimbaud's *Bateau Ivre!* Doomed to invisibility, and mystery, undecorated.

Valentina has a real ship, a real uniform, a real medal, a real, direct hero-worship from all. And I? I'm always in the *coulisses de l'âme.* I direct strange and ghostly battles with the unconscious.

I weary of the ghostliness of the soul's life, and wish to appear on the surface.

My telephone rings. "My mother is going to be operated on. I need a blood donor. Several blood donors." I offer myself and seek other volunteers.

Poor Captain Anaïs, deprived of the certitude of a concrete ship, a uniform, maps, technical knowledge.

In a Chinese shop I bought a Japanese paper parasol which I wear in my hair. So delicately made, with colored paper and fragile bamboo structure. It tore. I repaired it with tape.

When Samuel Goldberg took us to Chinatown for dinner I went into a shop to ask for parasols. The woman who received me was very agitated: "No, of course I don't carry those. They are Japanese. You bought them in a Chinese shop? Well, that may be, but they're Japanese just the same. Tear it up and throw it away."

I looked at the parasol in my hand, innocent and delicate, made in a moment of peace, outside of love and hatred, made by some skilled workman like a flower, lighter than love and hatred. I could not bring myself to throw it away. I folded it quietly, protectively. I folded up delicacy, peace, skill, humble work, I folded tender gardens, the fragile structure of human dreams, I folded the dream of peace, the frail paper shelter of peace, I folded innocent gardens and innocent music, innocence and the dream.

In times of war hatred confuses all things. Hatred falls upon cathedrals, paintings, and rare books, on Beethoven, Bach, Brahms, and the Japanese parasol. Hatred falls upon the innocent; children, workmen, women, dreamers, and Japanese parasols. In times of war souls are confused, I felt, as I folded the tiny Japanese parasol out of sight of hatred and revenge.

One cannot always keep time with the pulse of the world or its history, because there are small and large cycles and opposite cycles working themselves out at different times. Some are given to prepare the future, some of the truths I was given to protect because when everything will be blown away, it is a Japanese parasol which will raise its head to remind man of tenderness, peace and love, as the only antidote to poison, hatred, war.

This taste of happiness this morning on awakening. Like the miraculous new flavors of convalescence. After deep nightmares of the soul, the fever, the burn, the new dazzling appearance of the sun, new eyes, new vision, the new softness of the bedspring under a body which has recovered its aliveness, its sensory receptivity. The new taste of coffee on a feverless tongue. Floating on the cool blanket, bathing in the sun, because I had dragged my bed to the open porch last night.

A new joy which reminded me of the return to life after childbirth. I looked at the strip of sunlight turning the Venetian blind into a musical score in Venetian gold, marveling at its potency, at its power to pierce to the depths of human consciousness. When you possess light within, then you see it externally. It must have been there on other summer mornings but I did not receive it. This is the rebirth one can achieve over and over again by a revolution of the cells, a shock to the molecules, a rearrangement of the psyche by analysis. Analysis rescues the romantic.

[July, 1943]

Caresse persuaded me to go to Southampton. She found me an apartment above a plumber's house, across the street from the Old Post House, which she is managing. I have plenty of rooms, two bedrooms, sitting room, big kitchen and bathroom for the incredible sum of fifty dollars a month. The atmosphere of Southampton I don't like, it is ugly, chichi, snobbish. But I love the beach, the sun. And Caresse's friends stay at the Post, and there are many artists here.

Caresse takes me to the exclusive Beach Club, where at least there is a little beauty of decor. I sleep. Rest.

Friends. Dinners. Visitors. Hans Boeb, a German painter, Elie Aghnides, a Greek engineer, brother of the Greek Ambassador in England.

Caresse came to visit me. Charles Duits paid a few days' visit. My mother.

Matta, who drops in frequently, and I went sunbathing in the sand dunes. Charles Duits is not interested in sea or sand. He talks. He starts in the morning at breakfast. He writes intricate poems, long and complicated.

Luchita, a beautiful Chilean girl, came.

I meet other artists at the beach.

Pajarita is Matta's young wife, sweet, childlike, sensitive, silent. Matta is shocked and desperate at the idea of fatherhood. Twins! Pajarita asks me what can she say to reconcile him to the idea of fatherhood, which makes him feel old, a role he cannot, will not play.

I suggest that she tell him that having children reawakens one's own childhood and rejuvenates one, renews one, he will be rejuvenated through and by them.

Pajarita listens, as if I were Solomon. "Yes, yes. I will say that." A few days later she calls on me. "But when, exactly when should I say this to him?"

Helba, meanwhile, finds that the meat roast I sent her via Gonzalo is full of worms. I tell the butcher and he is horrified by the mad accusation, because it is impossible. It was fresh. Gonzalo said the incident sent her into a fit of madness. Worms, death. After much detective work, I realized what had happened: Gonzalo comes to visit on his bicycle. We shop together. On returning to his home, quite far away, he stopped at the beach, sat and rested. The meat was covered with ants! Charles Duits thinks this is a Dadaist story, and laughs.

Gathering strength to print *Under a Glass Bell*.

Gonzalo is terrified by women's new roles. Imagine kissing a corporal, a sniper, a captain, a welder! Imagine that! Impossible to regard them tenderly as women. Man's fear! But I say to Gonzalo (thinking of Helba): "Women are much more dangerous as thwarted wills, unfulfilled artists, frustrated mothers, perverted power-seekers, who seek to dominate indirectly, via man. Women of yesterday and their negative wills! Their will bending children, husbands, servants, gardeners, etc. Trying to fulfill themselves through others. . . ."

I would like to devote my life to the recognition of the Negro's quality, but I always feel ineffectual in political battles because it is a cynical world in which one can win only by force or trickery, and both are unnatural to me. I cannot adopt corny labels, practice the platitudes of propaganda. How can I help? I give my friendship. It is not enough. I open my home. It is not enough. When I approach one of the groups working for the Negro cause I find them talking, talking, talking, as the artists did in Paris cafés.

I cannot see the black and white drama as one of economic injustice. As a man in power enslaving a powerless primitive. I think when the first white man went to seek slaves for menial work and chose the Negro, there was a subconscious drama being played out below the practical need. He wanted to dominate his own instinctive primitive self, since the whole object of the white man's development was mastering and repudiating his primitive force, his nature.

When he invented sails, steam, electricity it was to master, enslave and prove himself a ruler over nature. When he enslaved the Negro it was to prove himself stronger than nature. And what a revenge nature wreaked upon the white man. For as he advanced into control of nature, he lost his natural vitality and power. In proportion to his mastery of the elements, he lost his other power as man; the more he invented, mechanized, made music boxes instead of playing instruments, the more impotent he grew in his body.

His senses are less keen, his muscles less enduring, his eyes less sharp, his hearing insensitive. He poured his blood into machines, bridges, and was left a robot with a brain. And meanwhile, while his humanity atrophied, his direct warm contact with human beings broken by his abstract way of life, the Negro, his slave, grew in beauty and natural strength and balance of body and mind and senses. Retained emotion. He lost none of his connection with nature, his own nature.

Before he left, Albert confided all his projects and plans. He wanted to bring back to Haiti his knowledge of architecture, all he had learned. He wanted to build inexpensive houses for peasants and workmen. He wanted to play a role in politics. And ironically, his handicap was his mixture of blood, the Spanish grandmother; he was too white, and the Haitians would not trust him wholeheartedly. His childhood sweetheart, approved by his family, was awaiting him. She had waited for all the years he was in college.

[Fall, 1943]

Return to New York. Activity. Work. Frances the most evolved of women, the most superior, a woman of wisdom, good for the altitudes.

Ideologically, what crystallized in one of our talks is the analogy between romanticism and neurosis. I see their connection. The result of both is self-destruction. I had not realized that they were synonymous. Frances made me read Denis de Rougemont's *Passion and Society*. Romanticism and neurosis destroy happiness. It is a quest for passion and intensity merely as a cure for anxiety.

"Write," says Frances.

"Come down from your stratosphere," says Olga. She feels a great uneasiness at my adventures. She cannot totally pass judgment on them because she feels some ultimate aim which she respects.

Olga tells me: "I always understood your emotions, but not your interpretation or analysis of these emotions."

"Without the second step there would be nothing learned, nothing gained," I said.

Contemplating fiction again. What happens if I leave myself out completely? Then everyone will be restored to his natural size, not mythical, not expanded, not symbolic. With me absent, and only the other characters present, I shall depict a human world, with other dimensions missing. I seem to be the conductor for an expanded vision. But my alchemy poetizes them all, translates them into myth.

I feel that the vision of others (Gonzalo's of Helba, Henry's of June, Sancho Panza's of Don Quixote, other people's vision of Gonzalo) is all limited. Nowhere can I find a limitless vision. I do not mean that mine is, but my own goes through a process of heightening by poetry, of white heat, of intensification, of an intuition of the potential which adds dimension to my characters. By themselves, swimming as it were in their own atmosphere, they seem constricted, limited, walled in.

Me absent, say, from the diary, and the fire crucible is gone in which all the lives melt and combine and produce another life. I'm the alchemist, not the ego. Every time I have written about a character to which I was unrelated, whom I did not know intimately, they seemed one-dimensional.

But I am tempted because these characters would relate to a diminished present, to the everyday present, whereas poetizing them places them in a timeless stream, and often destroys the ordinary and daily in favor of the eternal.

In maturity one has to rectify the errors made by the imagination, but the imagination also was the one which orchestrated and amplified its resonances.

I am ruminating my next book.

Theme one: There are very few human beings who receive the truth, complete and staggering, by instant illumination. Most of them acquire it fragment by fragment, on a small scale, by successive developments, cellularly, like a laborious mosaic.

Anonymous Portrait:
Because she felt insecure about her value, her appearance, it became absolutely essential for her to triumph in the smallest discussion. Every trifle became a matter of life and death. She could not bear to yield, to surrender, to be convinced, persuaded, swerved, because she considered these as defeats. She was afraid to yield to passion, to the feverish hunger of her body, and because she was so intent on controlling this larger impulse, it became essential not to yield in the small issues, as if she were constantly exercising her resistance rather than her power of surrender.

All her intensity was poured into the small battles because she had associated unconsciously the bigger resistance to the flow of life to the smaller resistance to the will of another. A difference of opinion, an affirmation, as if this were the proof of her rightness about right and wrong, in relation to taking or not taking a lover. She naturally derived no appeasement from these minor victories, because what she wanted deep down was to yield.

When one does not wish to face the darkness in one's self, one relates to the dark person who will represent this, and then one engages in a duel with that person, in place of a duel with one's own shadow self.

Some of the people I have liked have represented the dark Anaïs. The enemy is within me. Jaeger pointed out the inevitable suffering caused by idealization, dreaming, mirages, illusions. There is no happiness possible while dreaming. Jaeger has been concerned with my elusiveness. Everything I have placed outside of myself, in others. I could not bear to think I contained in myself any element of destruction. I suffered from this dark self at the hands of others. I must find this dark shadow in myself and not project onto others. I have never accepted any shadows in myself.

I feel like Don Quixote, awakening from his romanticism, a painful awakening.

Now to seize the dark Anaïs. She eludes detection. Recurrent dream of course. The diaries are burning. The dark Anaïs is locked away in the diaries. If she burns, I have no way to catch her.

"Stop fighting destructiveness in others," says Jaeger.

Josephine [Premice] and Charles Duits are so comically contrasted. Josephine all sunburn, all fire and vitality, Charles so pale, like a saint on a church window, illuminated ultramarine eyes, talking always in poetic abstractions, and yet both of them can be equally terrorized by *Dracula*. Josephine looks with wonder at Charles' eyes, at his remote expression, at his curly blond hair, disembodied Charles Duits, *poète maudit*, who refused the sea and the sun in Southampton, slept all day, and came out like a somnambulist only to ask for his dinner.

Josephine is puzzled by Charles, who is not fired by her voodoo dances. She is perplexed by this new species. But to me he is merely one of a long lineage of poets I have known; in the hierarchy and dynasty of poets, he is the palest flame of them all. I can detect his anemia. He dreams of vampires sucking blood. I held his transparent hand in mine, light and fragile, and Josephine cried out: "My God, you have no flesh at all!"

Josephine is teaching us dancing. She stretches her strong black legs and then prances like a highbred horse.

After that we sit in semidarkness, sometimes by the light of two candles, and we tell weird stories, trying to frighten each other as I did with my brothers when we were children. What terrified Josephine's childhood was the banana tree, which moved in the night like a woman waving her arms, the mapau tree of evil, which walks about at night, moving from place to place, sometimes so far one would never find it again. Josephine would stay awake to catch it moving away. She tells about the leaves one rubbed over one's arm, which caused a swelling and saved one from going to school. About the medicine a Negro took which turned him into an albino. About the voodoo priest who read your destiny in a glass of water and then ate the glass. About the voodoo magician who could place a lighted candle in water without drowning out the light. She tells about the test of fire, when the initiates must touch and hold live coals. If it burns them they are not ready, they are not believers.

Gonzalo has this gift for telling stories. The Haitians have it. And I love to tell myself stories, and I am about to write another. Stories are the only enchantment possible, for when we begin to see our suffering as a story, we are saved. It is the balm of the primitive, the way to exorcise a terrifying life.

For many days I lived without my drug, my secret vice, my diary. And then I found this: I could not bear the *loneliness*. That writing the novel about other women there were still so many things I could not give to them. I found that none of the composite characters could contain all of my experiences or awareness. That to stay within them meant a shrinking of horizons and perceptions, a restricted consciousness. I felt tight molds. I found that none of the invented characters could contain my obsession with a limitless, expanded life, its completion.

Integration. What I am experiencing now is like watching dispersed mercury magnetically gather itself into one unit. This moment is comparable to the difference between the telescope and the microscope. My wanderlust has quieted down. The near has become the marvelous. My vision, arranged to observe only the distant, focused on the immediate. I cleaned the apartment until it shone. I painted it. Fifth Avenue seemed animated, joyous. The hustle, the luxury, the rhythm were elating. I went to exhibits and looked at people as superficially as people looked at the exhibits, a passing glance. Learning to live superficially. Joy was not necessarily in the south of France, mystery in Morocco, art of storytelling in Haiti only, rhythm and music only in the Negro world, but might spring from one's own self.

I shall have to create it from within.

Letter from Henry:

I'm being offered an exhibition of my paintings here at two galleries next month. Wonder if you would care to lend me yours for the purpose, as the dealer would like to include a number of early ones. I've improved greatly in the last two months and have made many new ones, a number of which I've already sold at fairly good figures. The "open letter" I sent out brought excellent results—and then I had the good fortune to make friends with an Italian art store keeper who gave me materials, framed my pictures and exhibited them in his window. I sent you a little book the other day I thought would interest you. Hope you received it. I manage to get along. And you? How are you? Pierce Harwell gave me a lot of news, but I couldn't make head or tail of it.

Millicent's son was shot in a gang war. There is not enough blood to go around, not enough blood donors. I went up to the Harlem hospital to give blood. They turned down my "white blood." What a terrible place, with beds in the halls, overcrowded rooms. Bandages on the floor. Poor Leon breathing heavily through an oxygen mask. Millicent silently suffering.

Printed the first page of *Under a Glass Bell*.

My stories need to be placed in their light and time to be understood. They were written before the war. The fact that I describe adult fairytales, the fantasy, does not mean that I remain permanently with them.

A writer must be taken as a whole, as representative of history. No history is static and I am no longer inside this world I describe.

I want people to see the stories in relation to a changed world, as a part of their history and the history of their poets.

What emerged from the great underlying suffering, from an imperfect, unjust world was fantasy-making. The poet could not alter the suffering.

The guilt the poet has carried for working out his individual patterns and pleasures separately from the rest of the world is reflected in his anxiety and loneliness. It drove him mad, as in the story of Artaud, *"Je Suis le Plus Malade des Surréalistes,"* which is the true story of one of the best of the surrealist poets.

The loneliness of the aristocratic family drove the woman to madness.

Because the outer reality was monstrous, the poet turned to the construction of a fantasy world.

The whole duality lies between what is dreamt and what is actualized. The dreaming gives anxiety because it is lonely, ghostly, evanescent, unstable, fluid, but above all because it is lonely. No dream is shared. Reality is shared. People's dreams can be similar, as Frances' and mine are, but they do not create a human relationship by themselves. But similarities of human experience, war, birth, death, suffering, draw people together.

When Ramakrishna traveled through India, preaching ecstatically, someone cried out: "Do something for the suffering of the people." He answered: "I can do nothing." This was the position of the artist.

Reached page thirty-five of *Under a Glass Bell*. Received fifty-six subscriptions. I am printing three hundred copies.

When we are in conflict we tend to make such sharp oppositions between ideas and attitudes and get caught and entangled in what seems to be a hopeless choice, but when the neurotic ambivalence is resolved one tends to move beyond sharp differences, sharply defined boundaries and begins to see the interaction between everything, the relation between everything.

I opposed subjective to objective, imagination to realism. I thought that having gone so deeply into my own feelings and dramas I could never again reach objectivity and knowledge of others. But now I know that any experience carried out deeply to its ultimate leads you beyond yourself into a larger relation to the experience of others. If you intensify and *complete* your subjective emotions, visions, you see their relation to others' emotions. It is not a question of choosing between them, one at the cost of another, but a matter of completion, of inclusion, an encompassing, unifying, and integrating which makes maturity.

What I condemn now is not my tendency to live by my imagination, but the fact that I did not always see that when I concretized a fantasy (as for example the houseboat) it was not a single, unique, isolated experience.

To relate to others' dreams, I myself had to see that the houseboat was more than a houseboat, it had a meaning, it represented the quest for independence (between Left Bank and Right Bank), the need to imagine one's self traveling, moving in experience and not static, and that this unconscious myth had been dreamed by other men as they dream of desert islands, the heart of Africa, sailing a boat alone, etc.

By the time I write the story I am aware that this is a myth that comes from an unconscious which is not isolated, or unique, but universal. When Rousseau said he had a right to paint a sofa in the middle of the jungle, and added he had a right to paint his dreams, I might have known (but I didn't at the time) that I was living out a dream that was not mine alone. I sought detachment from a chaotic, confusing, battling world, and sought it in a houseboat.

True, I focused intensely on a few characters at first, those I knew deeply. But now I am completing the characterizations. I now see the relation of dreams to our lives (they are the key to it) and I see that to divorce them is a dangerous act.

What the surrealists did was to situate themselves within the unconscious and not relate it to action. They cut the umbilical cord. But in antique cultures the dream was a part of life itself, influenced it. Everyone was engaged in unraveling the mysterious dreams which were an indication of a psychic life.

Those who built the cathedrals or the temples of India were not unaware of people's misery but simply believed that a religious myth could make their life bearable, for they never thought this misery had a practical solution.

America set about solving this in a practical way. But it went too far. It treats art with a contempt which is equal to those who call religion "the opium of the people."

I was not traveling away from human life, I was seeking my own fulfillment. Searching for heightened moments uninterrupted by life's daily exigencies. But a human life which conformed to my dream of the moment. In order not to be distracted either in ordinary life or by ordinary life from my search and my vision I left out a great deal, I seemed not to see what was there in reality. I did have a penetration into others' lives, but I did not spread it out, dissolve and disperse it in many characters. I focused intensely on a few. It was only this focus and separateness which was wrong, not what I brought to light by this focus. A sharp searchlight leaves everything else in darkness. There is no need to oppose this intensely personal lyrical reaction to other forms of experience. They are not irrevocably opposed. They cease to be opposed (and this opposition usually causes paralysis, the inability to act, produce; it creates the frequent static moods we suffer from), when we see the relation between them. I see the relation of the dream to our action, not as separate, divorced activities. They nourish each other. What the surrealists did was to negate the relation between them, to drop one in favor of the other, to cut off the umbilical cord between the real and the imagined. Thus, they often reached artifice and insanity. In ancient people this power of relating dream and action was the secret of their strength. It is only today that we separate everything into conflicting levels and layers. A symbol of our general disintegration. What turned me away from romanticism (neurosis in modern terms) was an obsession with the far in place of the near, with the unattainable in place of the attainable.

It was young poet Duits' reading *Dracula* to frighten himself when a greater terror was taking place in Leningrad. It was the passion for the myth and distance in place of the near as yet untransformed. Romanticism became clearly synonymous with neurosis. When we confuse dreams and reality, or action and poetry.

[January, 1944]

A New Year's Eve in Harlem. The genuine joys. Joy of dancing. No drinking allowed in the Savoy Ballroom. No drinking necessary. Just good music and good dancing. We warmed ourselves to the gaiety, the vitality and humanity. People look at each other frankly, the faces are open and expressive. The voices are warm. They dance wholeheartedly, they laugh wholeheartedly. It is intoxicating. The floor seems to vibrate under so many feet. Whirling abandon to music. Surrender. We took Moira there and she loved it.

The Negro has suffered humiliation without becoming neurotic, twisted, or ugly. He has kept his sensitivity, his emotional quality, his sincerity and simplicity. He is the only one with beautiful manners, with grace, with naturalness. The movements of his body are flowing and relaxed. He has a natural grace and manner. He knows how to greet, how to wish well, how to treat others humanly.

This weaving of a pattern. It is not made by the primitive. The primitive begins each day anew and does not relate today to yesterday, or envisage tomorrow. With lack of relatedness comes absence of pain. Pain comes from awareness.

He does not suffer except at the very moment of reality, of the drama, but does not foresee it or dread it ahead of time. This understanding we wrestle from events, in a supreme effort to defeat and control our destiny, is absent in them. It is our very efforts to escape or protect ourselves from pain and shock which create a new realm of anxiety unknown to the primitive. We live to defeat nature and they learn to live with it.

In our complex battle against fatality, we succumbed to a new illness. We fought the idea of death by asserting mystical continuity, and in turn these mystical worlds caused our death ("Don't worry how much you suffer on earth, heaven is awaiting you above").

There was never any battle won. When one kind of disease is

defeated a new one appears. This suffering of the imagination we called neurosis.

America is trying a new experiment: a practical, scientific war against poverty.

But the primitive had a natural paradise. We do not. We have to create an artificial one.

Reached page sixty-four. Joy at achievement and a certainty that the stories are poetically valuable. The severe test of typesetting failed to dissolve them. The words are as pure, as unalloyed, as meaningful, after all the scrutiny, the concretization in lead. I live for days with each page. I set each word. I bind each line. I print the page over and over again, proofread it, cut it, each time I cut it I read a few lines to break the monotony of the work.

Frances is struck by my use of the key word "associations," the word by which I synthesize a development of analysis, or meditation, or observation, or the writing of a theme in the novel. Say one week it was "submission"—a world of images, ideas, and experiences is evoked. Another was "effort." Another "elusive." When one follows where they lead, a whole skein is developed (as in word association made in analysis), a vital regrouping, or new construction. You follow the Key Word like a detective's clue. Finally you draw all the threads together, it crystallizes. It is a way of avoiding the cliché structures into which our thinking falls. Sometimes ideas need to be juggled out of their somnolescent railroad-track banality.

Moira dreamed that I drowned as I leaned over a lake to fetch something for her. She stopped analysis just at the time when she was undergoing the phase of inflation. Phase of physical exhibitionism to balance the physical restraints put on her. Whatever one understands, knows the underlying cause of, one cannot judge.

Everyone should possess this knowledge. Unless you know how veiled, restrained, dominated, Moira was by her background, one cannot understand what she is undergoing now; she wears transparent blouses without bras, she arranges her garter in the street, she opens her shirtwaist almost below the breast, she flirts with everyone and anyone. She praises herself.

Opening a can of spaghetti sauce and pouring it over the spaghetti she says: "No one makes spaghetti like Moira."

The ones who have traveled too far from their primitive self must retrace their steps and find it again. Moira was created artificially by her husband. She had to discard all the acquired Moira.

I subjugated my own nature so much I had to live it through others, through Henry and through Gonzalo. I wanted so much to be an ideal person, wise and evolved, and of course I wasn't. I would not allow myself the freedom to be capricious, jealous, angry, selfish or irresponsible. I was as bound by my ideal self as Moira by her traditions. To breathe freedom I had to live close to my shadows, my primitive shadows. They lived it all out for me. Deeply, I approved them.

The first steps towards freedom are defiant and awkward. Moira is caricaturing freedom. It is her way of reaching it.

One night we went to an Arabian restaurant, downtown, in the deserted business section full of sinister buildings. Under the wing of a tall building the small, dilapidated restaurant concealed itself. Only Arabs go there. We had a gingery dinner, much wine, many new flavors and new textures. Musicians came. Moira became very gay. In a mood of expansiveness she left the table and began to dance a native dance, undulating, shaking, and quivering. The men sitting there, instead of enjoying it, stared at her with the utmost contempt and severity. One of them, dark and fierce, walked up to her and insulted her. "Whore," he said, very loud. Their glances were so murderous, she stopped in the middle of her dance and returned to our table. She was weeping. "This is the way it was at home," she said. The rest of the evening she was quiet and subdued.

Joaquin is on his way back from Cuba, where he had been drafted into the Cuban army. He is back to his professorship at Williams College.

The Graphic Arts Society became interested in our press and the work we had done. Wanted to see it. They admired *Winter of Artifice* and had considered exhibiting it. But first they wanted to visit the press.

Miss Decker and Mr. Stricker came. He was dressed meticulously, and looked severely at the dark stairs, the shabby studio, the orange-crate boxes holding supplies, the obviously Bohemian atmosphere.

I suppose he expected a perfectly appointed print shop. Gonzalo is not a disciplined, orderly worker. Mr. Stricker was startled by his appearance, his height, his dark face. He overlooked the beauty of the work. We explained the Blake method of printing engravings and his comment was: "Why don't you offset instead of printing from the plate? Easier, cheaper."

"But not as beautiful."

Gonzalo crushed the end of his cigarette on the floor, trying to curb his anger.

Mr. Stricker looked disgusted.

"No one is interested in your books," he said. "You are an unknown writer."

"I thought you came here because you found *Winter of Artifice* a beautifully printed book."

Miss Decker was silent. I finally rebelled: "You have very bad manners," I said. "You're insensitive and patronizing."

And so it happened that the Graphic Arts Society never exhibited my books.

Letter from Henry:

I just mailed you back the pictures you lent me for the Hollywood exhibition. Hope they reach you in good shape. Your birthday is about at hand, and I want to send you a sincere message of congratulation. Well, I am about to leave now, for an extended vacation. I may never return to this place. I have no definite plans—only an urge to get out and relax.

The experiences I lived through here were of enormous value to me. By a strange irony of fate I was put in the situation which enabled me to realize, as I never could before, just how I must have appeared in your eyes. It makes your stature even grander. I learned the lesson.

Everything that you wished me to do I have done. I went through a veritable ordeal, for which I am most thankful. I hope your own struggles have proved as fruitful. I would like to know if you care to tell me. All my strength came from the example you set me. There is no one on earth I venerate more than you.

My address for the next few weeks will be care of Jean Varda in New Monterey. I would like to make you a gift of the handsome book which some friends have made for me: *The Angel Is My Watermark*. Would you accept it? You wouldn't get it immediately—each book is composed individually—but in the course of the next few weeks. Yes? I hope I hear from you. And more than anything I wish you would believe that my only desire is to be of help to you.

I have been waiting most impatiently to see the new book. All the important bookstores here have ordered copies and are also eagerly awaiting the book. I once—more than once—told you that if ever I had the money I would give it to you to publish the diary. I still mean that. Seventeen books are coming out this year, here and abroad. Should the windfall come, you will hear from me. I have repaid my most pressing debts with the unexpected returns from the sale of water colors. I wanted to clear all this off in order to leave a blank space for you. I hope you won't deny me this great privilege when the time comes. Bless you, dear Anaïs.

On my street lives a writer, Henrietta Weigel. She is tiny, and overflowing with love and the capacity to admire, with enthusiasm and faith.

She responded:

Many thanks for letting me read the story of Artaud. It moved me intensely. Of all your stories it seems the most powerful. The most deeply felt. It is beautifully written. So many, many people would have wanted to read it. It is to me a fable spun out of indestructible glass and stirs my sluggish memory to dreams and stories dreamed. The stone becomes flesh and the flesh leaps through its prison through imagination. I know you have the courage. One needs courage to write such a story. It is hard, I know to work without the light of understanding on the part of the people—but they are our sleeping selves fearing to wake, to look, to see. Gently we must rouse them, yet there is such a danger that if too gentle is the waking hand, sleep wins. All people dream but do not remember, do not remember that world of ice and burning heat. They live only in the deaths of grey wakefulness.

I nailed this letter to the wall above the typesetting table.

Neurosis causes loneliness. But there is also the loneliness of individuation.

A day before ending the printing of *Under a Glass Bell* I was ill with bronchitis. When anxiety sets in like a fever, cold and hot waves, chills, be calm. Know it for what it is: anxiety. Do not explain it away by blaming any particular incident, experience, for then it becomes magnified. When depression suffocates you like a London fog, think that the cause is not as great as you may think. A small defeat, a small frustration, a small discord may set it off. You must see the transitoriness of moods. Anaïs, beware of exaggerated reactions to harshness, brutality, ignorance, selfishness. Beware of allowing a tactless word, a rebuttal, a rejection to obliterate the whole sky.

The first copy of *Under a Glass Bell*. An exquisite piece of workmanship. Gonzalo has a gift for book designing. He took a copy to Hayter's Atelier 17 and it was admired by Hayter, Lipchitz, and other artists working there.

I meet Hayter on the street and he tells me how happy he is that Gonzalo created something he could be proud of, that he never thought Gonzalo could accomplish anything, and that it was a miracle.

But later Gonzalo surprised me by saying he had no satisfaction from this accomplishment.

"But why, Gonzalo, you always wanted to work with your hands, and this is both an artistic and a concrete achievement."

He looked depressed.

"What would give you a sense of fulfillment Gonzalo?"

"I wanted to be a pianist. I did not have the hands for it. My fingers were too short and stubby. Circumstances beyond my control."

When Gonzalo said he had no satisfaction from the printing of the book, I asked him if working with his hands, working at all, did not make him feel more like a Marxist, give him a link with the workman which was real rather than a purely intellectual one. Didn't he think he was putting Marxism into practice?

I felt utterly sad. Hayter was speaking admiringly of Gonzalo's work, amazed that he should work at all, and so giftedly. Is it guilt for his success? Can he not bear to excel in any way, to succeed? I confess that all my understanding is useless in the face of Gonzalo's intricate reactions. Perhaps because they are all negative, and the negative aspect of experience escapes me. My imagination cannot conceive of nothingness. *Le néant!*

My pleasure in Gonzalo's achievement was destroyed.

Another Marxist was converted: Olga. Speaking of *Under a Glass Bell*:

Every word you write is the purest poetry. I wish I had written it. I feel that you represent our poetic soul, and I regret having talked to you last summer about objective writing. I see now that you have to go on being the poet for all of us. I feel in contact with the movements of my own soul when I read you. You are my closest relative, though we appear so different, opposites, in fact. I feel every word you write so deeply. You put me in touch with my own soul.

Exhibit at Wakefield Gallery a great success. Ian Hugo's engravings keenly appreciated, and with them copies of *Under a Glass Bell*. Comments were warm and enthusiastic. Miss Decker, of the Graphic Arts Society, said it was marvelous.

In spite of this praise from friends, the money from the sale of the book did not relieve the economic pressures. I had to borrow money from the bank. Gonzalo's unfulfillment set me thinking that perhaps the romantic press was too much connected with my work, not businesslike enough to inspire confidence and orders, and that Gonzalo might feel happier to be the head of a commercial press, able to print whatever came his way. It would be his press, bear his name, and he would have the freedom to use it as he wished.

I felt this would appeal to his pride, and that he needed independence. The practical problems were enormous. We had to find a place which looked professional. We had to get a bigger press. Gonzalo ordered one to be delivered March first.

We found a small, two-story house vacated by a Greenwich Village newspaper. There is room on the ground floor for the press, and room on the second floor for the engraving press. It is on Thirteenth Street, across the way from Schrafft's. The large window would allow us to expose the books. The back door opens on a dismal back yard, the water closet is as dilapidated as any Bohemian place, the small spiral staircase is difficult for visitors to the engraving studio, but with all that it looks more businesslike and may attract work.

Gonzalo did not realize how difficult it was for me to relinquish the intimate personal press, not open to the public. But I think it was necessary for him to be free and dissociated from my work and romantic projects. He needed the respect of his friends and a sense of rulership. He would have it.

His friends will say: That is Gonzalo's press. It would no longer seem like an extension of my work.

Letter from Henry:

Your book just came, as I am about to leave for Big Sur, where I hope to stay a month at least. Varda and Virginia are delighted. More than that. You will hear from them. They are preparing a little surprise for you. Meanwhile, won't you send them an autographed copy. I will send you a money order for it from Big Sur. Have no time to run to the post office now. The format, the paper, the type, the engraving, all are beautiful, striking.

I have only been able to glance at it, to read the Foreword. I like the way you close the Foreword. I must tell you that you have some staunch admirers here in the West. I have heard you spoken of in the most remote spots. Your name is already legendary. I had heard that you had lost faith in the publishing and printing of your own books. I hope that is not so. It would be just at the wrong moment. It is your weakness, if I may say so delicately, to lose faith at the wrong moment. I beg you, be firm. Part of the act of creating is in discovering your own kind. They are everywhere. But don't look for them in the wrong places. In Varda you have one of your greatest admirers and believers. I will not go into elaborate details. But he is close to you in many ways. He is thoroughly Neptunian, an artist, a doer to the finger tips. Like you also, he leaves no dust behind. He executes everything with ease, lives in the miracle. One day you will meet. I believe he plans a trip to New York in the summer. His gallery is Marion Willard. My stay with him has been inspiring. From the living statue, Dudley, to the dynamo.

I am offered a cottage for a while at Big Sur, which is a site I find magnificent (just as Robinson Jeffers describes it). I have much work to finish and am seeking peace and isolation. I am completely out of the world there. The stores are thirty-five miles away. I have no car. Depend on the mailman to bring food—mail twice a week. Precisely what I want. This is a strange year for me—begun, say, three months back—of realization on all levels. I am suddenly quite free. And I have the sense to enjoy it. The help I have received from many quarters has been overwhelming. It does seem a solid law, that the more one believes in oneself, the more the world believes in you. I hope in mentioning these things I waft some good fortune in your direction. I have found no security outwardly, but observe with joy that I need it less and less. Everything that the soothsayers told me (all of them) seems coming through.

Edmund Wilson, in *The New Yorker;*

The pieces in this collection belong to a peculiar genre sometimes cultivated by the late Virginia Woolf. They are half short stories, half dreams, and they mix a sometimes exquisite poetry with a homely realistic observation. They take place in a special world, a world of feminine perception and fancy, which is all the more curious and charming for being innocently international.

Miss Nin is the daughter of a Spanish musician, but has spent much of her life in France and in the United States. She writes English, but mostly about Paris, though you occasionally find yourself in other countries.

There are passages in her prose which may suffer a little from an hallucinatory vein of writing which the Surrealists have overdone: a mere reeling-out of images, each of which is designed to be surprising but which strung together, simply fatigue. In Miss Nin's case, however, the imagery does convey something and is always appropriate. The spun glass is also alive: it is the abode of a secret creature. Half woman, half childlike spirit, she shops, employs servants, wears dresses, suffers the pains of childbirth, yet is likely at any moment to be volatilized into a superterrestrial being who feels things that we cannot feel.

But perhaps the main thing to say is that Miss Nin is a very good artist, as perhaps none of the literary Surrealists is. "The Mouse," "Under a Glass Bell," "Rag Time," and "Birth" are really beautiful little pieces.

The connection I made with a few people from the publication of *Under a Glass Bell* seemed like the breaking of a shell (how many shells?), a second birth (how many births?), a becoming visible and tangible. My feeling of being merely a mysterious influence upon others ceased. I felt out in the daylight.

First of all, Paul Rosenfeld mentioned me to Edmund Wilson, who went to the Gotham Book Mart, where Frances Steloff talked of me, and he went home with a copy of *Under a Glass Bell* and wrote a review which appeared in *The New Yorker* of April 1.

The morning *The New Yorker* appeared I was being photographed by the photographer of *Town and Country* in a dress by Henry La Pensée. A very formal, very elegant photograph.

John Stroup wrote a review of *Under a Glass Bell* in *Town and Country*. This started a rumor that I had arrived! *The New Yorker* was lying there, with the review by Edmund Wilson, who is the highest authority among the critics. Telephone calls, letters.

One morning what appeared in place of a letter was a big square package, one yard around. I opened it and it was a collage by Jean Varda. He calls it "Women Reconstructing the World."

Against a background of sand the color of champagne, with its tiny grains of sparkling glass, five women in airy cutouts. The middle one is the strongest, with her abstract labyrinth of black-and-red stripes; on her left walks an Ophelia in a trailing white dress of clouds and lace, dancing not walking. And on her right a sturdy woman in white and blue, carrying a piece of music on her head. But it does not weigh her down. It gives a rhythm to her stance. A smaller woman in the distance is pierced with diamond-shaped apertures through which shine faith. A still smaller woman wears a merry dress of stripes. In the back are four small houses, all façades, pierced with smiling, askew windows; one can easily walk in and out of them, as lightly and airily as the women walk toward us with the grace of the rites of spring.

All of woman is enclosed in a dance of forms, squares, diamonds, rectangles, parallelograms of moods and sidereal delights, subtle harmonies and pliant mysteries. They are made of intangibles, lights and space, labyrinths, and molecules which may change as you look at them. Elusive and free of gravity. They bring freedom by transcendence.

Having gathered together the fevers, the conquests, the passions, having pulled in the sails of my ever-restless, ever-wandering ships of dreams (Henry will be a famous writer; Gonzalo will accomplish something of which he can be proud; Moira will be unveiled and become a modern woman; Frances will escape tuberculosis and enter a full life; the press will publish marvelous books and will triumph over the underworld, lower-depths writing), having garnered, collected, called back from the Tibetan desert my ever roaming soul, having rescued my spirit from the webs of the past, from the stranglehold of responsibility for the lives of others, having cured myself of the drugs of romanticism, surrendered the impossible dreams and called back an exhausted Don Quixote, I close the window, and the door, and open the diary once more.

I call back from its consultations with the oracle analyst, a weeping dreamer, disconsolate idealist, a seeker of heightened moments only, and take her for a tour of home, the softly lit studio, the present, the bed, the food, the rest. The dissolved, the dispersed, the given Anaïs must rest from pyres of sacrifice, from holocausts of possessions, wishes, and planning of other lives. Focus on the present. Accept a quiet happiness, the absence of fever.

Even an obsessed adventurer, always seeking for expansion and unchartered land, must come to terms with happiness, pale flame after heightened moments, but unconsuming, a pale flame which resembles the dawn rather than the fiery sunsets of tropical countries, dawns I perceived and longed for at times when caught in the infernal chambers of atonement. Passionate living is heaven and hell, and this homecoming felicity.

The body and soul rest in their moorings, the anchor is no longer being dragged against its will through an uprooted life which must learn both to keep afloat and to stay moored without pulling unreasonably at the forces of gravity which keep it from shipwreck.

Sancho Panza, the diary, grows fat and well-nourished, but the Quixote cannot alone carry out its vision of a perfect and human world.

For the first time I have conquered restlessness, my imagination does not wander to all the far places and towards all the far strangers, questing, expecting what?

For the first time my body and soul are together, and the sound of a window closing, a door closing, is no more alarming than the wings of an icon closing over a figure praying.

I can bear to listen to music, it is not a provocation to more adventures, a pursuit of ghosts, a tracking down of mirages, an embracing of the void. This is no mere interlude to an uneasing hunger and curiosity but a possession of the present and the near I have neglected, and now for the first time I appreciate the haven, the repose, the softly closed window and door which say: "Everything is here, in the present, on earth." Let distant ecstasies and imaginings no longer lure me on.

With the Haitians, with oracle analyst, I recaptured my own nature and the sources of joy. The Haitians came to remind me that the telling of stories is the only balm, the only drug, the only permanent, indestructible, constant, ever-inhabitable island. The long, protracted farewell to Henry, who sought his Shangri-La in California, the difficult act of setting each other free, all of us who had lived in a little Paris cell of fraternity, setting Gonzalo free of shame, and relinquishing those who could not be rescued, the building of the press to sustain the writing and to by-pass all bitterness, self-sufficiency, the telling of the adventures and the printing of them, cell and nucleus of imagining, acting, carrying out the visions, balanced by a pause, by a recognition that storytelling diverted one's attention from loss, partings, hurts.

It was not necessary to stay awake all night, like the children in Haiti, to catch the mapau tree which moves in the night. The mobile mapau tree is the storyteller's game with his memory album, his moving around the characters to see them from all sides. Close the door and window upon the world for a moment, turn to the diary for all its musical notations, and begin another novel.

Index

Abramson, Benjamin, 104
Acropolis, 8
Admiral, Virginia, 18, 70, 72–73, 89,
  93, 111, 124, 128, 129, 151, 247–48
Agee, James, 256
Aghnides, Elie, 290
Air-Conditioned Nightmare, The,
  178
Albuquerque, N.M., 108
Alemany, 196
Alianza Interamericana (magazine),
  199
Allendy, Dr. René, ix, 16, 76, 77,
  260; dying in France, 121
Alvin, 155
America: artists in, vis-à-vis Europe,
  120; contempt for art in, 300–01;
  experience of "new world", v; first
  journey to, v; immaturity of, x;
  looms as refuge, 3; luxury of, 11;
  new awareness of, in Europe, viii;
  narcicism in, 271; poetry in, 175;
  rejecting European influence, xi;
  relationship to, viii; rhythm in,
  45; seeks devil inside, 229; spiritual needs of, 28; success in, ix;
  third confrontation with, v; war
  on poverty in, 303
American Astrology (magazine), 25
Anderson, Sherwood, 28; visit to, 28
Angel Is My Watermark, The, 306
Anteros, 6
anxiety: experience of, 275–76
Aquatic Park (San Francisco), 118
Aran Islands, 162
Arcachon (France), vi

Arensberg, Walter, 119
Arequipa (Peru), 172
Ariadne, 242
Art and Artist, 257
Artaud, Antonin, ix, 19, 65, 74, 76,
  137, 299, 306; quote from letter,
  183–84; story about, 47; working
  on story about, 183–85
Atelier 17, 126, 307
Atlantis, 4, 10, 42, 218, 264
Attica, 8
Auden, W. H., 270
Azores, 4, 5, 218

Bach, Johann Sebastian, 288
Bailly, Auguste, 229; quoted on
  Joyce, 229–30
Baker, Josephine, 255
Bali, 188, 191
Balzac, Honoré de, 119
Barcelona, v, vi
Barker, George, 70, 150–51, 156, 157,
  162, 166, 175, 177, 181, 190, 267;
  on Catholicism, 150–51; visit from,
  197–98
Barnes, Djuna, 150, 185, 186, 188,
  259
Barrie, Sir James Matthew, 137
Barrymore, John, 118
Basie, Count, 106
Bateau Ivre, Le, 287
Baudelaire, Charles, 280
Beach, Sylvia, 11
Beatrice Cenci (play), 19, 184
beds: reflections on, 70–71
Beethoven, Ludwig van, 30, 210, 288